2016

"Son of Wales Award" for best new author and poet
"Excellence of Literature Award" for the outstanding achievement of the epic autobiography *Cave Days*

2017

"Best Adventure Autobiography" for Great Britain and Ireland King of the Castle Publishing.

"Best Adventure and Historical Award" for the outstanding autobiography *Gower of the Hills*, King of the Castle Publishing

Winner of West Wales, Excellence of Literature Award for *Nan's Nan, and the Pirates of Port Eynon*

Al Cole Interview, CBS radio, People of Great Distinction book interview for *Cave Days*, 2019

Nan's Nan, and the Pirates of Port Eynon

KINGSLEY R. HILL

Copyright © 2021 by Kingsley Ross Hill

All rights reserved. Written permission must be secured from the publisher to use or reproduce any part of this book, except for brief quotations in critical reviews or article.

Published in Swansea Wales by King of the Castle Publishing.

ISBN 978-0-9879493-6-3 (paperback) ISBN 978-0-9879493-7-0 (ebook)

Front Cover Artwork by Sylvia Nicholson, A Touch of Art, Victoria, BC

Unless otherwise noted, scripture quotations and verses are from the HOLY BIBLE, New Living Translation. Tyndale House Publishers, Inc. Copyright 2015

And New International Version Copyright, 1973, 1978, 1984 by International Bible Society. Used by permission of Zondervan Publishing House, all rights reserved.

To contact Kingsley Hill email at gowerofthehills@gmail.com

Book design by SpicaBookDesign, Victoria, BC

Printed and bound with IngramSpark

This book is dedicated to my beautiful wife, Janet Hill.

∽

*"You burst forth into my life
like the rising of the Sun!
And you "Danced just for me,"
an audience of One.*

They Made a Day

*O*nce upon a time, there was a man who lived in the dawn and the day. He walked about and said "This must be the way." But he felt alone, and thought: "I wish I had someone to walk with me in the dawn and the day." Upon his walk, he met a woman named Janet. And he said to her, "Would you please come for a walk with me along the way, and I'll show you my life in the dawn and the day?" The woman agreed, and said: "Yes, I'd like to come for a walk and see your dawn and day, but I walk in the twilight, and the night hours of the day. If I walk with you, will you walk with me? And, I will show you my way." And a walk was arranged with the night and the day.

First the man took the woman's hand and showed her the dawn and the bright of the day. And the woman said, "You have woken me, and made my spirit come alive and be free! Now come with me!" The woman now took the man's hand, and showed him her twilight shimmering sea, and as they walked, a different energy the man began to see, and no longer did he want to leave, because she was so different from he. She took him out, to sit underneath the stars and showed him things that could be, and they went to sit under a tree.

Gower Peninsula Adventure Series

"You have shown me so much with your poems and flowers, and you have changed me. I just want to bask in your sunshine for hours and run with you through the springtime showers. You have taught me so much too," the man said, "and you have changed me, for in your eyes I can see a missing part of me, your soul touches mine, and I am free."

"I have not changed you," the woman said, "I have just shown you who you are, and who you have always been, sometimes we need each other to be seen."

As time went on the man did not want to live in the dawn and daytime alone, not now, with everything he had been shown, for in the woman's heart he had found his home. And he longed for the twilight to come again, his way. Sometimes, he waited all day, until the sun closed the curtain's all the way. And the woman no longer wanted to walk in the twilight and nighttime alone, for in the man's heart she had found her home.

And under the crescent moon, she sat and thought, I will wait for the dawn, he will come soon, because he lives in my heart that no longer has a spare room. And he did! He held her, and kissed her, holding her tight, carrying her all through the lonely night. When the dawn came, they sat in loves glorious light, deciding to marry uniting the day, with the night. Oh, my darling, I shall make you a love-spoon because my sunshine could not live without your moon.

© Kingsley Ross Hill.

About the Author

𝒦ingsley Ross Hill, was born near the city of Swansea, in Glamorganshire, South Wales and grew up in the village of Pennard, on the Gower Peninsula. [The word Pennard, means "village without a gate" in the Welsh language]. Kingsley, describes growing up in Pennard, and on the Gower Peninsula, as "living this most wonderful adventure, with no gates."

It is interesting that the Gower Peninsula Series, which includes the books, "Cave Days," "Gower Of The Hills," and "Nan's Nan," all give the reader, such a sense of freedom and adventure; like walking through a land without gates or fences. The authors books are full of mystery and adventure and are extremely accurate in their betrayal of the history and geography of the Gower Peninsula itself.

The author is humble about his many awards. I am pleased that he is becoming well known in his native Wales, and throughout the United Kingdom, and more recently in Canada and the United States, for his unique style of writing and poetry.

Kingsley Hill, lives with his family in Creston, British Columbia. He is also a pastor and counsellor and works in youth outreach. He has a prison ministry, sharing his faith with others.

Table of Contents

1	Return to Canaan	1
2	Winters Long	34
3	Love and Bluebells	52
4	Two Pennies of Treasure	68
5	The Pirates of Port Eynon	80
6	Hunts Bay	101
7	A Taliath Tale	116
8	Happy Birthday Gay	134
9	Nan's Nan	148
10	Tuesday	182
11	It's 11 a.m., Lets Go!	228
12	Summer's Gold	265
13	Number 8 and Number 12	290

Chapter One

Return to Canaan

Canaan is what I named Vancouver Island when I immigrated to Canada over twenty years ago. And it became my "promised land."

♪※

PROMISED LAND

A POEM

Oh, God, what a mysterious and
wonderful Land my eyes have seen.
My soul is thrilled, as it wakens
from my sleeping childhood dreams, and
shouts 'It's real. I'm here, come and see!'
I sing and dance within, as I swim with the
whales and stand amongst the giant trees.
New dreams are falling,
falling with your golden leaves, and
you will be mine forever, is my song.

Today I have entered the promised land.
You belong to me, given by God's own hand.

I come to claim you,
to touch and caress your soul,
like a lover I will get to know you,
my promised land,
as I put my ring upon your hand.
Now take me, Kingsley.
You whisper, Welcome, welcome,
to your promised land.

© *Kingsley Ross Hill*

As my plane sat on the runway at Gatwick International Airport, with its engines revving and warming up for takeoff, I thought about the things that had made Vancouver Island become my promised land. It had certainly lived up to my boyhood hopes and dreams of finding a wild and adventurous land where I could hunt and fish and explore the untameable ocean and mountain wilderness, to build a life that suited my passion for exploring and discovering what was left of a great frontier.

I have climbed many mountains in British Columbia, and I have explored islands and secret beaches, and the sacred rainforests of the old growth trees. What fool's men have been to cut down so much of the old sacred forests – you can hear the "giant firs" calling out their stories along the paths of the forest to any soul who might be listening. I have seen the "great whales" as they travel along their ocean paths amidst the wild crashing waves of the Pacific Rim. I have looked down on the soaring eagles from the mountain heights and I have danced with the ravens and the wolves. I tamed a wolf once, as much as he could be tamed, as he traveled with me for a month through the mountains, and we shared a cave together and kept warm in a blizzard of snow.

And I made friends with a tribe of indigenous people – "the First Nations people," as they call themselves today. What a great people they are, and so misunderstood. They are indeed the first and original people of my promised land. They taught me how to spear salmon in the rushing rivers, and how to track and hunt bear and make clothing from their fur pelts. We made fires of cedar and hemlock and danced around the flames; my friends dressed in their native attire. They taught me how to carve wood and to shape the stones of the river. I learned what their ceremonies and customs meant in relation to their lives – past, present, and future. They told me the stories of their ancestors and what their lives were like before the white man intruded into their land.

I was humbled and privileged to be accepted by these great people, and even befriended by them, as I am a white man and not born in the land of their ancestors. I will never forget the time that a Chief and some of the Elders of his tribe took me thousands of miles northwards into the Arctic tundra to see the Northern Lights. We traveled by sleds that were pulled by the strong sled dogs, and we built igloos to sleep in and shelter from the arctic storms. We drilled holes in the ice to fish and we kept warm in the animal furs of the wild animals that we hunted. The Aurora Borealis crackled and danced over our heads with greens, purples, and yellows, and colours I had never seen before lighting up the cold crystal air. And deep in a forest at the singing river falls, I saw a white bear! The natives call them "Spirit Bears," and they are sacred! Some evenings I was invited into their teepee, and I would share stories of my life adventures. This was an amazing experience for me as I shared what I felt in my heart, and at the same time we smoked the pipe that was part of their tradition, passing it around in a circle of brotherhood that welcomed me.

This experience took me back to a time when I had lived in my cave "Bacon Hole" on the Gower Peninsula, and sat around the campfire with my three best friends, smoking Martin's father's pipe. Coming to explore Canada was only a dream then. But it is a dream that I have lived out! And the "oneness" that my soul experienced with my indigenous friends was wonderful, and I shall remember their friendship and fellowship all my life! And it was during the season of the Popping Seeds that the Chief sent a woman to my tent as a gift for me to keep me warm and comfortable. She could only understand a few words I spoke but answered every need of my body and every question in my heart. Thank you, Chief White Wolf, for your wonderful gift of "Shining Heart" – she still shines in my heart.

I stayed with my indigenous brothers and sisters for three large moon tides and left in the season of the Melting Snow. And when I arrived back in Vancouver, I walked into the waiting Spring with a Grizzly Bear fur and a tooth necklace. Thank you, Wind On A Hill, for teaching me how to track and hunt. I will never forget you!

Today however, I was returning to Canada, in hope of leaving its wild shores, giant trees, and native people behind, and returning as soon as I was able to the "land of my fathers," my beloved Wales! And to my beloved Gay and Melody!

"Godspeed your return," the Red Kite had wished me as he glided over the singing hills of Wales.

Suddenly we were racing down the runway, and leaving behind the grey clouded, wind blowing – rubbish smelling – seagull squawking – pigeon shitting -east Indian speaking – Chinese spitting-turban wearing – Brexit fighting -blocked toilet of a God Save the Queen London day!

The mighty Rolls Royce engines thrust us into the air, arresting any other thought other than holding on tight, as bump-bump through the dark clouds we went, and the London afternoon was left further and further behind.

We soon reached our cruising altitude and the pilot turned off the seatbelt sign. I undid my seatbelt and tilted my seat back as far as it would go. Gosh, we were seated like sardines in a can, there was hardly any leg room, and they call this comfort! Anyway, there was lots to think about to help pass the time. God had blessed me and made me fruitful in my adopted land of Canada, but in my heart, it was time to go home to Wales and to the Gower Peninsula – "the land of the setting suns." I was a married man now. I had found again the love of my life! And I pictured the smiling faces of Gay and Melody as we said goodbye at the airport.

I closed my eyes and tried to rest. I had a ten-hour flight ahead of me to Vancouver, and then a half-hour flight to Victoria on Vancouver Island. I thought of Gay and our last day together at the caravan when we had opened the rest of our wedding presents. We had only opened one as we went to bed as husband and wife. There were far more exciting things to do, even more than opening presents! And I laughed at the thought of us having spent three days in bed and then opening the rest of our presents when we were not looking into each other's eyes or eating chocolates and strawberries with Devonshire cream.

There was one present however, that was only addressed to me. It was from my dad. He had given Gay and I one to open as our official wedding gift, but as for this present, he said he had been waiting for a long time to give it to me. Gay had packed it in my carry-on luggage, so that I would have something to look forward to on the flight. I will wait until we reach Greenland, I thought, and then open it.

The hours seemed to be going by so slowly, even though I relived, over and over in my mind, the events of my wonderful experience finding Gay again, and our beautiful wedding. Finally, we were flying over the icefields of Greenland, and I stood up and opened the overhead storage locker to get my carry-on case. I pulled out the large box, which was wrapped in brown paper and tied with a string bow, and then I put my case back in the locker and sat down. What could it be, I thought, as I rolled it over on my lap and felt the weight of it. It was not very heavy considering the size of the box. I pulled on the string to release the knot, and then began to pull away the brown paper that revealed a slightly smaller round white box. It was kind of like an old hat box, the kind my grandmother would keep one of her best church hats in. "It can't be one of grandma's feather hats," I said, as I pulled off the top of the box. The lady sitting next to me smiled and then giggled, and by the look on her face I think she was enjoying this mystery as much as I was. To my surprise, there was an oblong-shaped parcel inside, wrapped in burgundy and yellow tissue paper, and there was a card.

Dear Kings,

No doubt you and Gay have opened all your wedding presents by now, but I have wanted to give you this for a long time. The present inside the tissue paper belongs to you. You found it when you were twelve years old. I decided to wait until you were grown up and had become a responsible young man before I gave it to you. Now, if you have not already opened the parcel before reading the card, please open the card and read the letter inside. It will explain the uniqueness and the value of what is inside the parcel.

I opened the card and started to read the letter...

Kingsley, I don't know how much you remember of the day you found this in the grounds of Pennard Castle. I took you and Fraser over to the Three Cliffs Valley with my metal detector, to try and find some coins or other artifacts. We didn't find much in the valley that day – only bottle caps and old pop cans, so we went up to the grounds of the castle to try there. Using the metal detector, we didn't find anything there either. But then you started digging in the sand in front of those rocks that look a bit like an altar or perhaps some official site that the inhabitants of the castle might have used for their ancient ceremonies. Do you remember those rocks in the middle of the grounds? And do you remember what you found that day?

∽

I could not wait any longer to open the parcel – this was all so exciting! I quickly pulled away at the colourful paper to find what looked like an ancient book between two pieces of animal fur that had been woven together. Suddenly, the memories of that warm spring day, that I had spent 'metal detecting' with my father and brother, came galloping through the pages of my mind. I can remember pulling the animal fur out of the sand and brushing it off with my fingers to see what it was. It was in the shape of a book, and the fur felt cool and oily. It was bound together with what appeared to be some type of grass or reed thread, and on one side the binding had disintegrated. I can remember opening the book and finding what looked to be an ancient document of some kind. There was writing that I could not understand, and the words were written on a thick form of paper that felt more like the bark of a tree.

On that day, after smelling the fur and rubbing it with my hands, I remember feeling a wind that seemed to come from nowhere. It swirled around my head and through my hair, like a gentle whirlwind. It was very strange, as there was only a tiny breath of wind that day, and I felt a presence around me that came with the wind.

"Dad! Look what I found!" I exclaimed.

"Let me have a look, Son. Come on, stop smelling it and let me have a look!"

I smelled the cool oily fur again before handing it over to my father, who was as excited as I was. I was still thinking about the strange presence that I had felt in the wind.

"Look, Kings," he said, "the writing is written in an ancient language, and it isn't written on paper as we know it today; it is written on pieces of tree bark. And the fur looks like it is from a bear or wolf, both of which would have been around in the ancient days when this manuscript was written."

Return to Canaan

Back to the present time for now. I continued to read Dad's letter, and he said that he had already started to translate the manuscript and that it was a "diary." It was the diary of a "Clan Queen" who had ruled her clan in the year 970 and some years beyond.

"Kings," my dad continued in his letter, "this is an actual story of a Clan Queen and her family, and their lives within the clan. You will now understand why I did not let you have it when you were only twelve. It is a priceless piece of history – a historical account of a Queen's life and her people. You are now mature and wise enough to have this. I am going to give you the responsibility of translating it from its original ancient language to English so that you can understand it and you can tell the story of this woman's life in the year of 970 A.D."

Wow! I thought, as I lifted the diary up to my nose and smelled it. I could still smell and feel the oil and musk on the fur as I had done when I first found it. And now I had goose bumps on my skin as I pondered my amazing find from all those years ago in the grounds of Pennard Castle.

I could now make sense of why my dad had given Gay and I the two ancient Celtic language books with the English translation of the words. It had been a rather strange wedding gift, don't you think, dear reader? Along with a year's worth of passes to every museum in Wales. Nay, not a strange gift if you are a historian and a great explorer like my father is.

I now sat back in my seat and tried to rest for the remainder of the flight. I tried to think of ways that translating the diary could help keep Gay and I interested in something we could still do together, even with her being six thousand miles away. She has the Celtic translation books with her in Wales, and I have the diary.

How can we work together on this, and even include Melody if we can?

Suddenly it hit me! I can write out copies of the diary and send them several pages at a time to Gay, and she can interpret them from the books into English and send them back to me. And Melody can look forward to me sending a little something for her every few weeks when I send Gay my copies. Maybe there will be maps or descriptions of places recorded in the diary where Gay and Melody can go and explore? I became more and more excited at the prospect of this project. It was going to be a great way for us to stay connected.

We were now flying over the Coastal Mountains of British Columbia and would soon be making our descent into Vancouver International Airport. I packed the diary back into my carry-on case and sat back in my seat. I was not looking forward to going through customs at "unfriendly YVR." They have a horrible habit of making one feel "like a fugitive" even when I am a Canadian Citizen. At least that has been my experience. I much prefer flying from Victoria to Calgary and then over to Britain, and vice versa on the way back, and thus avoid YVR. altogether! I have always found the ground staff and the customs people at Calgary friendly, helpful, and efficient. But today I had to land in "Happyville" and connect to a regional flight to Victoria from there. I only received a few wounds going through customs at Happyville and then I made my flight to Victoria.

It was almost 1 a.m. when I arrived back in Sooke, and everyone was fast asleep, including the mouse. And there had only been a few "legends in their own minds" driving black Dodge pickup trucks on the Sooke Road toward where I lived. How those idiots got driving licences I will never know! They drive two feet behind your rear bumper and try to intimidate other drivers by the size of their trucks. My friend Karen says it's overcompensation for their very small penises, to be driving such large trucks. Anyway, there are less of these rednecks driving at night, and I arrived home safely.

No sooner had my head hit the pillow when I heard a voice say: "Dad! Dad!" It was my daughter Samantha Jade, as she jumped on my bed and proceeded to tell me all about her adventures since I had been away. And she had painted two more pictures – one of which was of 'Great Thunder' my wild and wonderful stallion; only she had painted him as a "Spirit Horse," galloping in from the crashing waves of the sea.

Jade, as my daughter prefers to be called, is truly a gifted artist. She often has her work displayed in galleries up and down Vancouver Island, and she paints amazing murals on people's walls. She is also a wonderful flute player and composes her own music.

My eldest son Jonathan was also home when I arrived, and he came over and gave me one of his famous bear hugs, which always say more than any words can say. "Great to have you back, Dad!" "Great to see you too, Son! How has Liverpool been doing? I've missed watching the games with you, Champ." "Me too, Dad, let's catch a game together on the weekend; I think we're playing Man United, and we can't miss that one! And then we can kick the ball around with Ben." "That's a plan," I said, and Jonathan headed off to bed.

My youngest son, Ben, was over at his friends having a sleepover, and I looked forward to seeing him on the morrow. Ben, just like his brother Jonathan, is a great football player, and he recently led his team to back-to-back "Championship titles" in the Vancouver Island Cup. Had my sons grown up in the United Kingdom, they both could have been professional football Players! "Real Football" that is! Not to be confused with American or Canadian football, which is a pansy's game! Enough said.

I have coached both my sons in football, here in Canada, ever since they could walk. And the game has become a great heritage in our family. We spend hours practicing and training together each week, and on the weekends, we watch our favorite Premiership teams on TV. It's not the same as going to a live game and experiencing the atmosphere at the stadium and the brotherhood between fans, but we have fun watching and playing the "beautiful game." And today, being home again with my children gives me such "Joy," and I am celebrating "the wonderful gift of fatherhood." Thank you, God, for making me the richest man in the world!

Return to Canaan

℘

WHEN IS A MAN RICH?
A POEM

A man is rich when God shows him
the miracle of birth, and
entrusts to him the honour and responsibility of
caring for a brand-new life
whether a Son or Daughter.
He is rich when he is loved by his wife,
and has the wisdom to love her back, and
remember that it was she who bore him children, and
it is she that is his helpmate and his equal.
He is rich when he feels her love in his heart,
and the love of his children that
comes radiating back to him,
and melts away the ice of any cold and rainy day.
Oh, how wonderful is the gift of fatherhood, that
in His immeasurable love,
God bestows this wonderful gift upon a man.
He is rich when his own children follow
their father's ways,
or don't, and thus teach a man something new
about the God who made them.
Deep within the secret place of their mother's womb
God fashions a life and soul unlike any other,
and a man is taught many things if he only listens.
He is rich when he hears his daughter sing, and
helps her pick bluebells

Nan's Nan, and the Pirates of Port-Eynon

for her mother as a song of love.
A Son to live a father's dream, or
to show him a new one that he has never seen.
In a Son's eye, the gift of love gleams,
as you climb with your children over the hills and
bubbling streams,
and help your children follow their dreams.
You learn and grow through the seasons together,
In sun and rain, you walk and smell,
the grass and pick the purple heather.
Fathers and children grow up together, and
God looks from heaven,
And he smiles and remembers.
He remembers when a father's mother counted
all her son's ten toes,
And thanked him for life and love, and
all the things that her soul knows.
God made man and woman, and proclaimed,
"This is very good!"
It's only the fool that misunderstood the wonderful gift of
motherhood and fatherhood.
The years they come and go,
And when your child is young, life seems to be slow,
then faster and faster, as you come to know,
And you want to hold on to the precious moments and
years that make your heart glow,
And you try to make life go slow and
pray that we can all stay like this forever.
My beloved children, I don't want to let go!
But time does not wait for us, you know,

and then one day one of you will let go,
and in my heart the summer will turn to snow.
Come on dad! It's time to let go!
And I will carry on with what you have
taught me to know.
Yesterday has gone, and tomorrow,
I just don't know...
There is only today and my memories to
remind me how when you were little
you made my heart glow.
But there is one thing a father can know, and
that is, that family and love is forever.
Once a father, always a father, and of that,
I can never let go.
And I am a rich man because
God allowed me to be your dad,
you know.
Yes, time will move along, but I will always love you,
my sons and my daughter,
And your love and your faith in me has changed my life forever.
And I am a rich man.

© *Kingsley Ross Hill*

    The days seemed to be going by quickly now as I got back to my daily routine of being a pastor and spending time with my children. But I felt torn in a way, torn between two lives. One with my new family in Wales, and one here with my children on Vancouver Island. I needed God's help in uniting these two lives.

It was going to take time, I understood that. But as the weeks and then the months passed, it became more evident how difficult it was, being away from Gay and Melody. And yet, when I am in Wales, I miss my children here in Canada so much. But God knows I need a wife. A companion and helpmate to help me navigate through this sometimes cold and cruel world. And I thank God for giving me my Gay.

Gay and I had made the commitment to talk twice a week on the phone, and we wrote letters and sent cards to each other. But most often we just needed to hear one another's voices, and share our hearts, and our struggles and longings and what being apart was teaching us. Our love seemed to grow stronger after each letter, and especially during our conversations on the phone. Oh, how I longed for her touch, and to hold her in my arms again.

It was important to include Melody in our conversation time over the phone, and to reassure my own children that God would somehow work all things out. Gay had shared in our last conversation that Melody was missing me a lot, and especially my walking her to school and telling her stories.

With the eight-hour time difference between Britain and here on the West Coast of British Columbia, I found that calling early in the morning, my time, was the best time to catch Gay on her lunch break at work. And if I wanted to talk to both Gay and Melody, then I stayed up late, usually until about midnight, and then I was able to catch them before work and school. Talking to Melody before she went to school was particularly encouraging and reassuring for her, Gay shared. I could hear the change of tone in Melody's voice once she knew that it was me on the phone – she always sounded excited. So,

I decided to call one extra time a week, just to remind her that she was my Princess, before she left for school. Gay shared that my phone call was like a kiss for Melody, and that it put my presence around her as she walked to school. God was helping us stay connected, all these miles apart.

My next letter from Gay was going to be a special one, not that they were not all special, but I had sent her my first copies of "The Clan Queen's Diary." I didn't understand most of the words that I was copying yet, but Gay was in the process of translating them from our ancient Celtic language books.

Sometimes we felt that it would be easier to discuss the diary over the phone, but we had agreed that we wanted to keep our commitment to its translation through our letters. This gave us something to look forward to, other than emailing and texting in our fast-paced culture. Somehow there is something more pleasant and personal about receiving a letter. Melody likes to skip down the road to the post-office to see if Mrs. Brown has a letter or a parcel for her. And I do the same on this side of the pond. My daughter, Samantha Jade, has also started writing to her new sister, which has made going to the post office even more exciting for Melody, who has always wanted a sister.

I like the scripture verse of Proverbs 25 verse 25, "Like cold water to a thirsty soul, so is good news from a far away land." I agree! Gay and Melody's letters water my soul.

On this morning of the 22nd day of November 2019, I received my first translation of the diary back from Gay. And it was amazing! The diary was started by a woman introducing herself as Taliath-Seren, which translated, means "Diadem Star." I shall call her Taliath for short. Taliath went on to say that her writings were a recording of her, and her family's lives, as members of "Clan number One Forty-Two," of the one hundred and forty-four established Coastal and Black Mountain Clans of South and West Wales.

Taliath, went on to name the title of her diary: "How I Became a Clan Queen, and the Priest Who Killed Me." What a title! On Saturday morning I called Dad, to thank him so much for giving us the language translation books. What a gift for us to be able to translate the story of her life and her family living in the time of the Welsh Celtic Clans.

As Dad and I continued to talk on the phone, he reminded me again about the responsibility of telling Taliath's story. And to also be careful whom I shared it with, especially at this early stage of its translation. Dad felt convinced, from just what he had translated himself, that this was a rare and missing piece of history that had happened on and around the Gower Peninsula, and that it had a special relation to Pennard Castle where I had found the manuscript.

"You must not call it a manuscript," he said. "It is a 'sacred diary,' and you get to tell Taliath's story."

At the risk of creating a book within a book, Dear Reader, I have decided to include these first few pages of translation. And yes, with my father's permission, of course. And I hope you get to experience even a little of the excitement that Gay and I have already experienced in translating and reading these first few pages.

Return to Canaan

♪✳

DARK

Dark, dark, always dark! I want to scream and run from the smoke and smell, but where to? If I run past the Balla [I believe this to be the word for executioner] and the evil Priest, there are three walls before I can escape the castle! And the smell of ceremonies and burning bodies makes me sick! And I wonder if I will ever see the light of day again? Or feel the soft grass beneath my feet, instead of this cold, cruel stone? Or will I be sacrificed and burned? Or enter yet into another lustful ceremony, where I can only think of today, for tomorrow never comes. And if it did what hope would I have? Sometimes I have a recurring dream, that I will one day forget that there is a world beyond this thick dark smoke that hangs like an angry demon, obscuring even the dull light from the barred windows of the ceremonial-room. Oh, to be free! To feel the wind blowing through my hair, and to run through the meadow with the sun on my face. I must not lose hope! For there is a world outside this darkness, and one day I will leave this awful place and be free!

The Balla has left, and the evil priest's lusts are satisfied, at least for today. The ceremonial candles have been put out, and the watchers have left the temple. And I may return to my living quarters, and hopefully my three sisters will all return safely. We never know if we are going to see each other again from one day to the next. And we all know the evil priest's desire to murder our mother, who resists his advances each day at the Temple. He can't have her, so he wants to kill her.

I arrive back at my quarters and wait nervously for my sister's return. Our mother is the "Clan Queen," and is performing her evening duties in one of the temple rooms, or so a watcher told me upon leaving the temple. I don't think we will see her until late tonight, until after we have eaten and taken our rest.

My body trembles as I continue to wait for my sisters. I wrestle with my thoughts and my imagination as I remember things that I saw in the temple today. Things I wish I had never seen! The heavy ankle bracelet that identifies me as part of my clan [Clan number one hundred and forty-two] is pressing hard upon my skin and reminds me that I am but property!

Mother says my sisters and I are fortunate, because we are the daughters of a "Clan Queen" and we are "Royalty" compared to the commoners. And I can read and write, because of an aunt who taught me such wonderful things. The common clan woman cannot read or write; it is forbidden unless you are of noble descent. And even then, it depends on what nobility you descend from, and what you do or don't do, that determines your status. Priests, for example, are most often lustful and land hungry, and can usually be bought with a bribe. And then there is the Balla, who everyone is afraid of! Except for the Princes. That dark figure can sentence you to death with a glance. They scheme and betray with the Nobles, who buy and sell land, people and animals. It is said that the Balla keep even the Princes in the dark as to what they really do with their authority.

The Nobles spend most of their time arguing over lands and title, rather than serving the people and implementing the laws of the Princes who gave them land and title in the first place.

The Princes, what can be said of them? How could I even approach a Prince? Even though I am the daughter of a Clan Queen. So how much less the commoner! Who are these phantom men called Princes? I have never seen one! Mother says they govern all the Clans, one hundred and forty-four of them, passing down laws that we lesser souls must live by.

Mysterious men these Princes may be, but the sting of their ruthless laws is real enough. We live and die by them every day.

Fourteen years, and four New Moons have passed since I started, and now I have finished my writings on how my sister's and I lived our lives in "Clan number one hundred and forty-two" of the established "Coastal and Black Mountain Clans of Wales. South, I believe. Not that my mother, sisters and I have ever left our village or clan lands. We just hear, from travelers and warring clans, that there is a North and West Wales, but no East. How can that be? The sun rises in the East. And crosses the sky, as radiant and as excited as a young Clan Queen dressing for her first love ceremony.

Can there be a hidden land that my eyes have not seen? The place that at night my heart dreams of. Beyond these cold stone walls, and our village overlooking the valley and the winding stream below the Castle.

Over the distant hills, whispers of knowledge come to us like seedlings upon the wind and tell us of a land called England to the east. I know that it is there. That this place of my dreams exists. I have this "knowing." Yes, it's knowing that it is out there, waiting for me to come and find it. And it is this hope that keeps me going and gives me the will to keep living.

It is the year 970, and the second moon of the large sea. I have bound our writings in animal fur, and buried them in the Castle grounds, near the altar where my mother, sisters and I played, and they dreamed of marrying a handsome warrior, who would take us away from this place. To the land that we go to each night in our dreams.

It is my hope that one day our writings will be found. And the story of my sister's lives and mine will be told to a future people of understanding – who will think about us and remember our lives, and the ways in which we lived and died. Surely if our words are found and understood, our lives will not have been lived in vain.

Return to Canaan

♪⁎

That is all we have translated from the diary so far, dear reader, and I hope you enjoyed it.

∽

So, what do we know about Taliath's story in relation to Pennard Castle? The most exciting part for me, was reading about her putting her writings between animal fur and burying them in the Castle grounds, near what she describes as an altar. That is exactly where I found the diary when I was twelve years old. And as Dad shared on the phone, her writing mentions "the Castle on the hill overlooking the valley, and the winding stream below." This describes what one can see looking out from the Castle walls.

It seems obvious to me that she is writing about the Three Cliffs Valley and the Pennard Pill winding its way to the sea. And yet she does not mention the wide expanse of the bay, and the rocky headlands of the Great Tor and Oxwich Point in the distance…? And no reference is made to the most striking view of the Three Cliffs themselves, with their distinctive grey limestone peaks, that rise from the sands like three twin sisters. We shall have to wait and see, as the translation of the diary unfolds, if any more detail of the area is disclosed.

Pennard Castle has always had a special connection with me. It started when I was about five years old, while pretending to be a knight and fighting battles on its sacred grounds; and climbing its storytelling walls – which told me many things. Including that I was a real knight! And I didn't have to pretend. Later it became a sacred place for Gay and I as we shared many experiences there.

Very little is known about the history of Pennard Castle, or its inhabitants. There are a number of myths and legends about it. But I am only going to share with you what I know. Taught to me by one of the greatest historians of all, and the idol of a young boy – my Dad!

My Dad taught me that knowing history about a place is not enough to make it sacred. You have to make history with it yourself, just like with a person that becomes a friend. Then it becomes sacred and more valuable. A friend that you can go and visit at any time or season of your life and experience the connection. When I was eight, my father bought me a compass and taught me how to use it. The coordinates of the Pennard Castle area are 51.5766 degrees North and 4.1023 degrees West. It commands the view over my beloved Three Cliffs Bay, and it was built as one of a series of fortifications that secured Norman control over the Lordship of Gower. The Normans began to make intrusions into South Wales from the late 1060s onwards, advancing westwards from their bases in recently occupied England.

The castle was built on a limestone spur, overlooking the mouth of the Pennard Pill stream and Three Cliffs Bay. It is protected to the north and west by the surrounding cliffs. The fortification initially took the form of an oval-shaped ringwork [112 by 92 feet], with a defensive ditch and ramparts around the outside, and a hall made of timber in the center.

A local church, St. Mary's, was built just to the east of the castle, and a settlement was developed around the site. A rabbit warren was established in the nearby sand dunes. When

I was a boy, my dad would take my brother and I "rabbiting" in this area, and many of the burrows are still there. We put purse sets over the entrances of the rabbit burrows, and then put a ferret down one of the burrows to chase the rabbits out. Dad, my brother, and I each stood beside a burrow and as the ferret chased the rabbits out into the nets, we clubbed the rabbits and took them home to Mom and Grandma who made rabbit pie or stew. It was the smell of the ferret that frightened the rabbits, Dad said, and they started bolting out of their burrows as soon as they smelt him. The ferret "Ripper" was also my pet, and I handled him so much that I stunk like a ferret, grandmother said, suggesting that I take a bath. This worked out well for me, because my brother and I only got to have one bath a week before Ripper came to live with us, and now I got to wallow in the bath twice a week because I stunk of ferret. Maybe that's why the girl next door lost interest in me shortly after I got my ferret? Thanks Rip – I didn't really fancy her anyway!

In the early 13th century, a stone hall, approximately 61ft by 25ft, was built on the site of the older timber building, using red-purple sandstone with white limestone decoration. This part of the building's history, my dad and I can relate to personally. When I was growing up in Pennard, and went exploring with my father, the castle and its history records were mostly lost in the mists of time. But we found many wonderful things that over the years have only added to the mystery and the unknown past of my 'great friend,' Pennard Castle, whose crumbling walls still tell stories of centuries gone by. And if you listen carefully between the sweet songs of the skylarks, and the dancing spring winds that descend upon the castle from high on Cefn Bryn, secrets are still whispered from past times and past lives. And young girls in summer dresses have dreams that are born in the sacred castle grounds, and young men are told that "yes," they can still become real knights of the Gower Peninsula.

My dad and I still have a collection of the red-purple sandstone that we found in a sand dune, and it does have a white limestone detailing on each piece of stone. And it shimmers when the sun is on it, and with certain shades of light during even dull days of autumn and winter, it sparkles, which makes the rock seem like a treasure. It was for me when I first saw it sparkling in the sand. When I first showed these stones to Gay, when we were teenagers, she thought the white limestone flickers within the red-purple rocks were like the stars in the night sky. And they were! We snuggled in a sleeping bag in our sacred castle room and watched the movements of the romantic heavens shooting stars at the silver moon above.

As I said, knowing some of the history about a place is not enough to make it sacred. You must go and make a history with it yourself. Just like you would get to know a friend. Ring its ancient doorbell and wait for the draw-gates to open, and even if you can't see the gates, and only the ghosts open the door, go inside, and you will be told wonderful stories.

In 1107, Henry de Beaumont, Earl of Warwick was granted the Lordship of Gower by Henry the 1st. At this time, Wales was not a single political entity and instead was a series of independent kingdoms whose power and influence fluctuated, depending upon the strengths of their respective rulers. Whilst there was no centrally coordinated Norman invasion, magnates such as Henry de Beaumont were encouraged to seize what land they could, and in return they were rewarded by being given almost regal powers within their new territories. This strategy required a large number of castles to subdue the newly conquered regions, and the Gower Peninsula was no exception. Henry and his followers built at least seven substantial castles on the peninsula, including Pennard Castle.

When I played "Knights and Capture the Princess" with my brother and friends as a boy, I often thought about how well the castle was situated in fending off enemy armies. I would stand tall on the North-facing wall with my wooden sword in my hand, and I felt as proud of the castle as if I had built it myself; and I slammed my sword into the metal lids of garbage cans that my friends used for shields, and I ran and caught the prettiest girl. I also made spears and bows and arrows out of branches that I cut from the trees in Three Cliffs wood.

The cliffs to the north and west provided strong natural defences. And when you look out from the castle grounds at the breathtaking scenery of the Three Cliffs valley and the stream below, in the distance are the mysterious and beckoning headlands of the Great Tor and Oxwich Point that call out so loud! And you realize that the chief builder of Pennard Castle was both a romantic and a warrior. When I found a real metal sword with my father when I was twelve, I wished I could have used it on any enemy that dared attack my beloved castle.

In 1203, the Lordship of Gower was granted to the de Braose family by King John. At this time, the castle had been surpassed in style and design by others on and around the peninsula, especially Swansea and Oystermouth. Initially, the family made just a few modifications to the earthwork ring that was topped with a wooden palisade enclosing the courtyard and small stone hall. But around the late thirteenth century, the castle was rebuilt in stone. This rebuilding has been attributed to William de Braose, also known as Baron Braose. William was a powerful magnate within Edward the First's court, and he provided extensive military service to the King with his most notable achievements being the capture of the Welsh rebel William Cragh in 1290, and his participation in the battle of Falkirk in 1298, where the English defeated William Wallace. A sad season of events in my estimate! "I wish I could have fought alongside Cragh and Wallace," I said to my father as he taught me how to swing the sword we had found. "Especially Wallace – I'd love to have fought against the English!"

"We fight against them in Rugby now, Son," my dad said. "And we hammered them again this year to win the Triple Crown." Not as good as King John's head on a plate, but another Triple Crown will do!

As I am writing this, dear reader, a fond memory just galloped through the pages of my mind. I was about 13 at the time, and my father and I pushed metal rods through the thick sand that engulfed the castle grounds. And we felt what my father described as the floor of the stone hall that was built when the main structure of the castle was still made of wood. My father had made a map, and we pushed the metal rods through the sand every few feet. Anyway, it did not mean much to me at the time, but my father was ecstatic that he had found this stone floor underneath the dunes. It wasn't until I was about fifteen and a half that I began to appreciate this particular discovery, as I started to make maps myself of areas that I wanted to explore. But that is a chapter for another time. Back to the present...

Return to Canaan

His Lordship of Gower, where he exercised his extensive rights as a Marcher Lord, brought him into dispute with John de Monmouth, Bishop of Landaff. Whilst his relationship with the King enabled these issues to be resolved in his favor, it could have been this dispute that led to the upgrading of Pennard Castle. Utilizing local limestone and sandstone, the new building copied the line taken by the ringwork defence of the first castle. At this time, a twin towered gatehouse was added, as a small-scale imitation of the great Gatehouse Keeps that had recently been built in North Wales. My father and I believe that this new structure was likely aimed more at making an impression on the Bishop of Llandaff than actual defence, as it had a number of significant shortfalls. The portcullis grooves, for example, did not run all the way down to the ground, while the arrow slits were put at ineffectual positions along the castle walls. I remember Dad and I firing our arrows out of the arrow slits and trying to retrieve them from below the castle. Obviously, the flora and fauna of the landscape had changed over the centuries, along with significant trees and shrubbery, but the defence positions and layout of the arrow slits are unchanged, and it makes one ponder if indeed there was any thought of having to face an enemy setting upon the castle. I don't know how many arrows my father and I fired out of those slits, but we lost at least half of them. However, we had a lot of fun, and as a twelve-year-old boy, I wasn't just firing arrows out of the Pennard Castle walls; I was fighting against any enemy who would threaten my "great friend" Pennard Castle.

In 1320, Pennard Castle was confiscated by Edward ll. The King accused William of granting the castle to his son-in-law John de Mowbray without Royal permission. Hugh

Despenser was appointed as the Royal Warden of the castle, but as the troubles of Edward the ll's reign continued, the castle was eventually restored to de Braose, before returning to the Despensers once again, and eventually on to the Beauchamp family. However, by this time Pennard Castle was becoming overwhelmed with sand. The shifting dunes started to engulf the castle whilst the windswept sand eroded the masonry.

According to my father's studies, when exactly Pennard Castle was abandoned is unknown, but by the year 1400, there was no one there. And no one else ever moved in, probably due to its deteriorating condition. Today, there is no sign of the settlement and the church of St. Mary, and only part of a single wall of the castle remains standing.

What happened to Pennard Castle and the Settlement? According to ancient records, Pennard was never attacked, so why was it deserted? What made living conditions so unacceptable that the inhabitants left? Over the years, and during the countless hours that I played in the castle grounds as a boy and then grew into a young man who kissed a girl named Gay in our sacred castle room, I have thought about the many theories as to why the people left.

But once all the history has been said and done, I go back to that early experience of a five-year-old boy, when my mother first took me to the castle to play. There was "sand" everywhere! On the grounds and around the walls, and in my secret room. And all around the castle were the singing dunes to climb and conquer! The long sandy slopes where I raced my brother down to the valley below seemed to call to me. When the wild winds blew over the dunes, the sand stung my face and I closed my eyes, only to open them again to see my way between the gusts of the shouting winds that told me the stories of the past. There was no mistake about it! Pennard castle was abandoned to the sands. And for those who cannot understand the language of the winds, I will go on for a few more paragraphs.

My father took me to see the records of Kenfig. They state that further east on the coast of Glamorgan near Porthcawl, a succession of furious gales in the fourteenth century set the sands moving over a big area. The encroachment lasted over a hundred years and did not finally stabilize itself until well into Tudor times. The same thing must have happened at Pennard. The whole of the cliff and the high ground behind it was buried under the dunes. The inhabitants of the castle and those poor peasants of this part of Gower were driven away by the blowing, stinging sands.

'Those words that were spoken to you by the winds – they were right, boy!' Yes Sir, they were! 'The Gower has many secrets, boy. You just have to listen!' Yes Sir, I know! 'I'll see you on the next wind, boy.' Yes Sir, I'll look forward to it Sir!

Well, dear reader, that concludes my understanding so far of the history of Pennard Castle. But I am left with the wonderful mystery of Taliath's diary, and the fact that her diary entries start in the year 970, long before the presently known history of Pennard Castle ever begins. She even talks of stone walls and walking on a cold stone floor. The current recorded history of Pennard Castle states that it was built as an oval-shaped wooden ringwork structure, before at a later date being rebuilt of red-purple sandstone. So Taliath's diary contradicts the time of when it was believed to have been first built. Current records state that in the early 13th century, a stone hall was added to the existing old timber building.

Well, back to the present time.

Before dad and I had finished talking on the phone, he reminded me of the time when the police came to our door and demanded that we give them the artifacts that he and I had found. Dad had gotten hold of some ancient maps, and we had found all sorts of treasures using his metal detector. We found Roman coins, a Knight's sword and shield, and even a Viking helmet. I was eight years old when the police arrived at our house in the name of Queen Elizabeth and the Crown, and they demanded that my dad hand them over the treasures we had found. My father appeased them by giving them some old coins and the rusted sheath of a sword. I can remember crying at the door, and my father trying to console me. How dare they come and take my dad's and my treasure! It was ours! It didn't belong to some Queen in Buckingham Palace who had more treasures than she knew what to do with! And I will never forget what my dad said to me that day. He said, "Don't cry, old boy, I buried the good stuff at the bottom of the garden where no one can find it." Almost instantly my tears stopped flowing and a broad smile began to grow across my face. "Come on, blow your nose and wipe your eyes, Old Son; you don't think I would allow them to take what is ours, do you?" "No Dad, I don't!"

"Do you remember saying those things, Dad?" I asked him once. "Yes, Kings, I remember. Some experiences we remember all our lives and they become a part of us. And that is one of them."

He then said something that gave me goosebumps and sent a shiver up my spine. "Some of the treasures we found are still buried in the back garden of where we used to live on Brown's Drive."

At his words, a strong desire to go and dig them up was born right then, as I imagined who might be living in our old house, and how I could go about digging our treasures up…?

I didn't say any more to dad on the phone, but I pondered the thought of re-claiming our sacred treasures over the next few days. And when I called Gay, I told her what Dad had said. She seemed more excited than I was about going and retrieving our lost treasure. This pleased me no end, and I began to put our dastardly plan together in my mind. We would have to wait until spring though, until I returned home to Wales.

Meanwhile, I continued to copy Taliath's diary, and I sent Gay ten pages each week to translate. Slowly but surely, the wonderful tapestry of Taliath's life began to be woven together.

Chapter Two

Winters Long

Time seemed to be going by slowly now as the Canadian winter stared at us with its cold stone face, and in the shivers of the grey days of the west coast, I dreamed through the chilling mists of a faraway spring that would be coming to visit us again.

I kept myself busy, as always, by doing things with my children. My boys and I played football a lot, and we went fishing for crabs and chinook salmon in the Juan De Fuca Strait, close to where we lived in Sooke. Samantha Jade and I did a lot of walking and hiking as we explored the Southern Gulf Islands, which were only short ferry rides away from Vancouver Island.

Even with all the activities that the children and I did, winter seemed long here on the Island, especially with me so looking forward to returning to Wales. We even had a few weeks of snow! It was not cold compared with other parts of Canada, but for Vancouver Island folk, any snow is an adventure.

Across the Atlantic, Gay and Melody were having a particularly cold winter in Cardiff, and they too were looking forward to spring.

Winters Long

We continued to translate Taliath's diary, and she had even drawn a map and illustrations of landmarks on the Gower Peninsula, which included areas where castles were erected later during the Roman and Norman occupations of Gower – Swansea, Loughor, Oystermouth, Penrice, Penmaen, and specifically, Pennard! Dad was excited when I shared with him the news of Gay's latest translation and the discovery of the map. And he said that if Gay had translated the words correctly, the map would be unique, as it included the spot where St. Mary's Church was later built! Only one small fragment remains of the church today, and practically nothing is known about its history, other than it is believed to have been associated with Pennard Castle, and that it was part of a small settlement that grew up nearby and was then abandoned in 1532. I used to climb on it as a boy and play "battling knights" around it with my friends.

Dad thought we might have discovered a complete map of what he believed could be the church and lost village of St. Mary's. When I shared the news with Gay, she was excited! And we wondered if Taliath would share anything about the church later in her diary? We would have to wait and see.

I made two copies of the map, and I sent one out to Gay and another to Dad in Swansea. As I examined the map more closely, the illustrations, for the most part, were clear and easy to understand. There were buildings and what looked to be a whole village settlement around a significantly larger building. And there appeared to be a village square, a well, and animal pens.

I could not wait to receive word back from Dad and Gay. The time just could not go by quickly enough, until finally two weeks later I received letters back. Dad had also included his translations in the package, and he had written in pencil the translated English words beside the Celtic ones. They read: St. Mary's Church and village. Wow! Could this really be the map of St. Mary's Church and the settlement, when so little, if anything, was known about them?

On the top half of the map, Dad had translated the words around a large building, which by its illustration looked like a castle. It was some distance away from St. Mary's Church and the settlement. The more I looked at the drawing, the more convinced I became that it was Pennard Castle. It had to be! There were no more large buildings on that part of the map. And dad had translated the words to mean 'Pennard Castle.' A strange feeling of awe, and mystery, came over me, and it was as if I knew in my soul that I was staring at a map of the "fabled, lost-in-the-dunes-of-time, St. Mary's Church." Still, a part of me wrestled with the idea – could this really be true? But according to this map, and the translation of the words that identified those buildings, it was true! And my excitement was not over yet – there was more! Dad had also penciled in on the map something that Gay and I had missed. It was coordinated to an illustration of what Dad called a chest or trunk. The word in front of the illustration read "chest."

Dad had also sent a letter with his map, sharing that he did not want to miss out on the translation of the diary that Gay and I were working on, and would I please send him regular copies of the diary as I was doing with Gay? Of course, I agreed. With both Gay and Dad translating, the translation would likely be quicker and more accurate, I thought. Gay and I had already missed finding the coordinates to what might be a chest.

Winters Long

After reading Dad's letter, and studying the map several more times, I called him on the phone. I was far too excited to reply by letter, or even by email – I wanted to hear his voice.

He was pleased that I called, and he shared that he was looking forward to doing some more exploring around the castle with his metal detector, and of course near the remaining piece of wall of St. Mary's Church. He asked me to keep quiet about our map and to be careful not to tell anyone else about it, even in Canada.

I sensed the tone in my father's voice as being both excited and guarded. It was a reading of his voice that I had learned as a boy when he believed he was close to discovering something wonderful, like ancient coins, armour and swords. I remembered the day when we found the "Viking Helmet." For months, he was so protective of the area where we had found it, and he forbade me to say anything to my friends. "Not even your mother can be told," he said. "You know how those women talk at their weekly coffee hour."

Before we hung up the phone, we joked again about the time when the police came around and confiscated some of our finds. And Dad said, "I hope you're not planning to go digging at the back of our old house when you come back." I laughed and said, "What is ours is ours."

"I agree, Old Son," he replied, "but if you go digging in other people's gardens you will get in trouble." Dad always seemed to know when I was planning something mischievous in my heart, and this time was no exception.

"We will all meet at Pennard Castle when you come back in the spring, Kings."

"Yeah, that's right, Dad. I'll meet you at Pennard Castle.

Bye Dad, I'll send you copies of Taliath's Diary, and I'll call you in a few weeks."

I couldn't wait to tell Gay about Dad's translation of the map and what he said, and I called her in the middle of the night. "Wake up, lovely lady."

"What, my love, what is it? Is everything alright?"

"Yes, I just had to call you and tell you the news!"

She soon woke up and became excited as I told her about my conversation with Dad, even though it was two in the morning British time.

After we had expressed our excitement about the map, Gay shared that she was particularly glad I had called before morning. Why? I asked, as I heard an uneasy tone in her voice. "Melody is being teased again at school, and she is missing you walking her to the classroom. Can you call her again in the morning before she leaves for school? I think she just needs you to reassure her that you are coming back."

Gay's words tugged at my heart. I knew what it was like to be teased, and even bullied. "Of course, I will call in the morning," I replied. I set my alarm for midnight, which would be 8 a.m. British time, and I would catch Melody as she was having her breakfast.

I was awake before my alarm went off and I called right at midnight. "Dad, dad!" Melody's voice was full of excitement. "Yes, my Princess, what is going on?"

"There are two mean girls teasing me at school," she said. "They keep telling me that you are not coming back, and that I don't have a dad. I know that it's not true, and that you are coming back in the spring, but they keep saying it to me every day and it makes me sad."

Winters Long

"Oh, my Princess," I reassured her, "I will be coming home soon, and I can't wait to walk with you to school again and see what you have been doing in your classroom. Now you listen to me very carefully, Melody. I love you bunches and bunches!"

"Do you mean like more than all the bluebells on the path to Pobbles, where you and Mom kiss?" asked Melody.

"Yes, that's right. More than all the bluebells in the spring! Wait a minute, you sneaky Princess, how do you know that Mom and I kiss in the bluebells? Have you been spying?"

Melody began to laugh, and I could hear Gay laughing in the background.

"Okay, you two," Gay said. "It's time to hang up the phone. Otherwise, you will be late for school, Melody."

Melody giggled. "It's Princess Melody to you, Mom," she said.

"Oh, and there's one more thing I need to remind you about, Princess," I said.

"What is it, Dad? What is it?"

"I'm coming home in just seven more weekends!"

"Really? Really, Dad? Mom, Dad's coming home in just seven more weekends! And he loves me more than all the bluebells in the spring!"

As Gay took over the phone, I could hear Melody's excited voice continuing in the background. "Mom and I miss you like the springtime, Dad, and Grandma Helen misses you too!"

"Oh, thank you, my love," Gay said on the phone. "She's beaming now, with a big smile across her face. And I miss you too, my Prince. I don't know how Melody and I can go another seven weeks without you."

Gower Peninsula Adventure Series

And she wept as I told her that I could not wait to see them.

The following week, I booked my flight home for May 30th, landing at London's Gatwick Airport at 10:15 a.m. My children would join us later when their college and university classes were finished. It was going to be a lot of fun having us all together, and I looked forward to taking us on an adventure around the Gower. By the time college and university was out, it would be warm enough to swim and body surf in the sea.

The following Thursday, I phoned Melody again, and I told her I had bought my plane tickets to come home, and that my daughter, Samantha Jade, was looking forward to getting to know her new sister, and she wanted to build a sand boat with her on Pobbles Beach. Gay and her mom were getting excited about meeting my children too, which made me feel happy. There would be some adjusting to do as we all got to know each other, I thought. But with God's help and blessing, everything would work out in the best way it could.

Romans 8 verse 23, [And we know that God causes everything to work together for good for those who love God and are called according to his purpose.]

This was one of the Bible verses I had read each day after returning to Canada, and God was using it to encourage me and to grow my faith, as I put my trust in him to work everything out for Gay and I and our family.

Meanwhile, I had received a letter from my friends, David and Jackie Griffiths. David had offered me the youth pastor's position at his church in Swansea. It was only part time for the present, with me working two weekdays and Sunday mornings.

So, I would not have to commute every day from Cardiff. And he and Jackie had invited me to stay at their home on one of the weeknights, which would make things even easier. I was looking forward to spending more time with David and Jackie, and having them as mentors for Gay and I.

Eventually, Gay and I wanted to move back to the Gower, so we could give Melody the wonderful heritage that growing up on the Gower Peninsula gave to us.

Time was racing by now, and in another two weeks I would be on my way home to Wales.

Although the winter had been long, it had also been exciting for my children and I on Vancouver Island. My youngest son Ben and his team, the Lake Hill Reds, had won the Lower Island Soccer Cup, known locally as the "Lisa Cup." Ben had scored a lot of their goals, one of which was the defining goal to get the Reds into the Cup's final game. And then in the final, he scored two of the three goals to take the trophy! That is two years in a row that he's helped his team win the cup. Ben is following in the footsteps of his older brother, Jonathan, who holds the league record in most goals scored in a season – and the most hat-tricks scored in both league and cup competitions! And I got to be his coach. Yeah!

I must also share the success of my daughter Samantha Jade, with her "wonderful art." She has an amazing ability to inspire my writing through her pictures – they come alive to me and help birth the expression and passion of my stories. She is also at University, training to be an art therapist, and I know she will be so amazing at helping people through art. Yes, dear reader, my children have made me a proud dad!

Nan's Nan, and the Pirates of Port-Eynon

∽

The day of my flight arrived. And as much as I hated going through customs at Vancouver International, I had found a great deal on a flight departing from Vancouver, so I would grin and bear it. Or should I say, "frown and bare it." If you smile at them in Vancouver, they think you are an Islamic terrorist. That's alright with me. I don't want to smile at them anyway.

I had booked a BC Ferries Connector from Victoria to the airport in Vancouver. That way I could leave my suitcase on the coach while we made the ferry crossing to the Mainland and I wouldn't have the hassle of having to catch two regular and always over-crowded, transit buses to get me to Vancouver International Airport.

It is a long journey from Sooke on Vancouver Island to Swansea bus depot in South Wales. There is a saying: "The journey to a friend's house is never far." I beg to differ when one has been traveling for thirty hours straight! But I was traveling to be with "my love." That could never be too far.

My Son Jonathan drove me to the coach station, and with a bear hug and a promise to send him Liverpool's latest jersey, I was on my way. "Don't forget to watch the Rugby World Cup," he shouted, as the coach pulled away.

"I won't," I shouted back. "I'll call you after the first Wales game!"

"I hate to tell you, Dad, but I'm going for England this time!"

"You're not!" I shouted. "I won't let you!"

"I am, Dad, and I'm sure they are going to finally thrash those New Zealand All Blacks!"

Now the fight was on, as I stood up from my seat and shouted all the louder. But it was time to sit down and be quiet, the driver said. Those poofs play American football over here, I thought, as I obeyed the driver and sat down. Yeah, those Americans and Canadians could not play rugby if they tried! How did they ever even qualify for the World Cup? They won't even get out of the group stages. And they didn't!

We soon arrived at Swartz Bay ferry terminal and boarded the ferry. As soon as the coach driver parked and opened the doors, I headed up to the upper deck so I could sit outside and enjoy the spectacular views of the Southern Gulf Islands.

It was a beautiful day to travel as the sun kissed my face, and the cool wind gently blew through my hair beneath a blue sky. And I thought of my Gay and Melody, waiting for me in my beloved Wales, as I waltzed with the wind across the deck. "Who are you dancing with?" asked a seagull passing by. 'Why, the Spring Wind, of course!' "I see," he said, moving his head from side to side and then gliding off to Salt Spring Island.

♪※

IT IS SPRING ON THE GOWER AGAIN
A POEM, BY KINGSLEY AND SAMANTHA

Oh, how the music of spring refreshes and revives my wintered soul, as the sun kisses my face again, and I recognize my lover's taste and call out her name. The wind, which has only given me the warmth of a polite stranger, has become my playmate again, as he blows the veiling grey which has hung, oh so heavy, over the valley of Three Cliffs Bay – which has come alive again today!

Skylarks sing, honeybees buzz, and butterflies skip from heather to primrose and dance through the warm drops of rain. Behold, my soul, it is springtime on the Gower, and with the birds I sing a new song in the warmth of the falling shower, as I emerge from long shadows and I shout with the skylarks. 'I am ready to play again.' Yes, I am ready to dance and swim across Pobbles Bay, and to be told more ancient stories from the daffodils and the chatting stones along the high tide shore. Only a kiss and a wink from a girl could make it more!

Mr. Seagull listens, and I am ready to lose myself and find me again in the warm gentle breezes that blow through the dunes, and in the thousand different greens of Three Cliffs Woods, as I splash in the Pennard Pill, while Mr. Pennard Castle smiles and keeps still, as he looks down from his mighty hill. I will run down your golden sandy paths as fast as legs will carry. Oh, what a thrill! Hello everyone, I am Kingsley Hill! And I am King of the Castle! And I wish upon all the stars as they come out in their shiny jackets behind the westering sun, enough of them to twinkle and give new hope to everyone. The moon is rising and listens to his friend the sun, who makes promises of beautiful days and wonderful things to come, and he even has knowledge of the Holy One.

Winters Long

I am ready now for my journey between the moon and the setting sun, back to those longer days that lead me down those hidden and forgotten paths toward my dreams and a thousand new beginnings, as lovely as the spring and the golden dawn. Behold my soul, it is spring reborn on the Gower again!

© *Kingsley Ross Hill*

As the ferry passed the northern tip of Salt Spring Island, two bald eagles flew overhead, reminding me of my maiden voyage in taking the ferry from Tsawwassen on the mainland to Swartz Bay on Vancouver Island. Within minutes I realized that I was coming to my "promised land." The beauty of the Gulf Islands and the ocean wilderness are breathtaking! And like so many other things in life, we can take for granted their beauty and the people that are dear to us. Life is very fragile and goes by so quickly, cried the eagles that flew right over my head. "Indeed, it is, and it does, Mr. Eagle," I called back. And I vowed in my heart to try not to take for granted this wonderful life that I have been so blessed with. It was almost time to board the coach again as we were fast approaching the Tsawwassen ferry terminal. On the approach to Tsawwassen, if you look carefully into the ocean, you can see a distinct brown colouring of the water, which is caused by the mighty Fraser River gushing into the sea just south of Steveston, having dug up lots of mud and silt on its long journey. And today the muddy Fraser River sang loudly, contrasting with the clear blue/green each side of its flow into the Salish Sea.

The call to return to my coach was aired over the loud speaker as we arrived at Tsawwassen terminal. Tsawwassen is an Indian name meaning "the land facing the sea."

After a forty-minute coach ride, we arrived at the airport, which I had previously re-named "Happyville." And I wondered if it would yet again live up to its cheerful name.

I had plenty of time to spare before my flight departed for Gatwick, but I decided to check my luggage in right away and get through the hassle of security before it got too busy. The less stress the better. It is a long flight of nine-and-a-half to ten hours, as long we had a tail wind and little turbulence. And I wondered what was worse – going through heavy turbulence or going through security at YVR? I did not have to think too hard to answer that one; going through security at YVR was far worse! They treat people like fugitives, even if you are a Canadian citizen. And most of them have the personality of a "stop sign." Smile once in a while! It helps to put people at ease you know! Obviously, you don't! Are you afraid your teeth are going to fall out?

Today, surprisingly, wasn't so bad, and the woman reminded me of the episode on Winnie the Pooh when Eeyore almost smiled! Maybe she had won the lottery the night before, or had a romantic evening with her husband? Or maybe she was just thinking of Chinese New Year? Wonders will never cease. Finally, the hours turned to minutes and I boarded my plane. It was evening now, and we would be flying into the night. Maybe I would be able to get some sleep on the flight, but I generally only closed my eyes and rested when flying. And today, well, I was so excited thinking about seeing Gay and Melody.

As it turned out, it was a good flight, with very few bumps across the Atlantic and the Channel, and I surprised myself by getting a few hours sleep.

We landed at Gatwick right on time, and it was a cool London morning as I exited the plane.

As soon as I was through security, I saw Gay and Melody. Melody ran into my arms, almost knocking me over.

"Oh, Dad!" she cried, "I missed you so much!"

"I missed you so much too, my Princess! And this is a lovely surprise – I thought you would be at school."

"No. Mum and I wanted to surprise you! And she said I could have the day off school so I could come and meet you!"

"Well, this is extra, extra special to have you come with Mum to meet me!"

Melody beamed at my words.

As I looked up, I saw Gay's radiant face. She was wearing my favourite green and white dress, and high heel shoes, and her hair was long and flowing, and on her neck was the evening emerald necklace that I had given her when we had first met. Oh, you look so beautiful, my love! And as I looked into her eyes, they welled up with tears and she blushed as bright as the sunrise. And we just held each other for the longest time, as we melted the months and weeks and hours away.

"I couldn't have gone one more minute," Gay whispered.

"One more minute," Melody repeated, and then said, "Now that's love, if you and Mum couldn't go another minute."

Gay and I laughed and said, "Yes, its love, and we couldn't go another minute."

And what about me!" Melody exclaimed. "And I couldn't go another second before seeing you again," I said.

She giggled as she took my hand and then grinned like a Cheshire cat.

"Come on you two," Gay said, "let's get the suitcases back to the car and head home to Cardiff."

And soon we were on our way. As we drove through the London traffic and onto the motorway, the morning soon turned into a lovely spring day, and it was as if even the blue sky and the sunshine were welcoming me back, and indeed they were.

"Look, Dad," Melody said, "even the sunshine came out to see you!"

And I smiled at the world. Words could not describe how happy I felt inside, and then I felt Gay take my hand, and my heart danced.

After a three-hour journey, we arrived at our home in Cardiff. And Gay's mum, Helen, had come over and cooked us a lovely meal.

"Thank you, Helen," I said. "It's so nice to have a home-cooked meal instead of airplane food."

"I'm glad you're enjoying it, Kingsley, I knew you would be hungry after your long journey. And it's made with love."

"Made with love," Melody echoed with a giggle. "That's right, Melody!" Gay exclaimed. "Grandma made tea with love."

"And love makes the world go around, that's what my mum told me," I added.

Melody roared with laughter! "Did you hear that, Mum? Dad said love makes the world go around! Is that true, Grandma?"

"Yes, it's true," Grandma replied, and we all laughed.

After tea, Helen went home to her house, which was just a short walk from our home on Bute St.

"I will leave you three to rest, and I'll see you on the weekend," she said.

"Bye Mum, and thank you for making tea," Gay and I shouted out.

It had always felt strange for me to call Helen 'Mum.' She was still so young, far too young to be a grandmother, I thought. She looked like she was in her early forties. As soon as Gay and I had become engaged, she had invited me to call her 'Mum.' This was very dear to me, as my mum had only recently passed, and it felt good to say 'Mum' again.

After I told Melody a short bedtime story and promised her that I would walk her to school in the morning, we all headed off to bed. The next day was Friday, and Gay had taken the day off work so we could have a long weekend together.

"Oh, my love, I have waited so long to hold you in my arms again. It's so good to hold you," I told her. And as we made love, our bodies told what words could not say, healing our loneliness and relieving our deep need for one another.

"I can't get close enough to you either," she whispered.

And as we looked into each other's eyes, we traveled deep within each other's souls, and I said, "You are here within me."

"Yes," she whispered, "I can feel you inside my soul. You beat my heart, my love, and you are the song of my life."

And we sang together until dawn.

I awoke whole and refreshed, and I thanked my God for bringing me home!

Suddenly there was a thump on the door, and Melody came in and jumped onto our bed, and we all had a wrestling match until it was time for breakfast.

"Dad, did you let me win?"

"No, Princess, you have grown strong."

"Did you hear that, Mum? I'm a strong Princess!"

"Yes, you are, and Dad can see how much you've grown."

It was gammon, eggs, fried tomatoes, and toast with marmalade for breakfast. Yum! I had sure missed having a good British breakfast!

After Melody had put on her best dress and Gay had helped her with her hair, I walked her to school. She was so proud as she took my hand, and as we reached the playground, she looked around at her friends and peers, and said aloud, "See, here's my dad, and I'm his princess!"

And in my heart, I rejoiced at her victory! I knew that many of the girls had teased and made fun of her while I had been away. Now they stared at her with envy as she let go of my hand and did a spin in her new dress like a dancing butterfly.

"My, what a lovely dress! And I like your hair, Melody," said Miss Jones, her teacher. "And welcome back, Kingsley," she continued, having remembered me from the last time I had walked Melody to school. "Melody has been excited for months, and she's been talking about you walking her to class, and here you are!"

"And congratulations on your marriage to Gay," she added. "I'm happy for both of you, and I know that Melody is blessed to have a dad in her life."

"Thank you, Miss Jones."

"Oh, please call me Olivia."

"Alright. Thank you Olivia, I look forward to talking to you again soon."

"Bye, Melody, have a great day!"

The walk back to the house was just long enough for me to say my morning prayers, and I thanked God for Gay and Melody's love.

By the time I arrived at the house, Gay had already packed us a picnic, and she asked if I would like to go to Pobbles Beach for the day. And of course, I replied that I would love to!

"What a wonderful way to spend my first day back in Wales, a day at Pobbles Beach with you!" "I know what my man likes," she replied, her eyes dancing with excitement. And then as she retreated shyly, her lovely pink blush began to adorn her face as I looked deep into her violet eyes. "Oh, Kingsley," she sighed, "I love you so much!"

"I love you too!" I echoed.

Chapter Three

Love and Bluebells

It was an hour's drive from Cardiff to Swansea, and then another half an hour or so to Pennard Cliffs. And then a beautiful walk along the West Cliff path to Pobbles.

As we drove, Gay shared that Helen was picking Melody up from school and having her for the evening. This would give us time to spend the whole day and evening together, and I began to think of how wonderful it would be to watch the sunset.

When we reached Pennard Village, we decided to park the car there instead of continuing through the village and out to the cliffs. We would walk to Pobbles along the path beside the golf links, as this was the way we used to walk in the days of our youth. And today I felt like I was falling in love with Gay all over again. And in my heart, I wanted to court her again. We had been apart for so long, it seemed, and I wanted to make her feel special.

When we reach the bluebell meadow along the path, I thought, if the bluebells are in bloom, I will pick her one, and I will ask her if I can court her all over again, like I did when I was 15.

Love and Bluebells

We parked the car on Bendrick Drive and started our walk. At the bottom of Bendrick Drive are the remains of an ancient well, that once upon a time had provided all Pennard with water. It was still just as I remembered it – a little bog and a stream where the well had once stood, and then the stream disappeared underground into the passages of time. Sometimes during particularly wet weather, it would bubble up into a spring and form a pool. When I was a boy, it was not uncommon to find frogs and tadpoles in its shallow muddy waters. And today we saw three tadpoles and a baby frog. How wonderful in this ever-changing world to find something that stays the same, even if it is a little spring that bubbles up from the ground. It brings water and sustains life for little tadpoles and the wild Water Irises and Primroses that drink and smile from its banks. And we said hello to the little spring as if reacquainting with a lost friend, and then we carried on with our adventure.

Gay had always been so interested in my boyhood, and how special it was. I reveled in the glow of her interest, and when I had been fifteen, I wanted to kiss her just for that. And today, as I put my hand in hers, I felt again how wonderful it was to share one's life with another who is interested in your past as well as the present and the future.

I told her that, and she said, "It's all part of loving you, Kingsley." And I thought: 'how wonderful and mysterious it is, that being really loved in the present can somehow reach back into our past and heal us of the wounds that were inflicted there.'

As we continued along the path towards the beach, the sights and sounds of spring thrilled our senses, as if they were celebrating with us. The lush green bracken appeared on each side of the sandy path, and I remembered that in the autumn it turned the colour of flaming red, and before the November rains it becomes a soft nut brown.

Suddenly we heard the sharp "u-tick" and "u-tick-tick," coming from a small bird who was perched on the top of a high twig on a furze bush. The "u-tick" is his warning sound that someone is approaching. The bird is a Whinchat -rather smaller than a sparrow but it has a light-coloured eye strip and a delicately tinted buff-coloured breast – attracting our attention at the same time as he warned his mate of danger. When he has your attention, he flies to the top twig of another furze bush a short distance away and then repeats his warning. Gay and I literally played a game of hide and seek with the little Whinchat for quite some time along the path, and it was fun.

When I had lived in Bacon Hole on Pennard Cliffs, I would play with the Whinchats for hours in the early springtime. And I learned that this jumping from twig to twig goes on until the Whinchats ruse has succeeded and he has drawn you to what he thinks is a safe distance from his nest. He then will suddenly disappear, flying low behind the cover of the bushes and bracken and back to his first guard post.

No sooner had we finished our game of hide and seek with the Whinchat when we heard a "h-weet jur jur" sound.

"What's that sound?" Gay asked. It sounded like another warning sound, but different from the Whinchat's call.

"That's a Stonechat," I answered with pride. "And you are right. He is sending out an alarm that we are coming. There he is, can you see him? Look, he is similar to the Whinchat, but he has a black head and red breast. When I was a boy, we used to call Stonechats 'little Jacky-Tops.' Stonechats also dart from bush to bush and draw you away from their nests."

"Where's your nest?" I asked Gay with a cheeky smile. "Are you going to lead me away or let me into your feathered domain?"

"Come to my nest, you Jacky-Top," ordered Gay, as she smiled and pulled me down onto the sandy path where we kissed and twisted to the now loud calls of both the Whinchat and the Stonechat. "Do you think they approve?" Gay asked, wiping her lipstick from my face. "I think you look more like the Stonechat with the red," she said, laughing. "And are you going to protect me and warn me of danger like that little bird?"

"Yes," I replied, and I planted a passionate kiss on her lips.

"Mmm, my Prince, you are going to protect me, aren't you! I can tell just by the way you kiss me." I pulled Gay up from our sandy blanket, and we continued on our way.

Soon we arrived at one of our most sacred places. And we looked at one another with joy, as we were instantly taken back to that first spring that we spent together and fell in love.

It was our "bluebell meadow," a sea of blue gently rolling into the scotch pines. "Do you remember how you would hold me for hours, my Prince, as we sat in our meadow of waving dreams, listening to the birds and watching the butterflies and clouds?"

"Yes, my Princess, I could never forget. You would let your hair down for me and I would kiss your neck and get lost in your curls."

Gay blushed like a pink rose as I cupped her face in my hands and looked deep into her eyes; and they beckoned me to fall deeper and deeper, back in time to the souls of our youth.

I could feel my heart pounding as she took the ribbon from her hair, and gently shook her head as her flowing hair fell to her waist.

"Let us sit down, my love," she whispered, "here amongst the bluebells that tell the stories of our days." "Here in front of their watching eyes," I echoed, "for they keep our secrets safe within their bulbs through the long winter, and then they bring them out to us today, like a banquet all prepared for the celebration of our love."

I spread our picnic blanket upon the meadow and lay her gently down amidst the whispering and jealous flowers, and I pushed my fingers through her hair and smelled the faint perfume on her neck. She gave a sigh and trembled at my kiss and caress. From deep to deep, we fell into yesteryear even though it was today, and all the bluebells shouted hurray, hurray, hurray. Welcome Gay and Kingsley, back to your spring day.

On the hill I spotted some white bluebells. "Close your eyes, love, and stay here."

"What is it?" she asked.

"Wait and see, and keep your eyes closed…. Now open them!"

"They are white bluebells! And the little bells remind me of our wonderful wedding, and white is the colour of our marriage."

"And they remind me of you, my love," I echoed, "rare and more beautiful than all the others."

She wept at my words and I kissed her tears. "Oh, how I love you, my Gay. And there is something I want to ask you."

"What is it, my King? Tell me as we lie in our sacred meadow."

Love and Bluebells

"I want to court you all over again, just like I did in the days of our youth."

"Oh yes, please court me again. It is what my heart desires, for this is our first day together after such a long time."

Yes, I will court you, my love, and I will start today.

"Thank you, my King. There is none like you. You are gentle, and robed in kindness, and so handsome. Your eyes of green are deep, and they sparkle like the emerald sea, and reflect your beautiful soul. You are as brave as a lion to dwell in caves and live off the land and sea, and strong enough to be my man when you were yet a youth. And your heart still sings the song called Wild and Free, and like your galloping stallion, 'Great Thunder,' each new day you catch and captivate me."

"You have heard it said that a woman is most beautiful when she is in love. It is true. I am most beautiful when I am with you. You give me your courage and strength, and you keep my heart warm and alive in this dark and dangerous world. You have mined my heart and shown me my reflection within your own soul. I know that I am loved, and oh, so deeply. My heart kindles a fire for you that cannot be quenched. Let us lie in the dunes at sunset, my Prince, and celebrate our love."

"Yes, let us find our room in the dunes when the evening shadows fall upon the sands, and the night clouds march across the sky, and the sea turns to evening emerald." "Yes, my King, we shall find our room in the dunes where the long grasses grow. And look, I am wearing your necklace! 'Evening emerald,' the one that led you back to me."

"Do you remember when we first lay in our meadow, and there was only one white bluebell plant? And today there are seven."

"Yes, I remember. The seven plants symbolize our new family – You, Me, Melody and Mum, and now there are your children too, who I will love like my own."

"Yes, they do represent our family," I replied, breathing in the fresh spring air.

From the middle of our sacred meadow, we walked back to the winding sandy path toward Pobbles. Here and there, between the wild gorse and the happy hills, we saw glimpses of the sea, and then the limestone peaks of the Three Cliffs, and further in the distance the majestic headlands of the Great Tor and Oxwich Point. And it was as if all my Gower memories and adventures were traveling with me and singing in my heart with the happy spring.

What more could I want? My love is holding my hand, and her gentle caress, and her whispers and promises of oh, such wonderful things to come, as we waltz through our secret garden in our beloved Gower.

As we approached Pobbles, the sand dunes, with their golden paths and long grasses, rose high to greet us on our right, the peaks of the dunes contrasting with the deep blue sky. A kestrel hovered as it sought its prey, and two magpies jumped and cackled on the lower slopes. And in the distance, the roar of the tumbling waves welcomed us to our day on the beach.

And Gay looking up at the dunes, said what I was thinking. "Do you remember when we found our own room amongst the long grasses? We made love in the warm sand, and then went swimming in the sea."

"Yes, I remember, and tonight we will find our room underneath the stars."

Love and Bluebells

Gay began to blush, and she echoed: 'yes, we will find our room in the dunes and watch the sunset behind Oxwich Point.'

We arrived at the beach and climbed over the chatting pebbles at the top of the cove. The tide was a fair way out, and the sand was wet before the retreating surf.

"It's still going out!" Gay shouted excitedly. "We can explore our cave and walk through the archway at Three Cliffs."

"Yes, we can," I replied, and we looked around to find a place to put our towels and backpacks.

There are many little nooks and sandy dens between the rocks on Pobbles, where one can claim their own little spot. And as we looked around each little nook and corner, the rocks themselves seemed to call out, and they sang a sweet memory song that shook hands with my boyhood and teenage years. Sacred places are like friends, aren't they? – when they talk and converse with your memories.

Today Gay and I chose a place that was always one of "my best friends," a square of sand that lies against the rocks in front of the Dragon Pool, where Melody and I had started emptying its mysterious waters last summer, and we caught two seahorses.

Gay and I leaned over the rocks and peered into the Dragon Pool, but its waters were a deep emerald, and we couldn't see the bottom. On days like this, it appears to be bottomless, but in fact it is only four-and-a-half to five-and-a-half feet deep, depending on how much sand the tides and storms have pushed into the pool. Once I stood on its soft sand and it was only a few feet deep. This was after a strong westerly gale. The following week it was deep and murky again, and up to my chest.

"The Dragon Pool is even more sacred to me now, even more than on the day my father taught me how to dive into its depths," I said. "It's where I met Melody, and she led me back to you, my lovely lady."

Gay answered with a blush, and her eyes sparkled like the sun's rays that shimmered upon the surface of the pool.

We were hungry now, and we rested with our backpacks against the rocks to have our lunch. The smell of sea and salt filled the air, and the roar of the distant waves grew louder.

"I think the tide is coming in again, Kings… It is! Look at the swells building out on the bay. Let's have our lunch and then go exploring."

Gay had packed a wonderful lunch of crab sandwiches, cockles, and Welsh cakes for afters.

"Wow, love! This is the most amazing lunch!" She had always made these wonderful picnics, ever since we had first met, and I was living in Leathers Hole. We would climb the path to Cefn Bryn and sit on King Arthur's Stone, and eat our picnics amongst the ponies. And Gay changed the name of Arthur's Stone to "Kingsley's Stone," which I am still proud of to this day. Oh, where had the years gone? It is true that the days of our youth are special. But loving Gay as a mature woman seemed even more wonderful.

"It's the not having to say goodbye or goodnight, and then being apart, that makes it so wonderful," she said. "There is nothing more wonderful than holding you tight at night, my love. And saying nite-nite, and then waking up in your arms."

"Yes," I echoed, "there is nothing like it. And do you remember when we would kiss and cuddle in the warm dunes and wake all tangled up together?"

Love and Bluebells

"Yes," she giggled, "how could I forget? I burned for you like blazing June."

"And you are still my hot sunshine," I said, "and the warmth of my soul."

After we had finished our lunch, we went exploring our sacred haunts. First, we went to our family cave and re-lived our wedding day.

"Mum still talks about us getting married on the beach," said Gay, laughing. "I'll never forget her trying to walk along the sand in her high heels, and finally, after nearly falling over several times, taking them off and walking barefoot. She said that taking her heels off and walking across the sands was like losing her virginity."

We both roared with laughter.

"And do you remember Autumn Dancer?" I asked. "And how he came and stood at our side when we made our vows! That was so incredible! He knew that it was a sacred time, and that he was such a part of it. How many people have a wild stallion as their best man? This cave will always be our most sacred place."

"How many people get to experience what we did? Even in a whole lifetime?"

"The answer to your question is no one," squawked a passing gull. "You are the Cave Man and Cave Woman of Pennard Cliffs!"

"I like that title, don't you, my love?"

"We do indeed," we both agreed.

And I shouted out, "Thank you, Mr. Gull. Charlee, isn't it?"

"Yes, of course, don't you remember? I flew over your wedding – you did invite me, you know!"

"Yes, Charlee, of course we remember, and thank you for flying by. And please give our love to Sylvia."

"I will," he squawked, and then glided off.

After sitting in our cave and remembering our stories with our horse family, we headed toward Three Cliffs.

I piggy-backed Gay across the Killy Willy stream, just as I had done in our teens.

"Don't drop me Kings!" she screamed, as I wobbled my legs and pretended to fall. The tide had come in a fair way now, but we still had time to walk through the archway of the Three Cliffs Rock and explore the emerald pool, before the encroaching waves reached us.

"Come on, love," Gay shouted, pulling me through the archway to the pool. "Quick, let's go in for a swim before the waves reach us."

I quickly scanned the beach for other people. There was no one close by, only a man and his dog in the distance.

Gay stripped off her clothes and jumped in. "It's still got some warmth left from the afternoon sun," she shouted excitedly! "Come on in, my cave man!"

I quickly undressed and jumped in. "If this is warm, I hate to think what cold is!" I shouted. "It is refreshing though."

Gay laughed and swam over to me, and we kissed salty kisses and wallowed around like mermaid people in our emerald pool. Then the waves reclaimed the archway and came crashing into the pool. The sea was cold, and we were soon shivering.

I climbed out first and handed Gay her towel. We quickly dried each other and got dressed, just in time to wade around the point and back across the beach to Pobbles. We just got back to our backpacks as the waves reached our spot at the Dragon Pool.

Love and Bluebells

As I have mentioned before, the height and fall of the tides, and the speed in which they come in from the Bristol Channel are second only to the Bay of Fundy in Canada. So, one has to be wary of the tides when venturing on to certain beaches on the Gower Peninsula.

Gay took my hand and led me up into the dunes above Pobbles. The late afternoon sun still warmed the sand that stuck to our feet like velvet slippers. We soon found our room in the dunes, surrounded by the long grasses that whistled and danced in the high tide breeze. We lay down our towels and undressed. And as we lay on our warm blanket of sand, we felt like we were on our honeymoon again, as the sound of the surf and the skylarks sang a lullaby over our heads. And every fibre of my being joined the singing skylarks and the wild surf, and I sang a song called "I'm so glad to be alive." And we loved and laughed until our bodies were spent, and we fell asleep wrapped in arms and legs and dreamed of only this: "Kings and Gay in love's sweet bliss, and we dream of staying forever like this."

We woke to the stir of the evening breeze and its cool breath on our exposed skin. We cuddled tightly until we were warm again, and the sweet smell of the spring grasses and the salt-flavoured air greeted our nostrils as a magpie cackled on the hill above us. The chorus of the singing sea roared from a distance, as its receding waves retreated to their faraway dreams off Oxwich Point and Port Eynon Bay.

We continued to lie in our warm blanket of sand, and we looked deeply into each other's eyes. And we sang and danced in our sea of love, until the westering sun tilted his hat in the sky and our blanket grew slowly cold.

YOU DANCE UPON THE WATERS OF MY LIFE
A POEM FOR YOU, MY LOVE

Upon the waters of my life, there dances a beautiful light.
A light of awareness and shining truth.
She is as deep as the oceans and the mysteries thereof.
Who can know her eternal soul,
other than the God who lives within us?
Gay, you dance upon the waters of my life,
And like a crashing wave your love comes and fills me.
I love you my darling, for you dance
upon the waters of my life.

© *Kingsley Ross Hill*

We watched as the sun sank lower on the horizon, and the night clouds began their somber march across the sky, announcing the ending of the day. And I recited a poem I had written when I was the Caveman of Bacon Hole, many tides ago.

TWILIGHT STILL
A POEM

There is a time before the darkness,
and it is after the day's bright when my soul stands still.
Twilight Still.
The sun lays down her head,

Love and Bluebells

still glowing through her blankets
upon the western sky.
She is still before she dreams in the shadows.
Twilight Still.
The sleeping hours of the day
have been lived and have gone,
and they lie still in my memory song.
Twilight Still.
The night clouds they come,
wearing their silent silver gown
and the meadowlark is quiet below.
I watch as the moon and the owl,
race the silence over Cefn Bryn Hill.
It is now that my soul knows that it is,
Twilight Still,
Twilight Still, Twilight Still.

© *Kingsley Ross Hill*

Years ago, before I met Gay, it was a lonely time. For the sun and the day were my lovers, and when the night clouds came, they tried to steal my dreams away. But not today! For in my arms, I have my Gay, and her love makes the moonless night as warm as July's midday.

The evening's breath blew colder now, and we got dressed. We climbed up Great Thunder's hill, which is the highest hill overlooking the bay. And there was an area of the sea in front of Oxwich Point that shimmered orange and gold, and we sat and listened to sunset secrets untold.

"It's so beautiful up here, my Prince, I always remember that last sunset when we said goodbye, all those years ago. But there is one thing that I know now that I want to shout out to the whole world!"

"What is it that my Princess?"

Gay stood up where Great Thunder used to stand and she shouted: "I loved you so much, Kingsley Hill, when we were teenagers, so much that when I moved away to England, I thought I was going to die without you! But I love you more now than I did then!"

When she spoke, the wind blew and carried her words to the jealous mermaids far out to sea.

There was nothing for me to say with words, so I said what I felt in my heart with a kiss, which declared: "My love has always been with you, and you have never left my heart. I love you, Gay Hosannah Hill!" We continued to sit on Great Thunder's hill, and we played in the colours of the sunset. The Bell Rock, which was now an island on the sand, rang his bell and said goodnight to the red and orange tide that waved back to the long shadow of the Great Tor, and shook hands with the Killy Willy stream, who sang his glad song all the way to the dreaming sea.

The night clouds drew the curtains across our day, and we walked back along the path beside the golf links to our car on Bendrick Drive.

As we reached the car it was almost dark, and with at least an hour and a half drive back to Cardiff, Gay offered to drive, as I was still getting used to driving on the left side of the road again.

Love and Bluebells

"Thanks, my love," I replied, "I think it's a good idea that I get some more practice before driving the motorway at night."

It was a pleasant drive home, and we both glowed from our wonderful day together. We talked most of the way, discussing our plans for the coming weekend.

Chapter Four

Two Pennies of Treasure

Tomorrow was Friday, and we had arranged to meet Dad at Pennard Castle. He wanted to follow up on Taliath's diary and explore the landmarks that we had recognized from the illustrations to be in and around the areas of St. Mary's Church and the Castle. Dad was convinced that there had to be artifacts to find, if indeed there had been a settlement around St. Mary's Church. As I continued to talk to Gay about the illustrations, I felt like a part of me was trying to hold back my excitement. I didn't want to have high expectations of finding something and then be disappointed. And at the same time, my mind and heart were being bombarded by wonderful memories that I had spent with my father and brother, finding treasures with our metal detectors. We had found Roman coins, shields, and part of a knight's helmet. We had even found a Viking sword and a type of breastplate. So, I had reason to be excited! Gay, however, was more excited about what we were learning of Taliath's life and family, and the culture and time in which she had lived.

Gay didn't say much more about the diary, other than the responsibility she felt in translating something so sacred.

We were both spent when we arrived home, and I walked Helen home to her house. "Thank you, Kingsley, I am glad that you and Gay had such a lovely day to yourselves. You needed it after being away from each other for so long." She then gave me the biggest hug, and said: "I'm so glad you're here, Kings. We are a whole family again now that you are back."

"Thanks Helen, and thanks again for watching Melody for us. We will see you on the weekend."

It was so great having Helen living so close. Not just to watch Melody for us, but she brought a wonderful strength and wisdom to our family. She was for us what Nan's Nan is to the other horses at Three Cliffs Valley. I didn't tell her that, of course! Even though it was very definitely a compliment. There are two things one should not say to one's Mother-in-law. And that is: How old are you? and You remind me of a horse! Especially if you say them together! One could safely assume that if you did, she would kick like a stallion, and perhaps bite like a mule.

Helen is a gracious, classy, kind, and beautiful woman. And she can lead my herd anytime!

Before Gay and I went to bed, we quietly went into Melody's room to say nite-nite, but she was fast asleep. Kissing her gently on the cheek, I whispered, "Nite-nite, Princess. See you in the morning."

Gay and I were soon asleep, and next thing I remember was Melody bouncing onto our bed, whispering into my ear and asking if I would walk her to school.

"Of course, I will, Princess."

While we were having breakfast, Melody shared that she was now being teased by some of her peers because I was walking her to school.

Gay spoke up and said: "It wasn't that long ago when they were teasing you because you didn't have your dad walking you to school."

"That's right," I continued, "and now they are jealous because their moms and dads don't walk them to school."

"That's right," Gay said, "they are acting like silly cows."

Melody looked at me and then roared with laughter. "Can I call them jealous cows, Mom and Dad, can I?"

Gay and I looked at each other, and then Gay said, "If you call them names, Melody, you will be acting like them."

"You mean like a silly cow," said Melody. I looked at Melody and Gay, and we all roared with laughter.

"Come on Princess, finish your rice crispies and I'll walk you to school," I said.

Gay had taken the day off and we got ready to meet Dad at Pennard Castle as planned. He wanted to meet at 11:30, and he had asked us to bring our copy of Taliath's diary that had the illustrations in it. He said he was also going to bring his metal detectors so we could search for artifacts.

After Gay had made a picnic, we headed off to Swansea and the Gower. We arrived at Pennard Castle just before 11:30, and Dad was already there waiting for us.

"Good morning, you two – all ready to do some exploring?" "Yes!" we replied in unison.

"Well, first things first. We need to give Gay a lesson in using a metal detector."

Two Pennies of Treasure

He had brought three detectors so we each had one to use. As Dad showed Gay how to use one of his, he gave me my old detector that he'd given to me on my eleventh birthday. I had lost interest in metal detecting when I was about fifteen, but Dad had kept it for me all these years, even while I had been away in Canada.

I am sure glad that he kept it, I thought, as I turned it on and heard its familiar beeping noise. I threw some coins on the ground to practice, and the sound of my detector became higher pitched as I brought it closer and closer, and then right over the coins. The best way to use a metal detector is to swing it back and forth at a moderate speed over the area you are exploring. If you swing it too fast, you are less likely to pick up a signal, especially if it is a small piece of metal. And if you move it too slowly, it will take you a significantly longer time to cover any given area of ground. If you are looking for coins that are generally small, or the surface area you are exploring is rough terrain with long grass, or bushes or stones, then you want to swing your detector more slowly. The larger the metal or more dense it is, the louder the sound pitch is on your detector's sound system. The general exception to this rule is when the metal is deep in the ground – so your sound pitch is likely to be quieter, even with a relatively large piece of metal. I am speaking, however, as someone who has not been detecting for many years, and my detector is a dinosaur compared to the modern ones of today, as my father will attest to.

After reacquainting myself with my detector and listening to its conversation of beeps, I picked up the coins I had thrown on the ground and I tried an area of sand in front of the castle wall. It was a faint beep that I was picking up, so

I moved the detector in a slower circular movement over the area. I figured that it was either a small object, or something larger that was deeper in the sand. I put down my detector and began to dig. The digging – and not knowing what you are going to find – is the most exciting part for me. And, of course, when you unearth and see for the first time that ancient coin or other rare artifact that has been buried in the sands of time for centuries, maybe even thousands of years!

What would it be this time? I wondered, as I picked up an old bottle, its rusty cap having made my detector talk.

"What is it, Kings?" both Gay and Dad shouted. "Oh, it's just an old bottle of some sort. But until I dug in the ground and saw it, I thought it was an old Roman coin or ancient helmet or sword."

"That's the beauty of metal detecting, Kings, you never know what you're going to find!"

I may have found just an old bottle, but I was instantaneously taken back to yesteryear when Dad had first given me my metal detector, and for months on end, he and I would go exploring each weekend.

During the summer months, we would often go down to the most populated beaches, where both locals and holidaymakers spend their days on the golden sands of the Gower and go swimming in the sea.

In the late evenings when the crowds had left the sands, Dad and I would start our adventures. High above the tidelines in the soft sand, we would look for the stories written upon the beaches. If you look carefully, you can see where people and families have been sitting and playing in the sand. There are flat areas with half footprints and little mounds where people

Two Pennies of Treasure

have been lying on towels and digging their feet in while sunbathing. Other areas have multiple footprints of the bare feet of men and women, and small footprints of excited children dashing back and forth to their sandcastles and forts, with flags of seagull feathers and coloured seaweed proudly blowing in the wind.

Dad would always keep a diary of his finds, and he even recorded the markings on the beach, so he could pass the day's stories on to me.

Generally, we would find the most coins where families had been sitting or playing. Sometimes we found bracelets and wristwatches, though not very often. Mainly it was coins – ten and fifty-pence pieces, and hair clips of various designs. Families with young children often hid things in sandcastles, and once I found ten hot-wheel cars in one castle!

Dad once found a gold locket from the late 1700's on Port Eynon Beach. I was sure that it could tell some stories about the woman who wore it, and its adventures in the waves. And I found a beautiful silver pendant with a turquoise stone on Pobbles Beach. I have often wondered what happened to it. Dad said a mermaid had sneaked into my room while I was asleep, and then slipped back into the waves with it. More likely it had found its way to my father's box of treasures for safekeeping. Otherwise as a young boy, I would often trade my treasures with my friends. Now we do still have pirates on the Gower, so watch your purse dear reader. You might just lose its contents amongst the dunes.

Today we were looking for bigger things, like swords and shields, and other remnants from the ancient peoples that had once lived and battled on the Gower Peninsula. And with my detector in my hand, I became more and more excited! Especially when Dad showed me his new modern one.

"Look Kings!" he exclaimed. "It even measures the depth of the metal, and its size and density. And it has a built-in GPS memory so I can come back to exactly where I found the treasure. And it has a sensory camera!"

"Wow, Dad! That is some piece of equipment." "Only the best for your, Old Man!" My Dad grinned, his gold tooth sparkling in the sun.

"Your gold tooth is going to bring us luck," I said, and he and Gay both laughed. Gay was also getting more excited, and Dad threw some coins on the ground so she could hear and learn to differentiate the various sounds the detector made.

"Well, come on," Dad said, "let's start searching the area around the wall of St Mary's Church."

And as we walked over to the one piece of the remaining wall, I thought about how many ancient artifacts might be lying undiscovered in the general area.

"We'll split up so we can cover a larger area," Dad said. "And remember, Gay, to swing the detector from side-to-side like this…. And try to make a mental log of the area you have covered. Look at certain plants and landmarks that you can make a note of."

We all walked in a straight line about 30 feet apart so we could talk to each other when necessary. The old church wall is on the property of the Pennard golf course, so we had to be wary of golfers, and if you heard the word "Fore!" being shouted at you, you had to make sure you ducked quickly.

As a boy, I earned some of my pocket money by finding golf balls that had been lost in the grass or ferns beside the fairways. And on the days that I was a "bad boy," I hid behind the hills in front of where the golfers were teeing off, and as their shiny new balls came over the hill, I dashed out to get their balls before I could be seen. One day I waited for all four players to tee off, and I stole all four balls. The best day to steal golf balls was on Ladies Day, every Tuesday. In my experience, the ladies were far less likely than the men to chase you if they saw you stealing their balls. However, one lady chased me a quarter of a mile once, when I stole her shiny Slazenger number 3. She had even written her initials on it: S.R. And I kept that one for quite some time, as I had to outrun a pretty lady to get it. "And that adds value to the ball," I told my friends. And I knew for sure that she was pretty, because when I sold my other golf balls back to the pro shop, this same lovely lady came and served me from behind the counter. It was fortunate that she did not recognize me as the boy who had stolen her Slazenger number 3. Though maybe she did? She always smiled at me with a twinkle in her eye after that. And I finally gave that golf ball away to a girlfriend named Sandra Rodgers. I mean she did have her initials on it! But back to the metal detecting...

As we walked over the grass, a cool breeze refreshed my face, and the skylarks sang – oh, such a sweet song! – over our heads. And the silver sea that flooded the Three Cliffs Valley sparkled in the morning sun while the lonesome hill of Cefn Bryn waited like a friend and watched us from the distance. And my soul sang, and it flew with the skylarks and danced with the islands of heather that waved in the wind, as beautiful as bridesmaid's dresses. And I looked across at my Gay, who smiled back at me. And it mattered not if we did not find anything, for my treasure was Gay and my family. And my heart praised God for all he had given to me….

Then suddenly I was taken away from my conversation with Cefn Bryn by an excited shout from Gay.

"Look, everyone. I've found something!"

I made a mental note of the ground I had covered, put my detector down, and ran over to Gay. "Look, listen!" she said excitedly. "Listen to the beeping over this spot!"

"It's close to the surface," Dad said, recognizing the type of beep. "Here, take this, and dig right here." He handed her a small trowel, and she began to dig.

"The ground is hard," she said, "I can't break the turf."

"Keep going," I replied. "Once you get through the grass, it will be sand underneath."

Gay finally pushed through the turf and began lifting the sand.

"There it is!" Dad exclaimed. "It's a coin! Look, there's two!"

Gay had found two old pennies. Not Roman, or from any ancient people of the Gower, but old British pennies. Gay didn't care at all about that; for her, they were as precious as a valuable treasure!

"I've never found anything before!" she exclaimed. "This is my first-time metal detecting!"

She handed me the pennies to inspect. "What's the date on them?" Dad asked.

"One is 1935, and the other is 1921!" pronounced Gay, smiling as if they were gold.

"Not very valuable," Dad said, "but fun to collect. Keep going, Gay, I have found Roman coins near here."

At Dads words, she continued to swing her detector from side to side with great enthusiasm. Dad looked across at me and winked, as if to say: 'we will make a detectorist out of her yet!'

We continued searching the area around the old wall for another hour, and then Dad said it was time to break for lunch.

"I've made a picnic for the three of us," Gay stated. She was still excited about her find.

"You're going to make a good detectorist," Dad said, seeing her excitement. "You better keep this one, Kings!"

"I will, Dad! Don't you worry!"

Gay laughed and said, "I hope you will keep me."

Gay and I climbed up onto the wall, while Dad sat nearby, thinking about the next area we should search. Gay had made my favourite crab sandwiches again, and she had brought welsh cakes. They were delicious, and Dad and I wolfed them down.

"Okay, let's get back at it," Dad said after we had relaxed for a few minutes, "and thank you, my lovely daughter, the picnic was wonderful."

Gay gave me a gentle elbow and said, "Did you hear that, Kings? Your dad called me his daughter. It's been a long time since I felt like I had a dad."

"And I feel the same way about your mum," I replied, and we kissed.

"Come on, you two love birds, let's go and dig up some Vikings."

We continued our adventure walking back towards the castle, and Dad commented that he thought the settlement or village, according to Taliath's map, was right beneath us! At his words, expectation filled my veins, and I listened more intently as I swung my detector slowly from side to side.

"Okay, everyone," he said, "put your equipment down where you are, and let's study the illustrations. I know you are both waiting to see where these coordinates lead us to, and so am I."

We studied the map for about ten minutes, and the illustration of the chest and its coordinates, from where we were standing, seemed clear and concise to each of us – apart from one tree that on the map was described as a sycamore tree, but it was clearly an oak.

"Unless the sycamore tree is gone, and the oak tree has grown up in its place," Gay commented.

"Good point," Dad acknowledged, "and that's my main concern. If this oak tree has grown up at a later date than the illustrations of the original tree specify, then the coordinates for the chest could be way off…."

He paused for a few moments, and then he came up with a plan. "Let's give it a try. I brought three compasses so there is one each. Kings, you work with Gay and show her how to use the compass, and I will focus on the exact longitude and latitude."

We made several attempts from our starting point on the map and lined up the illustrated landmarks to the coordinates that led to where the chest was marked. But it was to no avail! Dad took the shovel off his back and we dug four holes, one exactly upon the coordinates and the other three nearby, but we found nothing. "It might be the tree, as we discussed before," he said, "but not to worry. We will keep at it, but I think that's enough for today. I will review the illustrations again tonight, and we will return in a week or so."

"Sorry the map didn't lead us to treasure," my father said as we all walked away, but I realized that he had given us a far greater treasure than finding a sword or ancient coins. We had done something special together as a family, and this heritage of metal detecting was something that Gay, Melody and I could do together, and my daughter Samantha Jade and the boys when they came to visit later in the year.

I thanked my dad for keeping my detector for me. "You always said that one day I would be interested in using it again. And today is that day!"

Dad wiped away a tear and said, "Glad to hear it, Old Son," with a proud look on his face.

Dad headed back to Swansea, and Gay and I headed home to Cardiff.

"Wow, what an exciting day!" we both exclaimed.

Chapter Five

The Pirates of Port Eynon

On the weekend, Gay and I, along with her mum Helen, took Melody to the Gower. Beautiful weather was in the forecast, so we planned to spend a full day at Port Eynon Beach on Saturday. Helen had rented a caravan for the day, so we didn't have to drive all the way home to Cardiff in the evening.

Once we were settled into the caravan, we headed down to the beach. The tide was falling, and it was already a long way out. Melody asked if we could go swimming in the sea.

"It's a bit cold yet," I said, "as it's still only spring. But we could build a sand boat on the beach; it's warm enough for that."

"A sand boat like we made last summer?" asked Melody.

"Yes, that's right, you remember, Princess." "Remember! I should say I do, Dad. We all got ship-wrecked when the waves came crashing into our boat, remember?"

We all laughed, and I said, "Yes, I remember, Melody, and this time we need to build an even better boat."

"Better than last time, Dad? We built a rather good boat last time..."

Then Melody shouted: "I know! I know! If Grandma Helen helps us, it will be better than our last one. Will you help us Grandma, please?"

"Alright," Helen said, kicking off her shoes. "I'm in. Now where are we going to build this boat?" "Close to the high tide mark – right, Dad?"

"Yes, that's right. That way we have enough time while the tide is coming in to build the boat before the pirate waves reach us."

"Pirate waves! Did you hear that Mum and Grandma? Dad said there's pirate waves. In that case we better get started..."

"Melody, look," I said. "I think the tide is already turning to come in!" Melody looked out to sea. "Pirates, pirates are coming!" she cried. "Come on everyone, let's get building our ship!"

"Now Melody, I'm going to test your knowledge and your memory," I said. "What is the first thing we do when building a ship?"

"Oh, that's easy! We find a stick and mark the shape of the boat we want to make on the sand."

"That's right, well done. How about you run up to the top of the beach and see if you can find a stick."

As Melody ran off, she said: "Grandma Helen, will you come with me...?"

"Alright," she said, "I will race you up the beach!"

And Gay shouted, "On your marks, get set, go!"

Helen and Melody returned with a good size stick.

"Now what do you think is the next step Melody?" I asked.

"It's choosing the best place to build the boat, of course."

"Right again."

Her beaming face looked at each of us, and then she ran back up to the top of the beach to find the tide line.

We soon followed her up, and I said, "I only have one more question for you to get three out of three right!"

"What's that, Dad?"

"Do you remember what I taught you last summer about finding the most recent tide line?"

"Yes, I remember. You walk along the beach and look for a line of seaweed and anything else the tide has brought in, but it must all be in a line that stretches the length of the beach. Sometimes it's a squiggly line because the waves come in at angles. And if there is more than one tide line, then you have to determine which is the most recent one."

"Wow!" Gay commented, looking at me. "You taught her that?"

"Yeah, mum, he did." Today, however, there were three tide lines close together.

"What does that mean, my caveman son-in-law?" Helen asked with a big smile.

"Well, if there are three fresh lines close together and they are high up the beach, it means, firstly, that the tides are high. It's a good size moon, and the gravitational pull of the moon upon the tide will pull it high up the beach. As the moon phases change, as in the case we have today, the moon is getting smaller, so each new tide line will be slightly less in height up the beach."

"Yeah, that's right, Dad, you tell them," said Melody, and she pointed out the three lines of the tide. "See, this is today, which is the lowest line on the beach, because we have a smaller moon. The second one here was the tide before that because it is higher up the beach. And this third one is the oldest tide – right Dad? – because it is the highest line." Gay and Helen were almost breaking their tummies laughing. Melody looked like a little professor pointing to the tidelines with her stick, and we were all students. And there was only one answer that I could give Melody, and that was an emphatic "yes!" She was right! And right again!

"Melody, I think you're going to be a cavewoman like your dad!" Helen declared. Melody replied, "There's only one thing wrong with that, Grandma, Dad is a caveman, not a cavewoman."

"That's right, Melody, you tell them," I said.

And she continued: "Yeah, Grandma. Dad is the caveman, mum is the cavewoman, his wife, and I'm the cave-girl, and you are a cave-Grandma."

"That makes us a cave family then, doesn't it," Helen concluded.

And this cave family began to build the boat. Melody got to mark out the boat on the sand with her cave stick because she had gotten all the questions right. Then Helen, Gay and I began to dig a trench with our hands in front of the lines Melody had drawn, and we threw the sand to the other side of the trench to build the walls.

Melody took the bucket and ran to the sea to get water. By the time she got back with the first bucket, we had a small pile of sand around the whole shape of the boat. "Shall I pour the water on the sand, dad? Or are the walls too small yet?"

"They are too small yet, so why don't you jump inside the walls with us and help us build them up."

We worked solid for about half an hour making the walls thick and high, and it was great to see Helen getting into it the way she was – high heels off, sand in her hair, and a determined look on her face to conquer the seven seas.

"Okay, Melody, you can pour the water onto the wall now – nice and slowly so we can shape the sand and make the design of the ship."

We shaped the bow into a point to streamline our vessel head-on into the incoming waves, rather than having a straight flat wall at the bow which is more easily and quickly penetrated by the surf.

"Wow, Mum and Grandma, it looks great!" exclaimed Melody. "I'm going to run down to the sea and get some more water."

"Hurry," I said, "the tide is coming in fast now. You only have about three trips of water left before the pirate waves reach us." Melody ran down to the waves like there was no tomorrow. The rest of us rested until she was in our sights again with the bucket. This continued for four more trips to the sea, and then the waves were upon us like vengeful pirates!

"Come on, Melody, jump into the ship," Gay ordered. "The pirate waves are upon us."

Port Eynon beach has a small hump for the waves to climb about three-quarters of the way up the beach, and then

The Pirates of Port Eynon

it is flat like Pobbles, and once over the hump the tide comes in fast.

We were soon surrounded by waves, a cave-family island in the sea.

"Come on, Melody," Helen shouted, "the walls are crumbling this side of the ship."

And with our bucket and hands, we poured and patted sand onto the crumbling walls.

"This side, this side," I shouted! "There is water coming in!"

"Pirates! pirates!" Melody shouted, as the waves came crashing over the sides. Gay grabbed Helen so she could stand up and escape the cold waves. Melody and I abandoned ship and jumped into the sea and ran up the beach to watch what was left of our sinking ship. Gay and Helen remained like two brave captains and screamed as the last wall came crashing in and the cold waves of Port Eynon Beach sunk our valiant ship!

Gay and Helen ran to catch us up at the top of the beach, and then we all ran shivering and laughing back to the caravan. I put on a pot of tea and I tried to warm up in the living room while the girls took turns jumping into the shower.

Finally, it was my turn, and the water was still hot. "Yes! Oh, that feels so good!" And I stayed in the shower until the chill of pirates left my shoulders.

Gay and Helen made a lovely tea, as Melody and I played cards in front of the small electric heater. It was small but warm, and it soon heated up the whole living room. Then after tea, we dressed warmly and went for a late afternoon walk on the beach. We followed the tideline looking for treasures the whole length of the beach, until we reached Horton.

Horton is the sister village to Port Eynon and is on its eastern side. The two villages are separated by the sand-dunes of the Burrows. And as we walked back from Horton to Port Eynon, I took my shoes off again to feel the fine white sand between my toes.

By the time we reached the far end of the beach, the tide had dropped low enough for us to go and explore Port Eynon Head. As the beach curves around before the point, there are the ruins of what is known as the Salt House. And we went over to explore the ruins. Helen asked me about its intriguing history, and I shared with her what I knew.

My father told me, "that in order to understand the history and wildness of this little piece of western Gower called Port Eynon and the Salt House, one has to know a little bit about the history of the Lucas family, and in particular a man named John Lucas." Port Eynon was certainly, in its early days, no quiet corner like it is today, especially when the boisterous, noisy holiday makers have left for their own corners of the country after summer's songs and July and August kisses have gone.

In the old days, Port Eynon seemed to breed a very wild race of men. And the most admired, but also the most feared, was a man described as having a magnetic personality and being a natural born leader. His name was John Lucas, and he built upon a great stone stronghold called the Salt House. The Salt House had battlements and walls all around it, even reaching into the cleft of the rocks. In the stronghold, Lucas stored arms and liquor. The Salt House is said to have a secret passage that leads to another building that Lucas rebuilt and repaired, called 'Kulverd Hall.' Over the years, many stories were told of the secret underground passage. One of the accounts is that Lucas, after a bout of heavy drinking one night, showed one of his partners in crime a large storage room full of pirate smuggled liquor. And in order to get to this room, they had to travel through an underground tunnel that was narrow in parts, and the sound of the angry waves could be heard as they roared and crashed and shook the walls of the tunnel in their disapproval of the life and times that Lucas lived.

John Lucas continued to defy the waves of the law for years, and he continued this way with enormous success. His illegal activities were kept safe and silent within his Salt House, while the wild wind-blown waves of Port Eynon crashed about the rocks, helping to keep his secrets.

The rocks known as Sedgers Bank and Skysea are at the foot of the two promontories forming Port Eynon Head, and they can only be reached at low water. And today the tide was low enough for us to go and explore these sinister rocks.

"Tell us more," Gay asked me, in her sweet but persuasive tone of voice.

"Yes, please do," Helen added, and Melody took my hand as if I was about to tell her a ghost story.

Alright, I shall continue.

"Local residents of Port Eynon tell a story about some bold and bad Buccaneers who were smugglers and ship-wreckers, and they lured ships to their doom on Sedgers Bank and Skysea."

"These rocks that we're standing on, Dad?" Melody asked, gripping my hand more tightly.

"Yes, right where we are standing now."

"How did they lure the ships?" Gay asked.

"They tied a lantern to a horse's head so that when the horse walked, the light from it gave the impression of a ship being tossed by the waves. And the passing ships would follow the light, thinking it was safe, and they would crash upon the rocks."

"They didn't put lamps on Nan's Nans head and bring the ships upon the rocks, did they Dad?"

"No, Princess. There have been horses on the Gower for hundreds of years, and these were horses that were owned by the smugglers and ship-wreckers, long before Nan's Nan was born."

"What happened to John Lucas?" Helen asked.

"Lucas was like a Gower Robin Hood and the country folk flocked to his side because he divided with them the spoils of his pirating ways, helping the less fortunate to live a better standard of life."

"And he passed on his pirating business and ways to his son, Phillip. The great cellars of the Salt House were kept full of illicit liquor and smuggled goods for many generations. The Lucas family held Port Eynon in their tight grip through the lifetimes of many a Gower man and their families, like a dictator or corrupt government that is both admired and feared. The end of the Salt House and the Lucas's of Port Eynon, came in the year 1703. And the end was very much in keeping with the wild, reckless, and romantic lives they led. It is said that John Lucas lay dying as the memorable storm of that year raged through the British Isles. It struck Gower with a tremendous force that has seldom been seen since. The waves of the huge seas came crashing in on the Salt House. John Lucas's skiffs were flung on shore, the cellars were flooded, and lightning struck the Salt House. The Lucas' stronghold and their fortunes perished like in the prophecy of a hell-and-brimstone preacher, and this prophecy came true! Now only the salt-encrusted, bramble-covered ruins remain."

"That's just what it looks like today," Helen said, moving a blackberry bramble from the wall.

"What about the story of Kulverd Hall?" Gay asked.

"That is one of the most intriguing mysteries of Gower," I answered. "But that's for another time."

"I'm hungry, let's go back to the caravan to eat," suggested Helen. We all agreed it was a good idea.

"We've had an early tea already," Gay reminded us. "Then we will have to have a giant snack," volunteered Melody.

The sun was westering in the sky as we arrived back at the caravan, and there was a beautiful sunset developing on the horizon behind Port Eynon Head.

We spent the evening relaxing and made tea and hot chocolate. And we sat and told stories at the front window of the caravan that faced the sunset and the sea, and we watched the changing colours that told their own stories of the day. And as darkness fell, the whites of the waves rode into the beach like galloping horses thundering up the sand. We opened the windows and fell asleep to the lullaby of the waves.

Sunday morning arrived as a gentle stir upon the beach of our happy lives, as I lay in bed with my lovely Gay and thought of what adventure might be waiting for us today. And after a lovely breakfast that Helen and Gay cooked together, we packed the car and headed for Pennard Cliffs. I decided to take the girls on a walk from Pobbles Beach to Hunts Bay, along the rocks and cliff paths. It was a walk that I had taken with my father when I was Melody's age. We bought drinks and sandwiches at Pennard Store, before making our way to Pobbles Bay. As we walked along the West Cliff path and watched the sea below, it was a falling tide, and by the time we arrived at the beach, the tide would be close to its low.

When we arrived, the waves were just receding from the rocks where we would be starting our walk.

"Before we start," I said, "we need to have a safety briefing, as it can be slippery and dangerous climbing over the rocks. We should walk in two's and stay close together, and not walk ahead too far on our own."

"Why are there pirates?" Melody asked with a smile.

"You might say that" I replied. "Pirates can come in many shapes and forms." Now I had her attention and Helen and Gay's nodding approvals.

"Now the first thing to remember is to watch our footing. The rocks and seaweed are slippery and wet, especially after they are first exposed from the receding waves. There are also deep rock pools and gullies. Don't try to step or jump over them if you're not sure you can, and even then, it's risky if the rocks are slippery. It is best to walk around them, rather than twist an ankle. And there are going to be some big boulders we are going to have to climb over later when we reach Fox Hole and Hunts Bay."

Melody was listening intently.

"And we are going to explore some caves too," I added, "and we need to climb some cliffs to get to them. Now are we all ready? Shoelaces tied?"

"Yes, we're ready!" came the chorus.

"Okay, Helen can walk with Gay, and Melody can walk with me. And one last thing! If someone needs to stop or rest, they put their hand up and call 'rest', and we will all stop. Okay, let's go."

The rocks at the eastern end of Pobbles Bay are for the most part quite flat, and we moved across them with relative ease, stepping over thin gullies and crevices and walking on mussel beds. There were a few larger rock pools and a deep gully that we had to walk around.

"This is one of the deep pools where I used to catch prawns when I lived on the cliffs," I shared.

And Helen said to Gay with a smile, "I can see why you found your caveman so intriguing, catching prawns and exploring beaches and caves, what fun!"

"It is," she said proudly.

"We are a cave family, aren't we mum!" Melody exclaimed.

"Yes, we are!"

We soon began to navigate some large boulders, and I had to help Melody up and over them with one hand and steady our grip with the other. Melody was a good sport, and although she scraped her knees a few times, she climbed very well and didn't complain. The other girls were doing well too, and we all stopped when one of us raised our hand. Our signal for needing a break was working well.

"Well done everyone! You are all doing well! Now let's take a water break, and I will tell you a bit about the Devil's Kitchen cave."

"Devil's Kitchen," Melody echoed, "that sounds like a scary place."

"It does sound intriguing," said Helen. "Are we going there next?"

"We are going there," I replied, "but first we are going to visit Ravenscliff cave."

"Tell us about Devil's Kitchen," Gay said. "I'm not ready to start walking again yet."

"Well, I first discovered Devil's Kitchen cave when I was living on the cliffs. I was walking along the rocks at the foot of the cliffs, and I came across quite a substantial stream of water coming out of a hole in the cliff."

"How big was the hole in the cliff?" Melody asked excitedly. "It was as big as a small cave," I replied, "and I decided to taste the water because I was thirsty. And do you know what? It was fresh water! And that stream coming out of the rocks became my fresh water supply for all the time that I lived in Bacon Hole."

Melody giggled and said, "Dad, you really are a real caveman!"

Gay and Helen continued to listen intently. "So, after I had drunk from the freshwater stream, I continued to climb up the cliff, and I discovered Devil's Kitchen cave. One of the most intriguing things about Devils Kitchen is that it has a chimney that opens out through a stratum of cemented sand. When you are in the cave looking up, it is like looking up at the sky through a tunnel in the earth. It's one of those places that you have to experience in person to appreciate its uniqueness."

We finished our break and continued to make our way up the cliff. "Don't forget to be careful of your footing and watch out for loose stones or gravel." I warned.

Melody continued to hold my hand while Gay and Helen walked close together. We followed a steep sheep track that led us up the cliff toward Ravenscliff cave. Melody held my hand tightly as we tackled more boulders and made it to the sheep path while Helen and Gay followed behind. Once upon the path, you realize how far up the cliff you actually are, and if you look back across the bay, you can see the magnificent stretch of sand of Three Cliffs Bay with the Three Cliffs rock projecting out from the mainland in the center. Helen put up her hand and we stopped to enjoy the amazing view. "It's so beautiful up here!" we all exclaimed. As we continued to the entrance of the cave, Melody shared that her legs were getting tired.

"It's only a few more feet to climb and we'll be there," I encouraged her.

"You can do it, Melody," Gay continued, "you are a great climber!"

Melody continued up the cliff, propelled by our encouragement, and we now arrived at the entrance of Ravenscliff cave. The cave from its outside appearance seems very uninteresting, but once you go inside, it has a wonderful atmosphere to it, and you can feel the past all around you. There is a loud hush, and the walls tell stories of thousands of years ago.

Melody seemed to sense this, and she asked me what had been found in the cave.

"Many wild animal bones have been found here, including lion, wild cat, hyena, hippopotamus, and mammoth, so it is well worth remembering this."

Helen reminded us that knowing the history of a place adds a special value in appreciating it, and we all had a wonderful discussion about what it would have been like living in a cave at the time of the cavemen on the Gower Peninsula, and to see all these wonderful animals, some of which are now extinct.

"You're a caveman, Dad," Melody giggled, "so you know what it was like."

"I do indeed!"

It was time to get back onto the path and make our way to Devil's Kitchen.

"I want to see the hole in the roof," Melody said, "and look up to the sky from inside the cave."

She needed no more encouragement for the rest of the hike to Devils Kitchen.

Melody and I arrived at the entrance first, while Gay and Helen continued to climb along the path behind us.

"Quick," Melody said, "let's go inside first before mum and grandma get here."

She pulled my hand, and we went inside. "Wow!" Melody shouted, "Look at the window to the sky! Oh, this is a magical place! It's like looking up to Heaven."

Then we heard Gay and Helen's voices coming in behind us.

"It is a tunnel to the sky!" Helen proclaimed.

Gay came over and took my hand. "Wow, this is a sacred place, my love!" And I kissed her.

Devil's Kitchen cave has more of an open-air feel to it, compared with many of the other caves I have explored. And I wondered when the chimney had first appeared in the roof? Was it during the time a Cave Family lived in the cave? Or did it happen only a few hundred years ago? We had some more

The Pirates of Port Eynon

to drink and a snack before continuing our way along the cliff path towards Hunts Bay.

We were making good time, so I decided to show the girls a few more of my special places along the way. We now looked down on a small inlet known as Heather Slade. Heather Slade has a small sandy beach, but you must wait until low water to access it. I have swum there a few times after Bass fishing from the rocks on a falling tide. But you only have about an hour or so to swim, as the tide comes in again quickly and re-claims the sand. There are some good shrimping pools there too at low water.

We now reached Fox Hole Bay, where the cliff path dips down and crosses another path that comes down from the cliff above. This path descends approximately to the middle of Fox Hole Bay, and people come down from the car park which is about a hundred yards up the cliff top. As we crossed the path coming down, we met a family on their way to spend some time on Fox Hole Bay. I call it a bay rather than a beach, because Fox Hole is very much like Heather Slade, in that it only has a relatively small strip of sand for people to paddle or go swimming. And this strip of sandy beach is only accessed at three-quarters to low tide. It is mainly a rocky beach, great for diving off the rocks, exploring rockpools, and catching crabs. And the convenience of Fox Hole is it is only a ten to fifteen-minute walk down from the cliff top, and Pennard Stores, so you can pick up a sandwich and refreshments and be on the beach in a matter of minutes. We were all getting hungry again now, so I we tried not to talk about food.

The cliff top above Fox Hole is called High Tor. And from here, we were able to look back westward and see how far we had come. I pointed out Ravenscliff, where we had first climbed up the sheep track from Pobbles, and in the distance we could see the Great Tor and the whole sweep of Oxwich Bay, where Great Thunder and I used to gallop across the sands.

"Wow, Dad, did we really come all this way?" Melody asked.

"Yes, we did Princess! And you're a great climber!"

Melody beamed at my words, and Gay and Helen both smiled.

"And Dad is a great tour guide," Gay added.

"He is, indeed," Helen echoed.

And with that much affirmation coming from my girls, I was up again and leading the way.

"Shall we visit one more cave before Hunts Bay?" I asked, "or shall we head straight to Hunts?"

Everyone put their hands up to visit one more cave first, so I decided to take us to Mitchin Hole.

"Mitchin Hole doesn't sound as scary as Devils Kitchen, Dad, but I liked it with the hole to the sky. What's Mitchin Hole like?" asked Melody.

"You wait and see," I replied. "It's one of my favourite caves, and I know you are all going to like it!"

We kept heading east on the cliff path, which was now heading back down towards the heaving sea. Much of the narrow path was overgrown with new growth gorse, with its lovely yellow flower – and its fragrance thrilled our nostrils as we walked. Finches and warblers sang their sweet songs, along with a yellowhammer and a blackcap, as spring bloomed around us. Here and there, bramble bushes intruded across our path, and Melody and I beat them back with two sticks we had found.

"This is tough going," I said, "but it will be worth it." We were soon at a low point on the path, one that I was familiar with. "Okay everyone, we are close to the entrance. Look carefully down along the sea-washed rocks at the foot of the Tor."

"I can see something down there, Dad! Like a ledge sticking out."

"Good spotting, Melody, I think that's the entrance." We scrambled down a sheep path to find a narrow cleft out of which the cave proper opens. Melody and I waited for Gay and Helen to catch up before we went inside.

"Look at this," I said. "We are standing on something quite remarkable! We are on a piece of raised beach that's clinging to the rock surface at the entrance."

"This is quite remarkable!" Helen stated. "If you stand here, Gay, at the side of the cliff, you can see that it is an actual piece of the beach!"

"Yes Mum, it's amazing how it has stayed attached to the main rock surface. I can see why this is one of your favourite caves, Kings."

"Come on," I said, "let's go inside." Melody took my hand and we climbed in. The floor of the cave slopes up very steeply, and we found it slippery in places.

"Gay and Helen, hold hands," I called back, and Melody echoed my words, as if enjoying the opportunity to boss her mum and her grandma.

"Are you giving me orders?" Helen called back.

"Yes, only because I don't want you to fall," Melody shouted.

"Good answer," I whispered, and Melody giggled.

"Why is the floor so uneven?" Helen asked.

"A good question. It is in part because of all the excavation that has taken place."

"When was it first excavated?"

"A man named Colonel Wood arrived first in the 1850s, and he found the remains of two types of fauna. One was temperate and interglacial, and included bones of the narrow-nosed rhinoceros and the straight-tusked elephant; the other colder, and therefore more favourable to the mammoth and the woolly rhinoceros."

Melody laughed and repeated the name "narrow-nosed rhinoceros."

"How did you know he was narrow-nosed, Dad?" she asked.

"Quiet, Melody," Gay said, "and listen to Dad. It's interesting."

"It's alright," I said. "Melody was just comparing the rhinoceros with one of her narrow-nosed friends at school!"

Melody began to laugh uncontrollably, and Helen looked away and giggled.

"Come on," I said, "let's all go to the back of the cave and look out."

From there, we looked back through the narrow cleft of the entrance. And a strange 'feeling' of being carried back thousands of years into a remote, mysterious past, visited us all like a story-telling ghost.

And in the eerie half light of the cave, I pictured a skin-clad family crouching around a fire, awaiting the return of the hunters from the cold, hostile world outside, and the ceremonies that were carried out in the depths of the cave in hopes of warding off the dangers that beset our early forefathers. And I wished I had my rabbit-pelt robe to wear as I stood here thousands of years back in time. And for a few minutes I thought of Taliath's Diary, and I wondered what ancient ceremonies I might read about as I continued to work on the translation of her life in a Celtic Clan.

Suddenly, I was wonderfully woken from my daydream, here in Mitchin Hole, as Gay walked up to me and whispered in my ear: "I want to sleep in this cave with you, Kingsley, and make love in front of a fire."

"Now, that's my cavewoman," I whispered back. "Let's plan it soon." Gay's eyes danced with mine in excitement, and I wished for the moment when only the two of us would be here.

Melody asked if I would tell her a story while we were all in the cave, and I told her not now because we needed to continue to Hunt's Bay, and then walk back along East Cliff path to Pennard Stores, so we had time for some supper before we traveled home to Cardiff. "But I will tell you what it was like on a cool misty day, when I lived in Bacon Hole," I said.

"Oh, yes please!" everyone whispered. "On the chilly autumn days, when the sun is dulled in the sky and it only seems to get to a half-light, and the mists are blowing in from the channel, you can feel those Palaeolithic hunters coming in on the mysterious winds, and sitting down beside you at the fire, and the flames flicker on the walls and dance with the shouting shadows, and they tell the stories of the hunters day. The logs seem to move on the fire, and whispers on a gentle wind tell you that you are not alone in the cave."

"Marvelous!" Helen said. "Now let's get out of here before those Palaeolithic hunters get back and find us in their cave."

As we came out of the half-light of the cave into the clear Gower sunshine again, it was a strange feeling to be suddenly back in the modern world and leave behind our lives that we lived thousands of years ago.

Chapter Six

Hunts Bay

We continued eastwards on the cliff path and arrived at Hunts Bay.

The tide had come up quite a way since we had left Pobbles Beach over three hours ago. The sea was calm with small rollers and gentle swells that swirled around the rockpools and glided up the gullies, lifting the large seaweeds that waved back and forth like mermaid's hair. Melody and I lay on a flat rock and peered into the mysterious deep. Hermit crabs scurried back and forth, carrying their homes on their backs at the bottom of the long-tunneled pool, and a large edible crab hurried along with no suitcase searching for its lunch. Rock gobies swam quickly from side to side disappearing into the cracks and crevices of underwater hotels, while orange-faced starfish hung to the rocks like art in these mermaid rooms. And the waiting, dreaming, gleaming pool shook hands with the white-gloved wave that brought yesterday's news, and today's shoes, to a Black Backed Gull that stunk of booze. Cuttle-fish rolled, and the shrimp became bold as the rising tide told stories yet untold, and Gay and Helen gave Melody and I a sandwich to hold, and welcome reader to our family fold.

After eating what was left of our food and snacks, my throat was dry, like after sucking on one of my grandmother's black hacks. We explored the rocks at the top of the bay.

"Hey look," Gay said. "Someone has had a campfire on the beach." And Helen found a wine bottle that still had the cork in its neck.

"Let me smell the cork," I said, as she handed me the bottle. "It still has the smell and colour of the wine on it. It's not that old and was probably consumed sometime over the last few weeks." "Kingsley has a story about a wine bottle, don't you my love," Gay said with a soft smile.

"Will you tell us a story now, Dad, will you?" Melody asked expectantly.

"Yes, finding this wine bottle reminds me of the last morning I spent at Bacon Hole before I moved into my new home in Leathers Hole on the Great Tor. I decided to take one last walk on Hunts Beach."

"Oh, tell it like a story dad! Not just thinking back out loud," Melody said.

"Alright, I'll try! But I need to think back in order to tell the story."

Melody sat on Gay's lap, and Helen sat on a nearby rock. And the only sound was the gentle waves, and the squawk of the Black Backed Gull, whose friend had arrived. Maybe they were here to listen to the story too?

"The tide lay low, and there was only a gentle swell on the water. I sat on my throne for the last time as 'the caveman of Bacon Hole.' 'Today is moving day,' I announced, as I looked out at the Emerald Sea."

Hunts Bay

At my words, Melody nudged her mum with her elbow and then gazed out to sea. And Helen looked as excited and expectant as a little girl. "I will continue," I said.

'What better way to end my time here at Bacon Hole, than a walk on Hunts Bay!' I said to a seagull, who said good morning and hurray!

'I climbed down the narrow path and on to the rocky shore. It was the lowest tide I had seen since coming to the cave to live, and I was able to walk out to the only sandy part of the beach. Everywhere else there were rocks and gullies. Wait a minute, what was that bobbing in the water? An old bottle! And there was something in it! I moved to the edge of the rocks to take a closer look. It was a message in a bottle! The gentle swell of the tide moved the bottle back and forth in the gully, and I began to get excited – what could it be? A letter from a beautiful girl looking for her Prince? Or was it from some sailor marooned on an island? I couldn't wait to find out, so I ran back to the cave to get my prawning net; I could reach the bottle with the net and scoop it out of the water. But by the time I got back, there was no need for the net, as the tide had brought the bottle up the gully to the shore. It dragged back and forth making a scraping noise on the small pebbles. I picked it up and sat on a rock to inspect it. It was a green glass bottle with the label long worn off. On one side, it had several barnacles on it; this told me that it had been at sea for some time. It was sealed with a cork well into its neck, and the top part of the cork had worn off, so I couldn't pry it out. I had no corkscrew, so I would have to break the bottle to read what was inside. Holding the bottle like a piece of treasure, I climbed back up the cliff to my throne. I would open it there.

With a small rock, I smashed the neck of the bottle. The note was tied up with a brown piece of string, and slowly I unravelled the tight scroll.'

"What was it? What was it?" Melody and Helen cried out at the same time! Gay, of course, knew my story.

'It wasn't a treasure map, or a letter from a Princess! It was scripture from the Bible! There were four Bible verses from God!'

"What did they say?" Melody asked.

"Yes, go on please," Helen chimed in. "Do you remember what they said?"

"Oh, yes," I replied. "I will never forget. They are written on my heart, and I will tell you two of them."

'I know what I am planning for you, declares the Lord. They are plans to prosper you and not to harm you, to give you hope and a good future.' Jeremiah 29 vs 11

'The word of the Lord came to me, saying, Before I formed you in the womb, I knew you; before you were born, I set you apart, and appointed you as a prophet to the nations.' Jeremiah 1 vs 4-5.

"When I read those verses, it was like God was putting his arms around me! And I knew in my heart that these words were a message from Him to me!" I said to Melody and Helen.

"When we pray to God, he hears us," I continued. "He knows what our hopes and dreams are, and sometimes we lose sight of them in this world. Or something happens and we stop believing that they will ever come true. But God keeps our dreams safe within his heart, and never forgets them. On the day that I found my message in a bottle, God told me what I needed to hear more than anything else in this world! And that was, that he still had plans for my life, and that he knew me and had a plan and purpose for my life before I was even born!"

"And finding Mum and I and Grandma were part of that plan, right Dad?!"

"Oh, yes, my Princess, finding Mum, you and Grandma was a big part of that plan."

Helen, with tears in her eyes, came and hugged me, and she said, "I don't know much about God's plans for me, Kingsley. But I do know that he brought you into our lives for a wonderful reason, and for that I am so thankful."

Gay came over and hugged and kissed me, and we all laughed and cried. And Melody laughed at us laughing and crying.

"There is something I want to do!" Helen exclaimed excitedly. "I want to write a message and send it in the wine bottle I found!"

"Me too, Grandma!" Melody shouted. "Can I send a message too?"

"Yes," Helen replied, "but we need a pen and paper."

"I have a pen and notebook in my backpack," Gay said. Gay helped Melody to write her letter, and Helen came over to talk to me.

"So, what are you going to write, lovely lady?" I asked. "Oh, I don't know, Kings. I would like to meet a nice gentleman who keeps himself fit and enjoys walking and exploring. Someone who has an interest in history and geography would be nice." She blushed as she added, "just like you." "Are you finished, Mum?" Gay asked. "Melody is ready to put her message in the bottle now." Helen looked at me and gently rubbed my arm. "Oh, I don't know what to say, Kings, can you write it?"

"Sure, alright, give me the pen."

I wrote: "Lovely, mature and family-orientated Lady. I enjoy walking and exploring new places. I have a keen interest in history and geography and in healthy living. Would like to meet a handsome gentleman with the same qualities and values."

"And we better write your phone number, or he won't be able to contact you even if he finds the bottle," I said. "No, let's give him your email, that's a safer way to correspond with someone until you know them."

Helen read it over, and she blushed again, almost as red as Gay does. Her big blue eyes looked deep into mine and revealed the young girl that still lived inside, and she gently kissed me on the cheek. It was a precious moment as my soul connected with this lovely woman.

"Okay, ready Melody," she called. "Let's put both our letters in, and we'll get Kingsley to push the cork back into the neck of the bottle."

"And I get to push it out to sea," Gay said.

I pushed the cork in firmly, and Gay and Melody walked out to the end of a high rock that jutted out into the waves. "Shall I just drop it into the sea or throw it out further?" Gay called back.

"You'd better throw it, as the tide is still coming in, and it will likely come right back onto this beach. Lob it out into the surf, and as soon as the tide changes, it will take it out to sea."

"Here goes!" she shouted. And the message in the bottle was on its way.

"Where do you think it will go, Dad?" Melody asked. "It could travel a long way, but it will most likely be washed up somewhere on the Gower Peninsula, or on the other side of the River Severn. What did you write in your letter, my Princess?"

"It's a secret, Dad," she whispered in my ear. "But I'll tell you after."

"Okay," I whispered back.

"Hey, no secrets!" Gay shouted. "I'm the only one allowed to whisper in Dad's ear!"

Melody laughed. "No, you're not, Mum."

We watched the bottle as it bobbed about in the waves, and it seemed to be far enough away from the sharp rocks of the reefs that ran out from Hunts Bay.

"Well, who's hungry?" Helen asked. We all put our hands up. "So let's all go and have supper at Pennard Stores," she suggested, and we all enthusiastically agreed.

Melody was tired as we started up the steep path from Hunts to the East Cliff Road above, so I put her on my back and off we went. By the time we reached the road, and walked another fifteen minutes to Pennard Stores, we were all really hungry and thirsty, and we sat down in the courtyard for an early tea.

"No dishes this evening," both Gay and Helen exclaimed. "Just a nice tea and a glass of wine."

"Sounds great!" I echoed, "and I'll have a glass of cider with my shrimp and tomato baguette."

"You can't have a cider, Melody, you're not old enough, so how about a Pepsi cola?" Gay asked.

Gay ordered the ploughman's lunch, and Helen had a bacon and cheese sandwich with a Caesar salad.

"What are you having, Melody?" I asked, seeing the waitress heading for our table. I was famished, and didn't want to wait a minute longer before we put in our order.

"Oh, I will have a plate of chips, Dad, and lots of ketchup."

"Come on, Melody," said Gay. "You must have more than chips. This is tea we are having now, and we won't be having anything else till we get home to Cardiff."

"Okay Mum, I'll have chips and a bacon sandwich."

"I should think so," Helen echoed, "A growing girl like you needs to eat a good tea, especially with all the hiking you have been doing."

The waitress took our order and I almost drooled as I looked around the other tables to see what other people were eating.

Gay looked at me and laughed! "It is better if you don't look," she said. "It only makes you -more-hungry."

"Yeah, stop biting at the bit!" Melody laughed, and I gave her a sip of my cider. Melody and I played a game of "guessing if the next order is ours," as we watched the two waitresses going back and forth and bringing the plates of food out to the courtyard. "This is ours, Dad, I'm sure of it!" And it was! "Hurray, hurray mum, it's here!"

Then there was silence, as we all wolfed down our food. Melody belched, and I tried not to laugh! "That's polite in Japan," I pointed out. "That's how you let them know you enjoyed the meal."

Melody burped again. "You're as bad as each other," Gay said with a smile.

And with a great look of pride on her face, Melody said, "Hear that, Dad? We're as bad as each other."

"They call tea 'supper' in Canada, don't they, Kingsley?" Helen asked.

"Yes, they are a bit backwards over there, and they think that 'tea' is only a 'cuppa-tea'."

"Then they need to go to finishing school if they don't know what the difference is," she replied.

And I loved the way she said it! Helen has this wonderful way of combining what I would call 'sobering truth with compassion.' She tells it the way it is, and she will say what other people would only think! And yet she is a ray of kindness and she would give the coat off her back to a person in need. I don't know why I find her speech and mannerisms so attractive; maybe it's because of the sense of justice and right vs. wrong that we both try to live by.

Our table in the courtyard faced Southgate Road, and we watched some ponies on the green. Birds sang loudly with the excitement of spring in their songs, while dogs took their owners for walks, and sometimes let them off their leash. Even the number 14, green, single-decker bus looked friendly as it pulled up to the terminus and the fat driver climbed out and lit a cigarette. It was the number 64 when I was a bad boy growing up in Pennard Village. Pennard boys are the worst behaved of all the schoolboys, Mr. Merals, the bus conductor, told my mother. But Helen says that I have turned out to be a wonderful young man! And that is what counts, doesn't it?

As we continued to look out over the village green, and the houses along Southgate Road, Helen noticed that one of them was for sale, and it had a sign saying "Open House today".

"Let's go and have a look at the Open House," she said.

I lifted my eyes to see which house it was. Why, that's Grandma and Grandpa's old house, I thought to myself, and I haven't been inside it for years! "Yes, let's go and have a look," I echoed. And we walked across the road to the driveway.

The realtor welcomed us inside and began to show us around. "You seem to know your way around," she said, giving me with a puzzled look. "Have you been here before?" Helen and Melody followed her upstairs, while Gay stayed with me as I stood in one of the bedrooms.

"Why do you think she asked you that?" Gay asked.

"Because it is true, I have been here before. This is my Grandma and Grandpa's old house. This was my bedroom every second weekend for over a decade. I also spent a large part of my summer and Christmas holidays here in this house. It has five bedrooms and three bathrooms. And I can almost smell ‹Pat›, my Grandmother's dog, who used to climb up onto the bed and sleep beside me each night."

Gay's face lit up at my words, and she called out to her mum and Melody. "Mum, Melody," she exclaimed, "This is Kingsley's grandparents old house, and he spent much of his boyhood staying here."

"Really, Dad, really?" asked Melody excitedly. Helen seemed to give me this knowing look which said 'That's nice, but I'm not surprised.'

"That's wonderful," Carol the realtor replied. "You certainly know your way around." I smiled. "Would you like to look at the garden now?" she asked everyone, and we followed her outside.

Suddenly, I was back in yesteryear, standing in Grandma and Grandpa's front garden. There were the yellow and mauve rose vines, thicker now and still growing up the wooden trellis. Bees buzzed, and butterflies danced from flower to flower.

"Are you alright, my love?" Gay spoke softly, so only she and I could hear.

"Yes, love, I'm more than alright. I feel like I am walking in a dream back in time. Look, there's the old swing set, where I swung so high – I went right over the top bar!"

Gay nodded her head. "Yeah, I can see you and your brother doing that."

"And there's the old stone bird bath that I pulled over on top of myself trying to climb up it when I was six years old. I remember doing that as if it were yesterday. Grandma and Grandpa, who were gardening nearby, came running over and pulled it off me. Fortunately, I had not been hurt, but I wasn't able to play in the garden on my own for the rest of that day. They had me pulling weeds and planting flowers with them, if I remember rightly."

"Are you two alright?" Helen asked, as she walked over with Melody and the realtor.

"Yes, I'm fine," I replied, waking from my wonderful daydream. Melody then left us to chase a large blue butterfly that was flitting from flower to flower at the bottom of the garden. I followed her back into my dream. And for a few wonderful moments, I dared to believe that this could be our family home one day!

"This is the perfect place for all of you," Helen exclaimed, as she watched Melody chasing the butterfly at the far wall.

"Yes, it's perfect," I echoed. "It's big enough for all of us, and it's in the heart of our beloved Pennard." I knew I was standing face to face with a "new dream" that I had already shaken hands within my heart.

I didn't say anything more to anybody. I just whispered to God in my heart and said, "What do you think? It's perfect!"

We thanked the realtor for showing us around and drove home to Cardiff.

Nothing more was said about the house until a few days later when Helen invited us over to her place for tea. As we sat at the table, she said that she had something to say to us all. What could it be? Gay and I wondered as we looked across the table at each other. Actually, I believed I already knew, only I wouldn't dare to say it. But my dream shouted out loud within my heart!

Helen offered to pay our down payment on the house, and she said we could pay her back when our house sold in Cardiff. "It would allow you all to go and live in Pennard," she said. "We practically spend every weekend on the Gower Peninsula as it is! And a house like that will not be on the market for long!"

Was I hearing this right? It must be a dream! But it wasn't! And the following Friday after work, we all drove out to Pennard and made an offer on the house.

David Griffiths, the lead pastor at the church where I worked in Swansea, said that they were happy with my youth ministry, and that within a year they would offer me a full-time position. Gay said that she would be happy to commute back and forth between Swansea and Cardiff. I could drop her off at Swansea train station before I started at the church at 9:00 am. And Melody didn't mind changing schools if we could go and live in Pennard.

Gay and I had always dreamed of coming back to Pennard to live and to be able to give our children the heritage of the Gower Peninsula that we had always enjoyed so much. Wow! This would be amazing if we could purchase Grandma and Grandpa's old house! And I prayed to God in my heart and asked him to give me the faith to believe that he would do this for us. All we had to do now was to pray, and to wait and see if our offer was accepted.

There is a wonderful verse in the Bible that my Grandmother gave me once when I was waiting for a prayer to be answered. It reads: "Commit your way upon the Lord, and trust also upon him, and He shall bring it to pass." Psalm 37 verse 5.

Whenever I think of that verse, I am reminded of the time I first learned to swim in the Black Pool at Pwlldu Bay. My father put me on his back with my hands grasping his shoulders, while he swam using the breaststroke around the deep pool. As I held tightly to his shoulders, I looked into the dark water and couldn't see the bottom, and I imagined what could be down there in the depths. Drowned sailors, a sea monster lurking, or a big crab ready to pinch my feet? If I slid off my Dad's shoulders, I would surely drown! My imagination went on and on. Then the moment I had been dreading came, when my father said, "Come on, Kings, I want you to try and swim on your own."

"I can't!" I protested. "What if I sink and you can't reach me?"

"You won't sink," he said, "you must have faith! The saltwater itself will hold you up with its buoyancy, and as you push and pull your arms through the water, you will have momentum and move across its surface. And I will be here swimming beside you, and I can reach you if you get tired."

"Remember, Kings," he added. "Faith is the substance of things hoped for, the evidence of things not seen." Hebrews 11 verse 1.

My hope was to swim around the scary Black Pool like my father and not drown! The evidence was to put my faith in what my father had told me. The saltwater and the momentum of pushing and pulling my arms back and forth would keep me afloat.

I will never forget letting go of my father's shoulders that day, and sliding into that deep black pool, and yes! that salt water held me up! I didn't sink and I didn't need my father's hand to reach out and save me. I did not even have to move my arms and swim. I could just lie on my back and float! And when I pushed and pulled my arms as my father had taught me, I could swim right across the pool!

"Well done, Kings!" he said. "Look at you!" And all my fears of the Black Pool fled away that day. For I believed in the evidence of what I could not see, and my faith became sight! God is like that, I remembered, we must let go of our own control and put our trust in Him. Then we will see the evidence of him working in our lives!

We made our offer on the house on Friday, as planned, and Carol introduced us to the owners, who seemed to be nice people. They said that if our offer is accepted, we would be able to move in within a month. It all seemed like a dream that I did not want to wake up from, and I tried not to get too excited. Easier said than done!

Each night before bed, Gay, Melody, and I prayed that God would give us the house and that we would have the faith to believe that he would do this for us. For it seemed such an incredible thing to ask for! To own Grandma and Grandpa's old house in Pennard! But then God had done great things in our lives before. He had helped Gay and I to find one another again after twenty plus years! He would not let us down, and if we did not get the house, then it would only be because he had something better in mind for us.

There were four other parties interested in the house, and we did not know what their offers were. Carol said that we could always make a counteroffer if one of their offers was higher than ours. But there was one thing that God had given to us already. And that was his promise that everything would work out in the way it was meant to. Gay and I were thankful for that. It surely is a blessing to have peace, and not to have the headache of needing to lean on one's own understanding.

Trust in the Lord with all your heart and lean not on your own understanding. Acknowledge him in all your ways, and he will make your paths straight.

Carol said we would know within a week if our offer was accepted.

Chapter Seven

A Taliath Tale

As we waited to hear about the house, another great event was upon us. Samantha called us from Canada and said she had been accepted into a student exchange program at Swansea University and would be coming out to Britain in the next few weeks to do some travelling before starting at the University in September. Wow, I thought! Wouldn't it be wonderful if we got the house and Samantha could stay with us in Pennard. That would be great, and I prayed another earnest prayer to God that Gay and I would get the house.

Our family routine in Cardiff continued. Melody was doing well in school, and my pastor's job in Swansea was going well. And pastor David and Jackie's hospitality in welcoming me to stay at their home once a week made my commute back and forth to Swansea a lot easier. I stayed over at their place on Monday nights after my day of work and went in with David on Tuesday mornings. And on Tuesday evenings, Gay drove down from Cardiff to pick me up, or I caught the train home. Every second Sunday, I taught at the church, and Gay and Melody would come with me.

We were particularly pleased that Melody was going to Sunday School again. She had been going to Jackie's class before I had left to go back to Canada. And now that I was back, she was enjoying going to Sunday School again and making some nice friends.

We heard back from Carol the following Friday after we had made our offer, and someone had offered a higher price. Carol had called us immediately upon hearing this, and we upped our offer. 'Well, this is it, God,' we prayed, 'we can't offer any higher.'

On the following Wednesday, we got a phone call saying that our offer had been accepted! Yes, thank you, Lord! Thank you for answering our prayers! This was such a blessing for our whole family! Now Gay and I could give our children the heritage of having a home on the Gower Peninsula.

The following weekend was Gay's birthday, and Helen and I decided to surprise her by renting a caravan in Port Eynon. We could celebrate Gay's birthday and the wonderful news of our offer being accepted for the house.

"You can't tell Mom!" Both Helen and I explained to Melody. "It's a surprise! We are going to leave right after you finish school on Friday." Melody took my hand, and we skipped all the way to school.

"Hello, Melody and Kingsley," Mrs. Jones said, "you look particularly happy today, Melody. It isn't your birthday today, is it?"

"No, Mrs. Jones, it is my mum's birthday tomorrow, and we're surprising her by taking her away to Port Eynon on Friday."

"Port Eynon. Oh, what a lovely surprise! I wish I was going to Port Eynon."

Melody dragged me by the hand into her classroom and showed me the paper for her special project that was in her desk. "We have a fortnight to finish the project, Dad," she said. "Can you and Mum help me?"

"If we're allowed to, we will," I whispered. "Sometimes Mrs. Jones likes her pupils to do projects on their own."

"Oh, you and Gay can help," Mrs. Jones, said, having overheard our conversation. "As long as the project is complete and handed in within a fortnight."

"Does that mean we have to find a fort and a knight in order to have it in a fortnight?" I joked with Melody.

"Don't be silly, Dad!" she replied, smiling. "Now give me a hug because class is starting."

"Okay, Princess, see you this evening."

"Love you Dad." "Love you too Princess. And don't forget that Mum will be picking you up from school because I'm spending some time with Grandpa."

Today was Thursday, and I had arranged to do some metal detecting with my father at Pennard Castle. He wanted to do some more digs and see if we could find the "treasure" that Taliath had illustrated on her map. Whether we found anything or not, I was looking forward to a relaxing day with Dad. Much as the last few weeks had been exciting, I sure needed some down time, to just process everything, such as my job at the church, and especially getting the house! And our move from Cardiff to Pennard. We had already put our house on the market, and Helen was also considering selling her house and moving to Pennard.

A Taliath Tale

What better way to relax than a day on Pennard Burrows, metal detecting with my dad, I thought. And I stopped for a cuppa-tea before I made my drive to Swansea. Dad said to meet him at his house, and he would drive us to the Gower. His partner, Mary, had made us sandwiches, he said, and he had also done some more translating of Taliath's Diary. I was sure glad that Gay and I had brought dad on board with the translating because we just hadn't had the time with our jobs and family life. And I was really looking forward to learning more about Taliath's life and the ancient culture in which she had lived.

It was a relaxing drive along the motorway to Swansea, and I was getting used to driving on the left-hand side of the road again. The morning commute was over, and I took my time as I drove by names and places that were all a part of my Welsh heritage. Margam and its endless sand dunes, Port Talbot with its famous smelly steel works, and there were the muddy waters of the river Neath making its way to the sea at Aberavon Beach. I could see the mudflats and marsh pools all the way to the sea as I crossed the Jersey Marine Bridge and then on past Swansea docks and the more recent university buildings. Welcome to Abertawe, the Welsh name for Swansea. I was almost there!

My father lived in Port Tennant, just outside the city of Abertawe. He had lived there since moving away from Pennard on the Gower, shortly after I stopped living in caves.

When I arrived, Dad was already loading the car with our metal detectors, "…and I've got Taliath's map," he said, and soon we were on our way to the Gower. We spoke Taliath's name as if she were a part of our family, and yet she remained such a mystery to me. Maybe not so much for Dad, who had translated the latest installment of her story. "Here Son, read this," he said, handing me the translation. "Go ahead, read it, it is very interesting!" And I did.

I am the youngest of four sisters. My name is Taliath-Saren, which means 'Diadem Star'. I may be the youngest, but my grandfather says, that I shine like a star! And my light shines upon my sisters guiding their paths. My eldest sister is Gwenhwyfar, who is training to become our next Clan Queen. Then there is Arlais, whose name means 'from the temple'. She is appropriately named, as she is training to be a "watcher" in the sacred ceremonial room. Then there is Tanwen, my sister who I am closest to. Her name means, 'shining or holy fire'. Grandfather says we have all grown into our names. It is believed to be part of our clan culture, to grow into our names. And if we don't, then we are of a dark spirit race, and are exiled from our family and clan! I don't know about that condemning law. Only that it was passed down from the Princes, who my sister, Tanwen, says, are suspicious of everything they don't understand or can't control! Tanwen, is the bravest of us all! And she says what the rest of us only dare to think. Mother says that her inner fire might one day cost her, her head. But it is Tanwen's passion and fire that I love! And if you ask me, she should be the one to become our next Clan Queen, not Gwenhwyfar. Maybe I am wrong about Gwenhwyfar? It is just that she is so gentle. And as our mother says, you must be tough skinned to be a Clan Queen. Grandfather says that Gwenhwyfar has a humble spirit, and a great inner strength, which will help her be a good Queen to our clan.

Our mother's name is Ebrill. And it means 'one born in April'. Grandfather always says with fondness, "Ebrill was born in the April rains, and her life as our Clan Queen waters everyone like the spring!" Our Aunt's name is Gwlithen, which means 'dewdrop'. Grandfather's face always lights up when he talks about Gwlithen. He says she glows like a fresh dewdrop on a thirsty flower. I love my aunt Gwlithen. She is more of a mother to me than Ebrill, for she is tender and kind and nourishes my heart.

Our mother was born a commoner, but not without beauty. And our father was put to death after participating in a Balwyn Stone Ceremony, which I will explain later in my diary of the various clan ceremonies. As I previously stated, my mother, sisters and I live as members of clan number one hundred and forty-two of the one hundred and forty-four established clans of the Coastal and Black Mountain Clans of South and West Wales.

In order to be an "established clan," the clan population must be between seventy and one hundred and forty members strong! This number does not include children, male or female, under the age of twelve, but able-bodied adults who can gather firewood, hunt, fight and protect the established clan from enemy clans, and from misplaced individuals of un-established clans.

If an established clan population drops below seventy members, it becomes an un-established clan. This happens as a result of disease, starvation, or attacks from enemy clans. And on occasion, the clan simply loses too many of its young warriors in battles or hunting expeditions, leaving its existing members unable to provide enough food to eat, furs for clothing, or to cut enough wood for fires, and gather stone for the repair of our settlements and huts. And we all pray to our Gods that we remain an established clan! Otherwise, we are plundered, raped, and murdered! Or bought and sold as slaves!

Every established clan has a Queen. The Queen of Clan, or "Clan Queen," as she is known in our clan. The Clan Queen is the most central figure in all of clan life and culture! Apart from the **Princes** and **Priests**, there is no one more powerful and important than the Clan Queen. The exception to this law is an evil **Priest** or **Balla**, both of whom are more dangerous than ten hungry lions!

Wicked priests can be bribed! The Balla, or "Death Kissers" as my sister Tanwen calls them, are greatly feared. They are said to have the keys of death! And if one of them wants you dead, you are as good as dead! And it is just a matter of time before he puts his evil plan into action. The Nobles argue and accomplish nothing! The Princes, as I have said, are rarely seen. And when they are, it is to end disputes between the common people and the priests, and to work with the nobles in passing laws that they are so far removed from, that they are scorned by the people. But the Clan Queen is loved and worshipped by the people.

My sisters all want to be like my mother, the Queen, and wear the sacred Surth and royal sandals. But I am last in line for such a title, so why should I squabble over what will never be mine.

My story starts when I was twelve years old. My Grandfather made shoes. He made strong animal hide shoes for the hunting and fighting clan warriors. And delicate, detailed sandals upon which he carved and coloured designs for people to wear at our ceremonies. Because of Grandfather's gift of shoemaking, my mother and us sisters were taken care of, and had status within our clan.

Grandfather would make his shoes and sit at the village well, and he sold or traded his sandals to the women coming to the well to fetch water. Priests put their monthly orders in for ceremonial slippers that the people were required to wear in the sacred temple rooms. Princes and Nobles ordered their shoes only once a year. Grandfather made them all with skill and pride!

I used to watch him for hours, and we would talk. It was here at the well where he taught me our people's laws. All laws, he said, were made by the bloodline Welsh Princes, who lived at the castle and owned most of the land. The Princes handed down the laws to the Nobles, who received both land and titles from the Princes to implement the laws among the people. And the Nobles ordained Priests and Ballas to uphold the laws and govern our clans.

I am my grandfather's favorite granddaughter, and my sisters all make fun of me, saying I should have been born a boy. But Grandfather always tells me to be happy with who I am. He says that he loves me more than any son! He has taught me many things about our people and culture. This includes our many Celtic Ceremonies that our mother oversees at the temple.

"Why is it important that I learn all this Grandfather," I asked? "Can't you tell me a story instead?" "No," he always replied, "learning these laws and ceremonies will teach you how to live and how to be wise among your people." So, I listened. And I am glad that I did. Some days he would joke with me and say, "Who knows, maybe one day you will rule your people."

And I would say, "Oh Grandad, if only I could be the Clan Queen, I would be a fair and just Queen." Gwenhwyfar and Arlais, would always laugh and tease. And mother would say, leave her alone, a girl can dream, can't she! And that is what I did when I was with my Grandfather. I listened and dreamed. I learned how to make sandals and carve symbols on them. And Grandfather told me again, as other men walked by proudly with their sons, that he was glad that I was not a boy, he loved me just the way I was. And when I made my first sandals, he was so proud of me! He showed everyone who came to the well and told them that I had made them!

Grandfather was the first man I ever loved. It is not that I do not love my father. As I wrote earlier, he was put to death when I was young. But he did make me a necklace, my mother said, and I wear it around my neck and imagine my father is with me. Grandfather says he is! He says he is with me in my heart and in the memory of my soul, that is separate from my thinking mind. "In this way we are all connected, Taliath," he said. "This is how we can feel good or harm from another person that we have not met before. Our soul memory remembers and recognize if a member of our ancestry has been harmed or blessed by them or by one of their relatives."]

"Well, what do you think, Kings?" Dad asked, as I finished reading the latest translation.

"Wow! That is great, dad! I feel really connected to Taliath, now. She does feel like one of the family, and I am looking forward to us translating more of her story."

"Take it home to Gay, Kings, I'm sure she'll like to catch up on the diary."

"So how is married life going, Old Son?"

A Taliath Tale

"Oh, it's great, Dad, we get on so well!"

"Good to hear. She is a lovely lady! And are you getting into a good routine with your work in Swansea and the commuting? And congratulations are in order, are they not! Congratulations on getting your house – and no ordinary house either! I am very pleased that you're going to be living in Grandma and Grandpa's old house. I have many happy memories in that house, as I am sure you do too!"

"We are all thrilled to be moving back to Pennard, Dad. It's going to be a great heritage for all of us."

"Did you put your house in Cardiff on the market yet, Kings?"

"Yes, just last week. I hope it will sell soon."

"I'm sure it will, Old Son. It is in a good location on Bute St, and it's a very nice house. When do you get possession of the new one?"

"In one month, so not too long to wait."

"Good, things are falling into place nicely, Kings."

We arrived at Bendrick Drive, where we parked the car and walked across the golf course to the castle.

"Let's have one more look at these coordinates on the map," Dad said, "and we'll get started and see what we can find. I am still puzzled about the tree, Kings. The sycamore tree that is illustrated on this map is long gone."

"Yeah, and this tree is an oak, Dad, and at most it looks to be about fifty to seventy years old. There is no way that it was around when the diary was written, although the coordinates on the map indicate that this is the exact spot." As I looked around, I could see the disturbed ground where we had dug holes the last time we were here.

"It's got to be here somewhere, Kings! But we can't just keep digging around like this, or people are going to get suspicious as to what we are doing."

"You're right, but there is one thing that we haven't considered yet."

"And what's that?" "Maybe someone has found it? They have done some excavating at the castle, and probably at St. Mary's Church wall as well," I replied.

"I try not to think like that, Kings! When you are metal detecting, you must believe that you are going to find that which you are searching for, otherwise it can get discouraging."

"True enough, Dad, let's carry on like we are going to find it then! Where shall we look next?"

"Let's look somewhere where we would least expect to find something, Kings. Just like when you found Taliath's diary. You were just digging in the sand, remember? How about we move away from the church wall and focus on the castle grounds again."

"Yeah, okay, like not bother with the map for a while."

"Yes," it hasn't done us much good so far, has it?"

"How about you start at the gate entrance of the castle, Kings, and have a go with my detector. It would be good if you get familiar with it, as it is so much more advanced than your old one. Here, let me show you a few things on these buttons. Turn this one about halfway to pick up depth, and this one should be turned up high for density, as there is a lot of stone and gravel with the sand. Your old one is still good at picking up larger objects closer to the surface, but I think we should be focusing on a fair depth."

"Right you are, Dad. I'll try at the gate entrance here, and you keep an eye out for people."

"Dogs walking their owners, you mean?"

I laughed, and I started swinging the detector from side to side with slow, wide movements. There seemed to be nothing right at the entrance, so I concentrated on an area of grass about thirty feet out from the entrance and just off the main path where people approach the castle from the east. I passed over a few bottle caps, and a fifty pence piece, which was nice, but nothing else. And as I looked across at Dad, he was fiddling around with my detector, and appeared to be bored.

"Are you going to use it, Dad?" I shouted across to him. "Yes," he replied, "I'm just adjusting it to its maximum depth sensitivity. I'd give this one to Melody, Kings, and get yourself a new one."

"That is a good idea, it's her birthday at the end of the summer. I'll give it to her on her birthday and keep it in the family." Dad nodded.

Suddenly, the detector beeped strongly, and I knelt to dig.

"Don't dig yet!" Dad shouted.

A dog and his owner were approaching from the north. "Good morning," the man said when they got closer, and his dog lifted his leg to pee. I was tempted to lift my leg, but I said good morning instead. People tend to mind their own business here on the Gower. The locals do anyway, but one can't be too careful when treasure hunting.

Once the man was a fair distance away, I started digging. There is nothing worse than digging for treasures and being joined by a dog, even if he has cleaned his teeth. And invariably, the owner soon follows, and has nothing better to say than "Can I help?"

Of course, you can't, you silly ass, now leave me alone, you and your dog! I don't say that of course. Unless he's a …. Ah, yeah, we'll leave it at that, I think.

"Hungry, Kings?" dad shouted.

"Yes," I replied as I pulled a Coca Cola bottle from the ground. It was an old bottle and with a rusted cap still on it.

"Let's have a look, Kings! It's a really old bottle, 1950's I'd say? Well, it wasn't a complete waste of a metal detecting morning. I'll put it with my other bottles. That's if you don't mind…"

"No, you can have it, put it with your collection."

We stopped in at the Southgate Pub for lunch and talked about old times. Much as I had been looking forward to finding Taliath's treasure chest, I wasn't disappointed. It had been a relaxing morning spending time with dad, and we had some great conversation on the way back to Port Tennant.

After a cuppa tea and a visit with Mary at Dad's house, I headed home to Cardiff. "See you next week Dad." "Yeah, see you Kings, and don't forget to give Gay the latest translation of the diary." "I won't, bye Dad."

When I got home, we all headed over to Helen's for tea. And Melody and I managed to keep our surprise for Gay quiet. Helen confirmed the plan with Melody and I while Gay was in the bathroom.

"We will leave my house at 6:00, and as far as Gay knows, you're all coming over here for tea tomorrow, so she won't suspect anything. And as soon as you arrive, we will leave for Port Eynon. I am packing a picnic for the journey, so we won't need to stop anywhere on the way for tea, other than a stretch of our legs when we reach Swansea. We can head right to the caravan and start our weekend."

"What about a cake for Mom?" Melody asked.

"You can help me make one, Melody, while Mom and Dad go for a walk on the beach." And our plan was in order.

"Shush, Grandma and Dad. Mom is coming back to the table."

"I feel like a pirate," Melody whispered in my ear, "making secret plans without Mum knowing."

"You are a pirate," I whispered back. "A very pretty one, mind you." And Melody laughed.

After a nice tea at Helen's and a long game of Scrabble, we headed home to bed.

Life is wonderful, I thought, as my head hit the pillow. Thank you, God, for blessing us with another wonderful day. "Goodnight my love" was the last thing I heard, and it was Friday.

Melody came bursting into our room and jumped onto the bed. And she whispered into my ear, "Today's the day, Dad, today's the day."

"It is," I whispered back, "but we have got to keep it a secret." And then I remembered that Melody and I had already told her teacher, Mrs. Jones at the school about the surprise. It was a good job that I was taking Melody to school today, and not Gay. I would have to pick her up too, otherwise one of her friends would likely say something to Gay.

"Bye you two," Gay said, as she kissed us and headed off to work.

"I'll pick Melody up from school!" I shouted.

"Thanks, see you both tonight."

"Perfect, Dad," Melody said excitedly! "She doesn't suspect anything is up!"

"Yes," I replied, and I walked Melody to school.

"Don't trade all your lunch," I said. "Unless it's for something really good."

"Like for a pony, you mean?" "Yeah, like a pony, my Princess. I love you and I'll see you this afternoon."

"Love you too, Dad. And remember, don't tell anyone!"

"I won't, only the Man on the Moon."

"You can tell the man on the moon," said Melody, and she was still giggling when Mrs. Jones called the class to attention, and I headed off for my day.

At 4:00 pm I picked Melody up from school as planned, and we met Gay at home.

"Come on, you two," Gay said. "Let's go over to Mum's for tea."

As we pulled up to Helen's house, she was in her own car waiting for us.

"What's Mum waiting in her car for?!" Gay exclaimed.

"I don't know," I said, and Melody began to laugh!

"What's going on? Something is up!"

"You bet something is up, Mum," Melody continued.

Just then Helen tapped on the window. "Come on then, are you all ready?" Gay rolled down her window and asked, "Ready for what, Mum?"

"Come and see," Helen said, and we all got into her car.

"Can I tell her, Grandma, can and I tell her?" asked Melody.

"Tell me what?" Gay pressed in her most persuasive tone.

"Yes, Melody, you can tell her," Helen answered.

"Guess where we're going, Mum, guess where we're going!" "I don't know. Where are we going?" Gay replied with what was now an excited and curious expression on her face.

"We are going to the caravan, Mum! Dad and Grandma hired a caravan in Port Eynon, for your birthday. Really! Really! I'm so excited!"

And we all shouted, "Happy Birthday Gay!"

"How long are we going for?" she asked, "and what about my clothes?"

"We're going for the weekend," Helen answered, "and I packed your clothes while you were at work."

"Oh, thank you. This is the best birthday surprise ever! You know how much I love Port Eynon. Thank you all so much!"

We drove as far as Swansea, and then stopped for our picnic that Helen had prepared. We were all too hungry to wait until we got to the caravan. And we sat on the clifftop at Bracelet Bay, watching the waves churning into the rocks below.

Gay took my hand and kissed me, and she said, "I sure missed you today, my love. It's been such a busy week, and I can't wait to spend some time with you."

"Me too," I said, smiling and pushing my fingers through her hair.

"Thanks for the picnic, Mum!" Gay and I said. "It's delicious."

"Thanks Grandma," Melody echoed. "I love egg and cheese sandwiches, and cockles, they're my favorite."

After all our thankyou's, it was Helen's turn to talk, and she asked me about the history of Bracelet Bay, and if I knew how it got its name.

"And what about the history of Culvert Hall?" Melody asked. "You said you would tell us part two of the story of John Lucas of Port Eynon?"

"Well, I can only tell you one story at a time, Melody, and Grandma asked first, so I will share what I know about Bracelet Bay, and then over the weekend I will tell you about Culvert Hall and the further adventures of John Lucas."

"Firstly, Bracelet Bay is not named after a bracelet, not that a bracelet hasn't been found amongst the rocks and pools at low water. Lots of people come here on hot summer evenings and cool off by diving off the rocks or going for a swim when the sea isn't too rough."

"Maybe a mermaid lost her bracelet there, Dad." "Maybe, Melody, the Gower has many stories and legends of mermaids and other sea creatures. But I will continue to tell you what I know about Bracelet Bay."

"After you pass the Mumbles Head, the two bays that lie immediately to the west are Bracelet Bay, where we are and then over that little tor to our left, there is another Bay called Limeslade. The tor is called Tutt Hill. Not named after me, because I am Kingsley Hill." Melody laughed, and Gay smiled, and Helen said, "Do continue."

"There is not much more to tell you about Bracelet Bay, other than, along with Limeslade Bay, it is here that begins the magnificent line of limestone cliffs and sandy bays that run for sixteen miles to the west and is the glory of Gower! Here also starts the wonderful cliff path that can take you all the way to the Worms Head at Rhossili Bay."

"And Dad and I have walked all the way to the Worms Head from here!" Gay, exclaimed proudly.

"I must do that some time," Helen said. "How long did it take you?"

"Kingsley and I took our time and hiked it in three full days, and we arrived at the Worms Head at dusk on the third day."

"Where do we get our word Slade from?" Helen asked.

"Slades are common along the Gower coast," I explained. "In addition to Limeslade, we also have Deep Slade."

"Which is also Hunts Bay, right dad?"

"Yes, Princess, I'm proud of you for remembering that!"

"Are there any more Slades, Dad?" Melody asked.

"Yes, there is Heatherslade, Rotherslade, and Mewslade. There are also others, known only by us locals. But the word 'slade' comes from the Old English slaed, which in place names, denotes a low valley, or a dell or dingle, or an open space between banks or woods."

"Well, it's time we were on our way," I announced. "We still have about a half an hour drive to the caravan in Port Eynon."

And with a full stomach and having stretched our legs, we continued our journey to Port Eynon. As we drove, it was nice to have the warmth and light of a late spring evening, and a beautiful sunset that promised a fair day on the morrow.

"Red sky at night, shepherds delight," Helen reminded us. "Or pink sky in morning, mermaids warning" – which is Melody's version of reading a new day.

We arrived at the caravan just as the sun was going down behind Port Eynon Point, and it was nite-nite to everyone as we all headed for bed.

Chapter Eight

Happy Birthday Gay

Saturday morning arrived, and it was my beloved Gay's birthday. And I wanted it to be a most special day for her! One of the reasons Helen and I had chosen this weekend to book a caravan, was because of the extreme low tides over the next few days and Gay's keen interest in exploring. She had wanted to explore the cave at Port Eynon Point, where on our last visit the tide did not go out far enough for us to reach the entrance and explore. It was low tide at about 1:15 this afternoon, and we would be able to reach the cave on the low and have just enough time to explore it before the waves claimed its entrance again.

After making Gay and I breakfast in bed, Helen and Melody packed us a lunch and snacks for the day.

"Where are we going today, my love?" she asked, as I continued to feed her breakfast. "Mmm, thank you, my Prince. I haven't had strawberries in chocolate since our wedding."

"I'm happy you're enjoying them," I said with a kiss. "I think it's almost time we had another wedding morning, don't you?"

Happy Birthday Gay

She pulled me onto the bed and said, "How about another wedding night tonight!"

"Oh, yes please!" I answered, breathing heavily. And our date for tonight was arranged. We would escape to the dunes when Helen and Melody had gone to bed.

"Have you two finished breakfast?" Helen shouted out. "Melody and I have made the lunches, and we're ready to start the day."

"Okay, just a minute," we called, and we stopped our kissing and got dressed.

Melody made sure all our water jugs were full, and we were on our way to Port Eynon Point.

When we reached the beach from the caravan site, the tide still had a fair way to go before it reached its low, which would give us time to explore some of Port Eynon's other secrets. The beauty of so many places on the Gower Peninsula is that you can visit them over again, and it still feels like the first time. They are fresh and new, and they always have something to say to you. Whether it is a silent reminiscing voice that connects you with the memories of your past experiences there, or a loud shout as you see something in a different form, or from a different light upon what is otherwise a familiar sacred sight, like the mist covering and hiding the walls of Pennard Castle.

The "Blue Pool," for example, changes colour under different skies and light. Rough tides churn up the sand to make its depths seem foggy and mysterious as the waves first retreat. And on sunny days, its waters are the darkest green or black, and it appears eerie and bottomless. My friends and I would have to coax or dare one another to jump in when it stared at us with its dark mysterious face and conversed with our imaginations and fears. Once you jumped in, it felt as if a sea monster would grab you by the leg and drag you down to its forbidden depths at any time. The reflections of the climbing sun above and the ripples upon the waters made pictures of flying sorcerers as they entered to and from their alien spaceship deep below.

But back to today.

We decided to walk out upon Sedgers Bank, on which the last Lucas was supposed to have been buried. And further out towards the sea's edge, we could see the group of lichen-covered rocks called Skysea. As we stared out at the forbidding shipwrecking rocks, Melody asked me again to tell the story of the pirates that lured the unsuspecting ships to their doom upon the cruel monster rocks of Sedgers Bank and Skysea.

"No, Dad, wait! I will tell you the story of the pirates – I remember it!"

"Go ahead, Melody, tell us."

"Some pirates, who were both smugglers and shipwreckers, lured ships to their doom on Sedgers Bank and Skysea by tying a lantern to a horse's head, so when the horse walked, the light from the lantern would move like a ship being tossed by the waves. And the light on the horse's head, looked like the light at the rear of a ship, and the ships would follow the light thinking it was safe, and then they would crash into the rocks!"

"Well done, Melody!" We all clapped, and I said, "Melody, you are getting to be a great storyteller!"

From where we stood, we could see the large mysterious entrance of Port Eynon Cave. "Is that where we are going, Dad?" Melody pointed, and she stared across at it with a look of intrigue upon her face.

Happy Birthday Gay

"Yes, that's where we're going."

We walked back inland from Sedgers Bank, and then made our way towards the point. By now the great wilderness of rockpools was becoming exposed, and we watched the gentle falling tide flow back and forth in the deep gullies and pools.

"Let's go for a swim," Gay said, as we came to a beautiful deep gully with large seaweeds swaying in the current.

"Not me!" Melody protested. "What if there is a sea monster in there, or a dead pirate!"

"There's no sea monster and no dead pirates," I assured her. "How about you hold onto my shoulders, and we can all swim around the gully?"

"Alright," she replied reluctantly, "if Mum and Grandma come in too."

Helen and Gay soon changed into their swimsuits and jumped in. "Come on in, you two, the water is lovely."

And I must admit, I was quite impressed that they were in and swimming around the gully so quickly.

"Hold on, Melody," I said, and I slid in slowly as she held onto my shoulders.

"Not too tight!" I cried, "or I can't breathe!"

"Don't hold Dad around the neck!" Gay shouted. "Just put your arms on his shoulders and ride on his back."

And when she did, I could breathe again.

"Did I almost drown you, Dad?"

"Almost! And I'm glad you didn't. Otherwise, we would have a drowned pirate on our hands!"

Melody giggled.

The water was so refreshing, and the gentle ebb and flow of the tide pulled us back and forth along the gully. The water was crystal clear, and we could see the various coloured seaweeds and the rocks on the bottom. Melody kept her eyes peeled for a sea monster as she clung on to my shoulders, and fortunately we did not see one; otherwise, I would surely have drowned. As the last of the small waves left the pool, we could feel the temperature warm up in the gully. It is amazing how much colder it is in the open sea. We wallowed around in the gully for about half an hour, and Helen and Gay dove down to pick up shells and fancy stones, and then handed them to Melody, who informed us that they were part of John Lucas' lost treasure.

We played in the gully until our goose bumps were as big as gold medallions, and then climbed out onto the warm sun-kissed rocks.

"Salt-water is so good for your skin and your soul," Helen exclaimed with a smile.

"And so, refreshing!" we all echoed.

"We can almost reach the point," I said, seeing that the tide had dropped even more. "Let's go, because we need to be at the entrance of the cave as soon as the waves have receded enough for us to get in. Remember, the tide will only remain low for an hour and then start coming in again."

We quickly dried ourselves and changed back into our walking gear, and then we were on our way to Port Eynon Point. The sea remained calm as there was but a whisper of a breeze – just enough to cool our faces as we skipped across the wet rocks and around the magic rock pools that glistened, like lost coins, in an undersea world that the ocean had left behind.

Soon the sea with its pirate waves would return like a frantic woman looking for her purse, and it would reclaim our treasure and cover our mysterious and sacred world with white-gloved breakers, returning our gully to yesterday's dream makers.

We soon reached the headland, where the cave lies on the southern tip of the point.

"This is going to be exciting!" Both Helen and Gay shouted out to Melody and I, who had gone on ahead. We stopped at the large entrance and waited for them to arrive. As one stands at the entrance, there is a feeling of remoteness! It comes from the cave, as one can hear the calls of the past that penetrate the present like an overpowering voice in an otherwise whispered conversation. And then there is the exposure to the wild crashing waves that sweep mercilessly across the iron rocks, that like soldiers stand on guard at the entrance – only to be overwhelmed by the charging white-robed horses that are pushed in by the angry swells of the drowned sailor's souls, still heard screaming in the winds of the bay.

"What is it, my love?" Gay whispered. "You're so quiet."
"I'm listening to the stories of the past. Can you hear them?"
"Yes, I can hear them!"
"No whispering!" Melody called upon the soft breeze. "Who are you talking to?"
"Oh, just an old pirate that once was lost upon a ship," I replied.
"A pirate! A pirate! Did you hear that, Grandma? Mom and Dad are talking to pirates!"
"I know," Helen replied, "Let's go and meet one!"
"No thank you, Grandma!"

We all entered the cave, and then as we penetrated further in, it became narrower and lower.

Nan's Nan, and the Pirates of Port-Eynon

"I don't like this," Melody said, as she clasped my hand. "It's getting darker and there might be a pirate."

There was no danger of that, so we reassured her and then continued to look around. Gay and I closed our eyes and felt the presence of the past that conversed with our exploring spirits.

"You can just feel that so much has happened here," Helen echoed, and the walls of the cave told us their stories. The remains of Lion, Cave Bear, Woolly Rhinoceros, Mammoth, and Red Deer have been found in Port Eynon Cave. And of course, there is also what the cave says to each of us, whether we choose to share it or not. And it tells its stories to the listening winds and tides that always hear its voice.

"How much time do we have until the tide turns and starts to come in?" Helen asked.

"About half an hour, I think. Before we head back to the beach, let's climb the path behind the Salt House up to the top of the headland and have our lunch."

We all agreed it was a good plan, and we made our way back to the old Salt House.

As we climbed up the path, we passed the old quarries where the scars have all been softened and mellowed by time, and we arrived at the open, breezy plateau of Port Eynon Head. Right on the edge of the cliff is a lookout, with a memorial stone dedicated to Dr. Gwent Jones and Steven Lee, the two founding members of the Gower Society. So many things that we enjoy today in Gower were saved by their efforts and those of the society they inspired.

Just beyond the monument, we walked over the top of the cliff, or so it seemed, for we followed a narrow path that almost plunged down a steep, limestone slope towards the sea,

Happy Birthday Gay

and then turned suddenly into a deep cleft in the rocks. We all held onto each other tightly as we made our descent. Melody needed me to pull her back a few times while she regained her balance, but she did well, keeping pace with the rest of us. Then suddenly we all looked up with a gasp! We were standing face-to-face with the celebrated Culver Hole!

The whole of the cleft, which reaches back almost to the top of the cliff, has been filled with a wall of masonry, pierced by two rectangular windows at the bottom and two circular windows at the top.

"Who built this? Was it pirates?" Gay and Helen asked in wonder! Melody was too in awe to say anything other than "Wow!" And I answered in the only way I could. "Some say it was built by John Lucas and his pirating buccaneers. And others say it was a pigeon loft for meat back in the early days…" And with a lot of coaxing from my girls, I shared what my father had passed down to me. And I must say, dear reader, that I thoroughly enjoy sharing with others the wonderful heritage of history that my father taught me, and I hope that you enjoy it.

There is nothing like 'Culver Hole' on the whole coast of Great Britain. It is an especially eerie place when the fog is thick, and the sea drives in through the cleft; and the wind cries through the bleak windows; and the sea spray is wet upon your brow. As I went on to describe a particular day when I took shelter in this haunting place, the girls listened intently.

"I struggled down the slippery path that was hemmed in from the sea by a thick wet fog, and I wormed my way into the Hole itself. In the semi-darkness, the air was filled with the smell of rotting seaweed as the wind howled outside. And as I looked out of the grey windows, the sea was the same colour as the sky, and I could not tell where one started and the other ended, as it was all dark and pirate grey."

"What do you think Culver Hole was?" Helen asked. Gay thought it was a smugglers lair, and Melody thought it was a pirate's den.

"By the nineteenth century, smuggling demanded secrecy as the essence of the business. And the inhabitants of Old Port Eynon knew every trick of the trade. I think the last place they would have chosen to hide their pirated goods would have been a structure like Culver Hole, which can be concealed on the landward side but could be seen for miles out to sea. Could the Lucas' have used it? Would they have needed it for piracy? Remember, Melody, what we learned about the Salt House. The Lucas' already had the Salt House nicely fortified, and they were brave as lionesses about their activities. In my view, they did not need another stronghold."

"What about those peculiar holes in the walls?" Gay asked. "What were they used for?"

"Perhaps those square holes in the walls give us a clue? Now, Culver is an old English word for Pigeon. Could Culver Hole have been a giant pigeon-loft for the Salt House? The Lucas' certainly had the power and resources to build it, and pigeons were a welcome addition of fresh meat. A change from beef, mutton, fish and rabbit. And in those days people had no means of keeping lots of cattle through the winter, so pigeons would have been a lucrative market of meat."

Helen thought that it was most likely built for pigeons, and not as a romantic smugglers lair for the Lucas'.

"What do you think, my love?" Gay asked.

Happy Birthday Gay

"Well, I really don't know... And in a way, I don't want to know. It's just like the Gower Peninsula itself – full of mystery and adventure!"

I deepened my voice: "Tis the Gower Boy! And she has many secrets! Yes sir, she does!"

"But," I continued, "I like to believe what an old man once told me when I was a boy..."

"According to an ancient account, John Lucas made a great stronghold of Ye Salt House, with its battlements and walls thereof all round, reaching even into the cliff and the rocks.... And storing the stronghold with arms, he rebuilt and repaired another stronghold called Kulvert Hall near there, in the rocks, and rendered both inaccessible, save for passage thereunto through the clift."

"Are you speaking in Old English, Dad?" Melanie asked.

"I am trying to, but I'm not doing a very good job, I'm afraid. Grandpa would not be best pleased!"

"And I like to believe that there is a secret passage underground, 'where no man was told the mouth thereof,' between the Salt House and Kulverd Hall."

"Is Dad speaking in pirate language now, Mum?"

"Yes, he is, Melody, pirate and Old English."

"I think we are all pirates!" said Helen. "Yes, we are the Pirates of Port Eynon!"

At her words, Melody tried to wrestle with me for any treasure we might find.

"Come on, you pirate girl!" I said. "We haven't found anything yet. You wrestle me when we find something."

"She's a dominant little mare," Helen shouted out, laughing.

Gower Peninsula Adventure Series

And then it was time for us pirates to go – before we got cut off by the waves that were now coming in and crashing against the rocks. "Come on everyone! Let's get back to the beach."

It was late afternoon by the time we got back to the golden sands of the beach, and we were hungry again.

"I've got an idea," Gay said, "as I'm the birthday girl, let's have fish and chips on the beach."

"Fish and chips, yeah!" Melody and I shouted out together.

There is nothing like fish and chips on the beach, I thought, as Helen and Melody went off to buy our meal, while Gay and I waited on the beach.

"Happy Birthday! my love. Are you having fun?" I whispered.

Gay smiled a big smile…. "I'm having a wonderful day, my Prince."

We all enjoyed an early tea on the beach, and we were surrounded by the happy sounds of summer, which seemed to have arrived today! It had done sot just for us, and I again looked forward to having a romantic evening on the sands with Gay.

After we had eaten our fish and chips, Helen and Melody said they had a surprise, and they had to go back to the caravan to get it.

"Gay and Kingsley, you stay here," she said. "Come on, Melody, let's go and get Mum's surprise."

"No peeking!" Melody shouted back, as they walked up the warm sand.

Gay and I watched the tide as it climbed the beach and got closer and closer.

Happy Birthday Gay

"We timed our walk perfectly," she said. "Look at the point. It's completely cut off now!"

"And only the ghosts of the long-lost Lucas' play in the wild waves," I said.

After about twenty minutes, Helen and Melody returned with a large chocolate birthday cake.

"Surprise! Surprise!" they called out.

They even had candles, which we lit, and Gay made a wish. Melody and I ate until we hurt!

"Gosh, that was good!" I exclaimed, and everyone echoed my enthusiasm.

"Fish and chips, and chocolate cake on the beach – you can't beat that!" Gay exclaimed, as she finished her lady-like mouthful, and Charlee the seagull swooped down to clear up any crumbs.

After tea, we all headed back to the caravan to change our salty clothes and have a rest. Then Helen and Melody stayed in for the rest of the evening, while Gay and I went back to the beach to watch the sunset.

We walked eastward across the sands towards Horton, while the incoming tide climbed higher up the beach. To our left, were the dunes that separate the two villages of Horton and Port Eynon. There was still plenty of light in the sky as the sun had not yet gone down behind the horizon.

"That gives us time to reach Horton and back," I said to Gay, who seemed to have her eyes fixed on the dunes. About halfway between Port Eynon and Horton are the biggest dunes, but there is one that is taller than all the others.

"Let's climb up there on the way back, and watch the sunset from the top," she said softly.

"Good idea, my love, that's exactly what I had in mind."

We held hands and paddled along in the waves until we reached Horton.

"I've missed you so much," she said softly, as she squeezed my fingers. "I've been looking forward to being alone with you all day."

"I can't wait to make love to you," I whispered, and I led her up the beach to the front of the tall dunes. The evening sun was warm between our toes as we climbed up to our high castle. It was almost high tide below, as the breakers rolled in and washed away the footprints of our day. But our memories were safe, locked away in our hearts forever where no storm could wash them away.

At the very top of the dune is a long grass 'room' where the entrance faces west. Gay stood still with her eyes fixed on mine as I undressed her and undid the ribbon from her hair. She gently shook her head and her long flowing hair fell to her waist. And I kissed her from her lips to her feet until she panted and streamed like a flowing brook.

"Oh, don't stop, my love, you're driving me wild," she moaned. She began to tear at my clothes as we crashed to the sand, kissing and rolling like the wild sea. Oh, my love, oh!

Oh, my love, oh! my body echoed back, exploding like the Blow Hole on the Worms Head, as we crashed and rolled down the storytelling dunes, while a man and his dog looked up from the beach to see where all the noise was coming from. And as we looked out across the bay to Port Eynon Head, our cries of joy shouted louder than the screams of the drowned sailors on the Sedgers and Skysea Rocks.

Happy Birthday Gay

The sun tilted and went down behind the headland, and the painting of our day glowed upon the western sky like licking flames from a fire of oranges, reds, and yellows.

"They are the colours of our love, you know..."

"Yes, my love I know. You are orange, and I am indigo. Kiss me my love, and taste me, and oh! Keep going so slow...."

We had rolled three quarters of the way down the sand dune, until we lay spent and glowing like the day, and Gay and I both shouted together: "Hurray, hurray!" for our lovely day! You may walk me home to our caravan, my love, before tonight turns into tomorrow's lovely day.

Good night, my love, hurray! Good night, my Princess, hurray!

Good night, Helen. Good night, Melody. Don't forget that tomorrow is a new day!

Chapter Nine

Nan's Nan

Sunday morning arrived and spoke with the seagulls out on the bay, and the rising sun welcomed us to another wonderful family day. The sound of laughter and the smell of bacon and toast greeted us from the kitchen. It was a wonderful day already, I thought, as I kissed Gay's cheek and smelled her hair.

"Breakfast is ready, my love, and would you like a cuppa tea?"

"Yes, my Prince, but give me another kiss first. And let's sit at the kitchen table with Mum and Melody and look out across the bay."

As we sipped our tea at the window, little did we know that today was going to be a day set apart in our lives like few others. There are things that happen to us that we always remember, whether good or bad, but some events change our lives, and even reach out and try to become a part of who we are.

After breakfast, Helen said that she was going to have a quiet day at the caravan and read a book that she had been looking forward to reading. Gay and I decided to take Melody

Nan's Nan

to the Three Cliffs Valley and try to find the horses so she could start work on her school project. Melody had chosen to do a study on Nan's Nan, the horse I had introduced her to last summer and whom she also got to ride.

"I want to find out all I can about her family," Melody announced excitedly. "Do you know when she was born, Dad? And who Nan's Nan's mother and father were?"

"We will go and find the horses first, and then I will share with you what I know about them. And Mum knows some of the horses too." Gay nodded in agreement, and we were soon on our way.

We drove from Port Eynon to Penmaen and then walked across the Burrows to Three Cliffs Valley. As we climbed down to the beach, we crossed the stepping-stones over the Killy Willy and on to the marsh grasses of the valley. We couldn't see any horses grazing below Pennard Castle, but there were muddy clouds in the water, which told us that some horses were drinking or crossing the stream around the corner.

"There they are!" Melody shouted. "Can you see Nan's Nan?"

"The main herd must be somewhere else," I said. "I don't see Nan's Nan. She's a chestnut brown with a white mark on her forehead."

As we approached, we could see that there were two cream-coloured mares, and a dark grey mare who looked to be the leader.

"Look at the two foals, Mum, when do you think they were born?"

"They were probably born in early May," Gay replied, looking across at me.

"Yes, I would say early May. And look, there are young stallions too!" I always get excited when I see newborn stallions, because they remind me of my great friend and companion "Great Thunder" and his son "Roaring Thunder." And I wondered if these young stallions would have to fight one day to become the dominant stallion of the herd. But today we were looking for the "Great Grandmother" of the Three Cliffs Valley Herd, Nan's Nan.

"I hope we can find her," Melody said. "I want to see her and then I can start writing about her."

"I've got an idea," Gay said. "How about you ask Dad about her family, and we can have a sit down here in the valley and you can write in your book what is most interesting about Nan's Nan's family…"

"Now that's a good idea," I announced, and we sat on the grass to start the project.

"Nan's Nan is certainly the Great Grandmother of the herd," I said. "She was born at least fifteen years before I left Wales to go and live in Canada. And I have been away for over twenty years!"

"So, she is more than thirty-five," Gay said, "and that is very old for a wild horse."

"Nan's Nan is the mother of Chestnut," I continued, "a reddish-brown stallion who had a foal with Stormy, who was a feisty mare that chased anyone who came near her little foal called Dune-Dune. That I can tell you from experience, Melody. Stormy chased me all over the valley and up to the castle."

Melody laughed and was amused at the thought of me being chased. She reminded me that she was writing everything down in her notebook.

"I can't wait for my teacher Mrs. Jones to read this! Tell

Nan's Nan

me more about Dune-Dune, Dad." "What was most interesting about Dune-Dune, was that he was born in the sand dunes, and he was the same colour as the sand. I saw him being born with my friend Debbie Jones. There was a big windstorm in the valley that day, and Stormy went into the sand dunes to find shelter, and that is where she gave birth.

When Dune-Dune was older and wanted a family of his own, he left the Three Cliffs herd, and he went over to Oxwich Marsh where he met a mare named Iris, who was named after the marsh flower water-iris."

Melody quickly wrote everything I was saying in her notebook, and Gay looked over and smiled at me.

"Go on, Dad, tell me more. Did Dune-Dune and Iris have a foal?"

"Yes, and I saw Iris give birth."

"Was their foal a mare or a stallion?"

"Iris gave birth to a mare named Smokey."

"Now Smokey has a special story related to her name. Iris gave birth in a lovely grass meadow in the middle of Oxwich Marsh."

"Is that the same meadow where we found all the stallions hanging out together, when we went on our journey around the Gower?" Gay asked.

"Yes, that's right, and you said all the stallions were members of the Gentlemen's Club, remember?"

Gay laughed. "Yes, I remember."

"Hey, come on you two," Melody complained, "we are supposed to be talking about Nan's Nan's history, not your journey around the Gower." "I can talk to dad too Melody, or do I need to ask your permission?" said Gay with a stern look.

Melody smiled and tried to be patient.

"Right, where were we? Smokey's story,"

"Yes, so when Smokey was born in the meadow, within just a few hours of her birth, there was a wildfire! And a large part of Oxwich Woods was burning, and the whole marsh was full of smoke. Now, you know how a horse can stand up and walk almost as soon as it is born, well Dune-Dune and Iris had to lead Smokey out of the marsh and through the smoke to safety on the beach. And that's how Smokey got her name after escaping through the smoke. Another amazing thing about Smokey was that she was born with a grey coat, the same colour as the smoke from the fire."

"Wow, Dad, how do you know all this?"

"Dad lived among the horses," Gay replied.

And I proudly continued: "Now Melody, you might have noticed that I have followed Nan's side of the family but not the family of her mate. Now I have a question for Mum: Why do you think I chose to talk about only Nan's side of the family?"

"Because a stallion is harder to track or keep connected with than a mare is," replied Gay.

"That's right," I said. "Well done, Gay!"

"You see, Melody, Mum knows a lot about horses too."

"What do you mean, Dad? I can't quite understand."

"Well, soon after Nan's Nan gave birth to her foal, the stallion who was her mate left to continue his leadership of the herd as they moved around the different areas of Gower. And stallions are a lot more elusive than the mares, who feed and nurture their foals, especially when they are very young and need their mother's milk."

Nan's Nan

"The stallion has his part to play in the foal's life too," Gay shared. "He watches over his family, just like Great Thunder watched over his mare, Thunder-Spring, and his foal, Little Thunder. He used to watch them from on top of a high hill, and whenever another stallion came too close, or there was danger near, Great Thunder would come charging down from the hill to protect his family."

"Oh, I know that story!" Melody exclaimed. "That's Little Thunder who had a fight with another stallion and won! And Dad changed his name to Roaring Thunder to remember his great victory."

"That's right!" Both Gay and I exclaimed together! And as we looked into each other's eyes we celebrated, in our hearts, the heritage that we were already passing on to Melody.

"Well, have you written all this in your notebook, Melody?"

"Yes, most of it, Dad." "Okay, there is one more thing that I remember. And that is – Nan's Nan's mate was called Clover. He used to watch Nan's Nan and Chestnut from up on top of Clover Hill."

"Right," Gay replied.

"Okay, let's have our lunch now," Gay suggested, "and then we can see if we can find Nan's Nan."

We sat on the bank of the Killy Willy stream below the castle and had our picnic. There was no sign of any other horses in the valley, so we decided to climb up the steep path to the castle grounds. Sometimes you can see the horses near the castle from the valley, and other times they are out of sight somewhere in the castle grounds.

"I hope she's there," Melody said in a tired voice as we climbed up the steep sandy path. Then suddenly we heard the neighing of a horse coming from behind the castle walls, and with a renewed spring in our steps we ascended the rest of the way to the castle.

"There are the horses!" Melody shouted. "And there's Nan's Nan over by the entrance to the castle gate." "It looks like her," Gay replied.

"Come on," I said, "let's get closer…."

It was Nan, alright! And she seemed to recognize Melody and me from last summer. She came right over to us, hoping we had something for her to eat.

"Can I give her my apple, Mum?" Melody asked.

"Yes, alright, but remember, our food has to last for the rest of the day!"

"I know, Mum, but I don't mind giving her my apple."

"The only problem with feeding Nan is – we are going to have the whole herd around us in no time," I said looking around.

And as soon as Gay had finished speaking, we were surrounded by the whole herd, wanting to look inside our backpacks.

"That's not yours!" Gay called out firmly, as a grey mare pushed her nose into Gay's backpack.

"Don't forget to hold the palm of your hand flat and keep your fingers together," I called out to Melody, who had already started feeding her apple to Nan.

"Her nose is warm, and she tickles when she eats out of my hand," said Melody, laughing.

"I'm sure she remembers you from riding her last summer. A horse will always remember your smell. That is how horses remember if a person is kind or mean to them. Do you remember how hard it was to get the saddle on to Nan's back, Melody?"

"Yes, Dad, I remember! And Nan bit Uncle Fraser when you and he were following her with the saddle. That must have been so funny, Dad!"

"I thought it was funny, but Uncle Fraser was not amused."

"And horses bite hard," Gay reminded us. "So be careful, Melody, and do what Dad said. Keep your hand flat and your fingers together."

As Nan finished her apple, she walked away to join the rest of the herd that had moved toward the back wall of the castle. Then suddenly the wind came up and there were dark clouds forming in the sky.

"I think there is going to be a storm," Gay said, as we watched several flashes of lightning and heard distant thunder out over the bay.

"Is the storm coming this way?" Melody asked. "It might be," I replied, "but it is still quite far away."

"It looks like the horses can sense the storm is coming this way," Gay said. "Look! Nan's Nan is leading the other horses into the castle room to take shelter. It's amazing how horses can know and sense things often before people can."

"Look, Mum and Dad," Melody said, "Nan has a limp in her left hind leg. How did she hurt her leg?"

"Well, part of it is old age, I'm sure," I replied. "But she was once hit by a car as she was trying to protect a young foal."

"Tells us the story…" Gay and Melody asked together.

Suddenly there was another rumble of thunder and a flash of lightning. This time, it sounded like the thunder was getting closer.

"I think it's coming this way," Gay said, "and that's why the horses are still in the castle room."

"I'm scared of thunder," Melody said with a concerned look on her face.

"Don't worry," I said. "There is nothing to be frightened of. And I'll tell you the story of how Nan's Nan got her leg injured."

"Wait Dad. I want to get my notebook out of my backpack so I can write the story down."

"Let's sit here on the wall," Gay said, "and listen to Dad's story."

"But what about the storm, Mum? Shouldn't we head to the castle room too? Dad said Nan is a wise horse and she knows things before people do, so she knows the storm is coming this way."

"Oh, I think we will be alright sitting here for now," replied Gay. "The storm is either going away or still a long way off. We haven't heard any more thunder over the last few minutes."

"Got your pen and notebook ready, Melody? I'm ready to start."

"Okay. An old man once told me that Nan's Nan was no ordinary horse, and that she had special powers of knowledge and discernment."

"What's discernment mean, Dad?"

"Well, if you're a horse, it means to sense something or know something is going to happen before it happens; or being able to know if a person is kind or cruel when you first meet them."

"Like Nan and the horses know that there is a storm coming, and they are already taking shelter in the castle room?" "Yes, well done Melody," Gay said, clapping her hands.

"What if you are a human, Dad? What does discernment mean then?"

"With human beings, it is more like intuition, but this is a conversation for another time. For now, I will continue on with what I know about Nan's Nan."

"The old man told me that Nan is able to connect with the past and discern the future," I stated.

"There is a girl in my class whose mum is a fortune teller, and she reads cards. Do you mean like that?" asked Melody.

"No, not like that, Princess. It's more of an instinct with Nan, like when we have a gut feeling about what someone is really like, even if other people think differently. Or when we go somewhere where we have not been before, and it is familiar to our soul."

I glanced across at Gay, desiring her help in explaining to Melody.

Gay smiled back and said, "It's like the saying a cat has nine lives. Like the animal has lived nine different lifetimes, so it has a lot of experience, and wisdom, in what it has learned during all those lives."

Now Gay and I started laughing, and Melody said, "I'm glad you two aren't my teachers at school. No one else in my class would be able to understand you, including Mrs. Jones." We all roared with laughter – and just then we heard a horse neighing from the castle room.

"It's Nan's Nan laughing," Gay exclaimed! And we all laughed some more.

There was no time for any more of my story, as the thunder and lightning was now getting much closer!

"Nan was right!" Melody said, and we joined the horses in the castle room.

The horses were quite accepting of us at such close quarters. The castle room is not big – about twenty square feet. Nan clearly felt comfortable with Melody, and she came right up to her and stood at her side. The other horses all stood facing towards each other at the east-facing wall of the room.

"She has discerned that I am good, and that I care for her," Melody shared, and Gay and I smiled back at each other. Our daughter was becoming just like us.

Suddenly there was a flash of lightning and a loud roar of thunder – very close!

"I told you that Nan was right!" Melody called out, in a rather nervous voice. "The storm is coming this way!"

Just then there was another flash and an even louder roar of thunder. "Let's move to the far end of the wall," I said, "and look away from the lightning." It looked like fork lightning now and it was crackling across the sky.

Melody took both Gay and my hands, and the horses moved toward the entrance of the room as if they were protecting us.

"Look, Melody," Gay said. "The horses are standing at the door like they are guarding us from the storm!"

"I'm sure they are," I echoed, before the next clout of thunder arrived, right over our heads! Melody and Gay both clasped my hands hard as the next series of clashes seemed to shake the whole castle!

"Look how calm the horses are!" Gay proclaimed, as she turned around and drew comfort from the herd.

"They are used to all types of weather and storms," I reassured, as the booms continued overhead.

Crash, boom! And then came the rain! Gay and I quickly took our jackets off and made an umbrella over our heads. It was a good job we had taken Helen's advice and brought our jackets otherwise we would have been soaked through.

Slowly the roars of thunder moved further and further away, and I began to count the time between the clashes as my Dad had taught me when I was a boy. Soon we were all counting, and Nan was neighing.

"I'm sure she is counting in horse language," Melody informed us, and I was sure she was right.

Eventually the thunder moved out across the bay and the rain stopped. And the horses looked totally unperturbed by the ordeal. As for us, it was time to make our way back to the caravan. The rain had stopped, and the dark clouds and thunder were moving out across the bay.

I helped Melody and Gay lift their backpacks back onto their backs and we were on our way.

"Come on, Old Girl," I said to Nan's Nan, who was still blocking the entrance of the castle room. "Come on, Old Girl! The other horses have moved out of the room, so why are you standing in our way?"

"She's acting very strange," Gay commented, as I continued to try and push past the mare.

"What about giving her some more of our food?" Melody suggested. "Maybe that's what she's waiting for."

"No, it's more than that," Gay discerned. "She's trying to tell us something."

I looked at Nan's Nan. "Is that right, Old Girl? Are you trying to tell us something? What is it, girl, what are you saying? Look Nan, it's stopped raining and the storm has gone now." And I tried one more time to push my way past her. This time she pushed me back with her nose and showed her teeth!

"Alright Old Girl, I get the message loud and clear – you want us to stay in the room for a while."

"She can sense something, Dad," Melody said, and Gay agreed that there had to be something that the mare was trying to tell us, but what?

Suddenly, the wind began to pick up, and the dark clouds were returning our way. Lightning flashed across the sky and the thunder roared again!

"It's coming back, Mum and Dad!" Melody shouted. "And Nan knew the storm was coming back – right, Nan?"

Nan quietly neighed, as if answering.

"She is talking to us," Gay said, "I can tell, and it's uncanny! I've connected with a lot of horses in my time, but Nan is something special…!"

Within minutes, the sky was as dark as if it were late evening, and the rain began to pour. Nan neighed again, and this time louder. Soon the other horses returned and entered the castle room.

"She was calling the others back, Mum," Melody said.

"She sure was," Gay replied.

Now there was a strong wind and stinging hail!

"Quick, let's turn toward the wall and kneel down," I called out. "Help me hold our coats over our heads, Melody."

Nan's Nan

"This is sure a freak storm for the middle of June," Gay said, giving me the most puzzled look.

The lightning crackled in the sky right over us, and the thunder boomed so loud that it scared some of the horses, who anxiously moved around the room, and I thought they might injure us!

Then Nan's Nan made a call that neither Gay nor I had ever heard before. It was a loud series of high-pitched neighs, in a sequence of different tones. "She is speaking to the others," Gay said. "She is trying to keep them calm."

"And us too!" Melody added.

The storm lasted for another twenty minutes before slowly moving out across the bay again. And in all my time living on the cliffs and in my caves, I had never experienced a thunderstorm as powerful as that one!

We were soaked through, and we needed to get back to the caravan for warmth. The other members of the herd left first, but Nan continued to stand in the doorway for some time. And none of us questioned her reasoning this time, for we had all learned a valuable lesson from Nan's Nan.

Finally, she moved away from the door of the room, and we didn't hear one more bout of thunder all day. But our day of learning from Nan was not over yet! We were about to experience an event that was going to change our lives forever.

As Nan moved away from the door and crossed the castle grounds, we followed her. The rain had been so heavy that the sandy paths leading down to the valley from the castle were like little streams, and Nan proceeded to walk down one of them.

"This is the path I would have chosen, Nan!" I shouted. "Lead us back down to the valley, Old Girl."

As we continued to follow behind her, the other horses seemed to have all disappeared.

"Probably gone to graze somewhere else," Gay said. "There were lots of new shoots of grass to eat coming up all over the burrows."

Suddenly, Nan stopped in the middle of the path.

"What is it, Old Girl? Can you sense something else?"

Nan's Nan neighed again, lifting her head up and down, and then she began to dig in the sand with her hoof.

"She answered you," Gay exclaimed, "and she wants to show us something she's found."

We all moved closer to look. Nan continued to dig with her front hoof, and to look back at us as if making sure we were taking notice of what she was doing.

"What is it?" we asked ourselves. "Wait a minute, what's that? It looks like a piece of old wood," I said. I moved closer and stood right next to Nan, and suddenly, her hoof scraped on something.

"It's the top of a box!" I exclaimed. "Gay, Melody, come here and look at this!" Nan continued to paw, and we could see now that it was the top of an old wooden box of some kind. She had led us to something buried in the sand! Nan then stopped suddenly, and continued walking down the path towards the valley, which gave us the opportunity to inspect her find.

I knelt and started brushing the sand off the box with my hand. Gay knelt on the other side and did the same.

"What is it? What is it?" Melody shouted in excitement! "It's a treasure chest, Dad, I bet it is! Nan's Nan wouldn't lead us to something that wasn't special!"

Suddenly, we could see that the top of the box was rounded, as more of the sand and mud fell away. "It's a chest alright," I said. "Look how the top is rounded and curves down to the sides. There doesn't seem to be any lock on it, but the top is stuck fast with hard clay."

In my excitement, I banged the top with my hands and then tried to pry it open with my fingers. "That's not going to open without a mallet or a screwdriver," I said, "and we don't have any tools."

Gay and I were silent now, almost disbelieving what was in front of us. We continued to dig around the sides of the chest, throwing the sand up on the bank beside the path until our fingers were sore. Melody joined in to help, and we soon removed all the sand from around it until we reached a coat of hard clay. This was so exciting! And we discussed what might be inside. "Could it be lost treasure or artifacts?" Melody wondered aloud. "If it's gold coins, we could pay Grandma back for loaning us the money for our house in Pennard."

"We could indeed," I replied, my spirit rising to the excitement in her voice.

Gay remained quiet, as if still contemplating what we had found.

"You're quiet, my love. What are you thinking?"

"I'm thinking about Nan's Nan. She knew the box was here! She didn't just stumble across it because of the rain. Horses don't do that – lead people to lost artifacts. But she knew the chest was here, and she wanted to make sure that we found it!"

"What's wrong with that, Mum? Nan has special powers," Melody said, with a puzzled look on her face, as if it was all the most natural thing in the world.

And I marveled at her simple faith in something she did not need to understand or have explained. It was time for me to say something. "Mum is just saying how unusual it is for a horse to lead us to find things," I stated.

"You mean like it's no coincidence?" queried Melody.

"Yes, that's right! And I agree with Mum. Nan knew it was here and she wanted us to find it. Remember the way she looked back at us when she was digging with her hoof? Then once she knew we had seen the chest, she continued on her way down the path."

"It is no use trying to dig around the chest anymore," I said. "We can't move the hard clay with our hands. Let's just concentrate on the top for a while and see if we can determine what type of wood it is. My guess is that it's oak – only a hard and durable wood would last in the sand and clay like this. It's probably been here for centuries!"

Gay checked the time, we had been digging around the chest for over two hours, so we needed to get back to Helen at the caravan and get ready to go home to Cardiff.

"What are we going to do with the chest?" Melody asked. "It's too heavy to carry."

"We will have to leave it here and come back with Grandpa and pick it up tomorrow," I said. "But we must bury it again – otherwise someone else will find it."

"Come on", Gay said, picking up the first handfuls of sand and throwing it back into the trench that we had dug around the chest.

"Let's not forget to cover the top," I said. "We need to make the sand look as undisturbed as possible. That way people are least likely to suspect there is something buried here."

Nan's Nan

It took us another 20 minutes to cover up the chest, and we headed back to the caravan. I was concerned that if we had more torrential rain, the top of the chest would become exposed again. "We will just have to trust that no one will find it, and then come back with Grandpa as soon as we can."

By the time we walked back down to the valley and up through the burrows to the car in Penmain, we were all tired, and I drove us back to the caravan in Port Eynon.

When we arrived, Helen had already cleaned up and packed up our clothes to leave.

"Oh, I'm so glad you're all back!" she said. "I've been worried that something might have happened. And did you get caught in the thunderstorm?"

"Yes!" we all replied together.

"And there is so much to tell you!" Gay added.

"So, you had a nice adventure then?"

"That would be an understatement!" Gay exclaimed. "You will never guess what we found!" "We found a treasure chest, Grandma, buried in the sand. I mean Nan's Nan found it. And she led us right to it after she had protected us from the storm."

"Nan's Nan, and treasure, Melody? That sounds intriguing! Nan's Nan is a horse, isn't she? She's the one you rode with Dad last summer...." "Yes, Grandma."

As we drove along towards Cardiff, we all filled Helen in as to what had happened. And once she understood the significance of us finding a chest in the sand, she became excited too.

"So how are you going to carry it back across the golf course if it's heavy?" she asked. "And are you going to get Grandpa Roger to bring out his tools and open it, so you can see what's inside?"

"I'm going to call him tonight, Helen," I replied. "And ask him to try to come out and get the chest as soon as possible."

"And before anyone else finds it and takes our treasure!" Melody interjected. "Are you sure there is treasure in there, Melody?" Grandma asked.

"Of course, Grandma! Nan's Nan would not have led us to the chest if there wasn't."

"Well, we will have to wait and see, you three. But one thing I do know for sure, is that the four of us are becoming more like pirates every weekend with our adventures on the Gower!"

Melody laughed, and Gay held my hand and smiled.

"So how was your book, Helen?" I asked, "And did you have a relaxing day?"

"Did I ever! I read my whole book and then I watched the storm in front of the fireplace with a hot cuppa tea. And in the afternoon, I walked from Port Eynon to Horton through the narrow lanes behind the village."

Helen looked around at the three of us. "Well, what would you three like to do for tea?" she asked. "We've eaten all the sandwiches and it will be quite late when we get back to Cardiff, so shall we stop somewhere on the way?"

"Fish and chips!" Both Gay and Melody, shouted.

"And Joe's Ice Cream for afters!" I added. "Mm, I can taste the salt and vinegar chips right now," Helen said, making our taste buds water. And I thought of that rich and creamy Joe's Ice Cream, dipped in chocolate sprinkles.

We ate our fish and chips overlooking Swansea Bay, and then got a tub of ice cream each, from the original Joe's Ice Cream parlour, just as my mother and father had done with my brother Fraser and I on so many occasions. And I thought: What a wonderful heritage I am continuing to enjoy and to pass on to my own family.

After we finished our ice cream at Joe's, we headed onto the motorway and made our way home to Cardiff.

"You soon won't have to drive all this way," Helen reminded us, "as you will be taking possession of your new house in Pennard at the end of the month."

It still felt like a dream to me, as I pondered the significance of living in my Grandparents old house.

We arrived home safely in Cardiff, and after saying goodnight to Helen, I carried Melody upstairs to her room and she fell asleep within minutes.

"No story for little Princess tonight," Gay said, walking quietly into the room. She then asked if she could talk to me about something.

"Of course, my love, what is it?"

"I hope you don't think this is weird or anything," she began, "but when we were kneeling and digging around the chest, I felt a presence around us. It wasn't something that frightened me like something evil, but rather it was a peaceful presence, and very strong! And I had the impression that it was a person who was concerned about the chest and its contents inside."

"You mean like the presence wanted us to find it?"

"Yes, in a way, and for us to understand and appreciate the importance of what we had found. Does that make sense, Kings? Or am I off the wall here?"

"You are making perfect sense, Gay."

Gay looked relieved.

"And by the way, I forgot to give you this to read. It's the latest translation of Taliath's Diary that Dad made. I meant to give it to you on Friday or Saturday but being so busy with our weekend I forgot."

"Do you mind if I read it now?" Gay asked. "My mind is far too stimulated to just go to bed." "A good idea," I replied. "It's quite amazing to learn more about Taliath's life! And I will give dad a ring and tell him about the chest."

"I hope this is important, Kings," Dad said. "I had just got into bed when the phone rang."

"It's important, Dad. You will never guess what we found near Pennard Castle this afternoon…" "A dead Viking! Or a sword? Coins? Come on, Old Son, don't keep your old man waiting – what did you find?"

"A chest, Dad!"

"You're joking! You're not being serious, Old Son!"

"I am, Dad, and that old mare Nan's Nan led us to the chest."

"So, you didn't use Taliath's map then?"

"No, the horse led us to the chest, which was buried on one of the slopes beside the castle."

"Well, did you bring it back? Where is it?"

"It was way too heavy to carry back, so we reburied it."

"What, you left it there?! Did you open it up and see what was inside?"

"No, the lid was stuck fast with clay. We had to dig away the sand around it, and then there are still layers of hard clay stuck to the wood. I didn't want to damage it, and I remembered you telling me that sand and clay can protect and preserve ancient wood."

"Yes, well done, Old Boy, you did the right thing. Otherwise, you might have damaged it."

"Now, did anyone see you digging there?" Dad continued. "And have you told anyone else about it?"

"For sure, no one saw us digging in the rain. And the only person we told is Helen, who was back at the caravan site when Gay, Melody and I found it."

"Good! Now we need to pick it up as soon as possible. Are you working tomorrow Kings?"

"Yes, I'm working until 4:00 at the church in Swansea, and Gay works until 4:30."

"Alright Kings, this is what we're going to do. You come over here after work, and we can wait for Gay to arrive. She should be able to get here by about six – what do you think?"

"Six will be fine," Gay called out, having finished reading and having heard part of our conversation.

"Good!" Dad said, "We have a plan then! You all have a good night, and I will see you at my place at 6:00 tomorrow."

"Are you sure that works, love?" I affirmed with Gay.

"Yes, that will work out well, because Melody and I were going to come and pick you up from work in Swansea anyway, so we may as well make an evening out of it. And I wouldn't miss picking up the chest for anything!"

Before we went to sleep, Gay shared how much she had enjoyed reading the latest translation of the diary.

"And there is one more thing I need to tell you before we go to sleep, my love," she said.

"What is it?" I asked expectantly. I was sure she was going to share something in relation to the diary. And she did.

"It's about Taliath, Kings. I believe that the presence I felt today was Taliath's spirit."

"Gay, there is something I want to share with you too. I might have actually told you this before, but when I first found Taliath's diary in the grounds of Pennard Castle, I felt a presence all around me, in a gentle wind that came from nowhere when I first held the diary in my hand."

"Yes, Kings, I remember you saying that."

"This is amazing! I can't wait to go and pick up the chest with Dad tomorrow. Maybe we will find more clues inside…?"

In the morning, Melody came jumping onto our bed as usual, and we told her about going over to Grandpa's and picking up the chest in the evening.

"Would you like to go over to Grandma's, Melody?"

"No, I want to come! Can I come?" she pleaded. "What about your class assignment on the horses?" Gay asked. "It's due to Mrs. Jones tomorrow, isn't it?"

"Yes, Mum, it is, but I still need to write about Nan's Nan leading us to the chest."

"Don't write about finding the chest," I said. "That's our secret."

"Yes, Dad's right, Melody. How about you write as far as Nan's Nan protecting us from the storm and finishing there. And if you promise to work on it tonight when we get home, and then go straight to bed, you can come with Dad and I to Grandpa's."

"Yes, yes!" Melody danced in excitement. A deal had been struck!

Gay and I looked at each other and laughed, and she whispered in my ear: "I think we are a bad influence on our daughter. We are going to make a pirate of her yet."

After breakfast, Gay took Melody to school, and I headed off to take the train to Swansea. "Don't forget to pick Melody up from school," I said to Gay, "and I will meet you at Dad's place at six."

"Bye Princess," I said, "You be good at school."

"Bye, Dad, see you tonight when we go to pick up our treasure." I smiled all the way to the station.

It was a busy day at work, but the time still didn't go by quickly enough. And a few times during the day, I pictured someone else finding our treasure and breaking into the chest to get what was inside. "It's going to be fine," I told myself, and I even went into the bathroom to pray on my break, and asked God to watch over it for us and not allow anyone else to find it.

Finally, the hands on the church clock read 4 o'clock, and David came into my office and said it was time to lock up. "Congratulations again on getting your house in Pennard," he said, "and Jackie and I want you all to come over for tea again soon."

"That would be nice," I said, "and we will look forward to it. See you at work on Thursday, David."

"Yes, you're off tomorrow and Wednesday, right. See you on Thursday, Kings, and say hi to Gay and Melody for us."

"I will, David, and say hi to Jackie."

Dad was already waiting in his car when we all arrived.

"Get in, you three," he said, "I've got a shovel and a spade in the back, and any other tools we might need."

As we drove along towards Pennard, Dad was as excited as we were, and we were soon at Bendrick Drive. Dad parked the car and we walked across the golf course to the castle.

There were golfers out enjoying the evening, and we heard a few shouts of 'four' as we hurried across the fairways, but we escaped being hit by a golf ball.

We arrived at the castle grounds and looked for the path beside the castle where Nan's Nan had led us to the chest. Melody was tired after walking across the golf course, but I kept her amused by playing a guessing game as to what we might find in the chest.

Dad reminded us that there was virtually no history known about Pennard Castle, apart from the approximate time it was built, and that the room we had sheltered in on Sunday with the horses was added to the original structure at a later date.

"And as far as St. Mary's Church is concerned," he added, "there is nothing known at all about its origin, other than what we are learning about the settlement that grew up there, through Taliath's diary."

At Dad's words, Gay and I looked across at each other in excitement. What would we discover today, we wondered? Could we learn more about Taliath's life and her people? Or would the chest have no connection with her at all?

"There's the path!" Gay exclaimed as she pointed, and we made our way down through the wet sand toward where we had re-buried the chest. Dad and Gay walked ahead as I lifted Melody up onto my back.

"Here it is!" Both Dad and Gay called out.

"It's a good job we came back tonight," I said. "Look, the horses have trodden over it and removed some of the sand."

"You're right," Dad said, "someone else could have easily found it." And he knelt to inspect our find.

Nan's Nan

"It's a chest alright!" His voice carried over the otherwise quiet valley. "Look at the top and how it rounds, and you can see the stain of mud in the wood. And I think it's oak," he said, tapping it gently.

"Just like you said, my love," Gay whispered as I lowered Melody off my back.

"It's been stuck deep in the clay for a long time," Dad continued, "and it has helped to preserve the wood in the ground."

"I'm so excited," Gay said, reaching out and taking my hand.

"Now I'll use the small trowel," Dad said, "and remove the clay to within an inch or so of the actual wood on the side of the chest until we can see what we are up against. I can see you have already removed a lot of the softer clay and sand with your hands, but this stuff is hard, and I don't want to push any metal against the wood. This clay may be the only thing holding it together."

After a pause, he continued: "Kings, you use this spade to dig deeper in the ground around the chest and gently break the clay. Gay and Melody, if you can just use your hands to remove the loose clay that I'm breaking off and throw it on the bank away from the chest…. That's great, nice and easy, it's coming away nicely now. Remember, we need to leave a layer of clay around its sides to protect it. Kings, how deep is the clay at the bottom of the chest?"

"Deep, Dad, and it's hard as a rock in places."

"I figured it might be. Use the miniature pickaxe I have in the backpack and see how that works."

I did as he suggested. "This is better, Dad, it's breaking off easier using the point…."

"Good. But watch you don't hit the side or the bottom. Remember, we just want to be able to lift it."

"This is more exciting than emptying the dragon pool," Melody shouted, rubbing her hands like a little pirate, as the rest of us remained silent in expectation.

Finally, we had dug a fair size hole around the chest, and it sat like an island in the middle of the path. It was time to take a rest, and we all knelt in the sand and wiped the top of the chest with our hands. For a few moments, there was silence between us as our hands rubbed the top of our treasure box, and each of us imagined what might be inside. Dad broke the silence by singing "Yo ho ho, and a bottle of rum."

"I'd better not sing that," he said. "We don't know what's inside yet."

"And that's a pirate song," Melody said, laughing. And then her face returned to an expression of deep contemplation as the skylarks hovered and sang their sweet songs above us, songs that seemed louder in the still, contemplating air. Were they excited and awaiting what was inside too?

Dad had brought a large flat-edged screwdriver and a putty knife, and he gently attempted to pry the lid open.

"You're right, Kings, there is no lock or keyhole on the chest, as far as I can see. Only two well-crafted wooden joints on what looks to be the back of the trunk."

"The clay in the joints is like rock," he said, pushing the screwdriver into the clay as hard as he dared and gently tapping it with the small mallet. "If we can't move the hinges, then the top won't open. I can't tap it any harder or it will damage the wood."

Nan's Nan

I felt the urge to force open the lid if we had to, just so we could see what was inside! And I could see disappointed looks growing across Gay and Melody's faces at the thought of not being able to open it. 'But I needed to be patient and be an example,' I said to myself. 'And besides, Dad knows what he's doing. And he said that the chest itself might be extremely valuable, regardless of its contents, so we can't force anything.'

Dad now tapped the clay on the front of the chest, and it came off a lot easier. Once the clay was off, we could see that the chest was braced by a metal support.

"Would you like to hear what I think so far?" he asked. "Yes!" we all replied eagerly.

"Well, the hinges, as you saw, are made of wood. This tells me that the chest is likely to be a lot older than one with metal hinges. And the metal on the front of the chest is likely for decoration rather than for support. This tells me that it is less likely to be a more common storage trunk, but rather a more prestigious chest with valuables or treasures inside!"

A renewed wave of excitement rolled over all of us as we pondered Dad's words. He now took a rag from his pocket and began to rub the metal brace. "You can see now that it's not so much for support, but rather for show," he reiterated, his voice sounding more excited as the metal began to gleam when he rubbed the mud stains away.

"I think it's silver," he said. "Yes, I think it's silver!" His voice became more excited… "Iron or steel would rust, and it certainly wouldn't shine like this! And it isn't copper or brass either!"

"Is it treasure?" Melody whispered in my ear. And Gay answered for us both: "We don't know yet, Melody, let's wait and see."

Dad continued to tap the clay away on all four sides of the chest now, but he pointed out little pieces of wood that were breaking off with the clay. "We are going to have to carry it back to the car and take it home to my workshop. Otherwise, we might collapse the wood and ruin the chest."

It was going to be a long haul across the golf course and along the beach path back to the car. But we all agreed that it was better than damaging it.

Dad and I took an end each and Gay and Melody helped to lift and steady the sides. It was tough going, traipsing back up the path through the deep sand, and we had to take several breaks until we reached the castle grounds. Dad encouraged us by saying that he was convinced that there were artifacts inside the chest, and there was no water dripping out of it, so they would probably be well preserved; and that even with the added weight of the clay, if there was nothing inside, it wouldn't be this heavy.

After taking another rest on the castle grounds and pondering Dad's words, we wobbled our way across the golf course with a renewed enthusiasm – up and down over the hills and far away, and we were glad that the light was fading fast, as there were still a few people left on the golf course and we looked most conspicuous waddling around with a large chest.

"We certainly look like pirates," Melody reminded us, and Dad almost dropped his end laughing.

"We look far more ridiculous than pirates," he said. "it looks like we are carrying some poor soul in a coffin."

That made us all laugh, and we almost dropped the chest to the ground. "Come on," Gay said, "we are almost to the beach path."

When we reached the path, we rested again before the final haul to the car on Bendrick Drive.

"Gosh! My arms are two foot longer," Dad said, as we lowered our treasure box to the ground. He opened the trunk of the car, and with one more final heave, we lowered it in. "Quick!" he said, "Let's get going! In case we were spotted, and someone called the police. The authorities don't take too kindly to people taking artifacts."

Gay gave me a knowing smile, as she remembered stories that I had told her of Dad's and my adventures with our metal detectors and the treasures we had found.

Much as we were all disappointed that we couldn't open the chest and see what was inside, it was a fun ride back to Swansea, as Dad shared about what he thought might be in the chest. And we played a rather more extensive game than what Melody and I had played earlier when we had been guessing what we thought might be inside. Dad made us guess what century we thought the chest was made in? and to what people it belonged? Gay and I both answered the 10th or 11th century, hoping, of course, that it would be connected in some way to Taliath's Diary, which was written in approximately 970 AD and onwards. Dad had always had this wonderful gift of making history come alive! And our guessing game was no exception, as Melody wanted to continue to play until we reached Dad's house in Port Tennant.

When we arrived at the house, we carried the trunk straight to his workshop and sat it on the table. He suggested that we wait until tomorrow before opening it, which would give him time to think about the best approach. I must admit, and I know I speak for Gay and Melody too, that we would much rather have opened the chest to find out what was inside, even if we did do some damage to the wood. But we wanted to respect Dad's knowledge, and his belief that the chest was very ancient, which meant we would later regret damaging it.

After a quick hello to Dad's partner Mary, and a drink of juice, Gay, Melody and I decided to head back to Cardiff as it was getting late.

"I promise I won't open the trunk without you," Dad said. "I am going to try and loosen the clay with a solution that won't damage the wood. Bye, you three, and drive safely on the motorway."

"Bye, Dad, see you tomorrow."

As we drove along towards Cardiff, Melody, who we thought was asleep, said, "At least our treasure is safe at Grandpa's, and no one else can find it and take it away from the path."

"That's right," Gay replied. "It's our treasure now, and we will soon be able to open it up and see what's inside!"

"That's right," I echoed, "and we have Nan's Nan to thank for it."

"I think she deserves a big carrot, and an apple," Gay said. "We will feed them to her next time we see her."

By the time we reached Port Talbot, Melody had fallen asleep, which gave Gay and I the opportunity to talk.

"I am glad that Melody is asleep," said Gay. "I really need to talk to you about Nan's Nan, again. I hope you don't mind, but I can't stop thinking about her!"

"No, I don't mind," I replied. "I know we talked a bit about her before, but what would you like to know?"

"Well, do you remember when you told me that she was alive before you left to go to Canada, and that you knew her

Nan's Nan

even before that? Before you went to live in Devonshire with your grandparents, that is."

"Yes, I remember, and we calculated that she was at least 35 years old, which is ancient for a horse living in the wild. Yes, I remember us talking about that."

"Kings, there is something I need to ask you."

"Yes, of course, go ahead, love."

"Well, you know how you and Melody have been working on her school project together, and you have been telling her stories of your experiences with Nan's Nan at bedtime…"

"Yes, she loves hearing about our adventures."

"Well, you know how you have both been writing in her diary…"

"Yes?"

"I know this might sound crazy, but I was reading some of the stories about Nan's Nan in Melody's diary, and there are two stories in there that are about events that happened during the time that you and I were together as teenagers. And I remember both of those stories because you introduced me to Nan's Nan over 35 years ago, when you and I went to Dumbarton House School together. What I am struggling to understand, Kings, is that the Nan's Nan, you introduced me to when we were kids was old then! And the horse that led us to the chest yesterday, was the same horse! She had the same colouring and the same markings on her forehead, the same temperament, the same limp in her left hind leg, and she appears human-like in her intellect. I recognized her yesterday, and she knew me! Is there something you're not telling me, Kings?"

"Yes, there is. And the reason I haven't told you is because it doesn't make sense. It's unbelievable, but it's true."

"Try me – have I ever not believed anything you have told me?"

"No, you have always believed and trusted what I've told you. It's just that I can hardly believe it myself, and yet I know it's true! And I will tell you about Nan's Nan if you like."

"Yes, I want to know everything about her, Kings. You know that you can talk to me – you can tell me anything! No secrets, remember – that's what we promised each other when we got married."

"Yes, no secrets! So, are you ready for this?"

"Yes, my love, I'm ready. Tell me."

"Okay, I first met Nan's Nan when I was seven years old, along with my friend Debbie Jones. Nan was the oldest horse in Pennard back then. And I once met an old man who told me that she was from a special lineage of horses that had special powers, including having as you said, human-like intellect."

"Yes, I remember you telling me about the old man. He was a tramp, right? And he lived in the forest, and sometimes in a cave like you. And he would just show up at different places around the Gower when you were a boy."

"Yes, that's right, and he would somehow always show up when I needed a friend or some special help in my life, and he had a special connection with the wild horses. He told me that Nan's Nan was over 600 years old. Everyone thought the old man was nuts, of course, but I didn't. I have always known that there is something special about that horse."

"The old man also told me that she was able to travel back and forth through time. That is a bit far-fetched, I know, but I liked the old man. He helped me during some hard times in my life, and he taught me a lot about the horses and the Gower. Maybe he was from another time?"

At my words, an uneasiness came over Gay, and there was an expression on her face that I had never seen before. Maybe she was tired.

"Are you alright, my love?"

"Yes, I'm alright."

As we continued our journey home to Cardiff, Gay put her car seat back and appeared to be contemplating what I had shared.

It had been an amazing day, I thought to myself, and the fact that Gay and Melody had spent this time with Dad made me feel happy. I felt such a sense of peace and joy.

I was tired when we reached home, and I carried Melody up the stairs to her room and tucked her in. Gay and I went to sleep almost immediately, and we both dreamed about what was in the chest.

Chapter Ten

Tuesday

The next thing I remembered was a gentle breeze on my face, coming in from the open window of our bedroom. Gay was still sleeping, so I lay there thinking of the events of yesterday and my plans for today.

I had the day off, so I would be able to walk Melody to school and drop Gay off at work. Dad was going to ring sometime this morning regarding how things were going with the chest. Gay and I were anticipating him inviting us over this evening for tea, so we could open the chest.

But before we left the house, Helen rang, and invited us over for tea at her place in the evening.

Gay laughed. "It's nice to be in demand," she said, and after a quick discussion, we accepted Helen's invitation and looked forward to sharing yesterday's events with her, and, of course, to talking more about our new home in Pennard. We were due to receive the keys and possession of the house on Friday. Not driving to Dad's in Swansea tonight would also give us time to help Melody complete her class project, which was now over due to be handed in. We were all so tired last night, we didn't work on it as we had originally planned.

Tuesday

It was time to walk Melody to school and be her "hero" again, and as we entered her classroom, she flung her arms around me and kissed me in front of her teacher and friends, having made sure of course, that they were watching.

"Love you Dad."

"Love you, Princess, see you this evening."

Yes, fatherhood is such a wonderful thing! Every mum and dad can be their kid's hero – if they can just open their hearts.

I called Dad when I got back to the house, to fill him in on our plans for the evening. And as much as I wanted to see the treasures that awaited us, I told him that tonight wouldn't work for us.

Dad was pleased that we'd wait at least another day before opening the chest, as this would give him time to talk to an archeologist friend of his who knew a lot about the care and preservation of wood. Dad said he would call in the evening and let us know how things had gone with his friend.

After driving Gay to work, I drove to the bottom of Bute St. and spent some time by myself. A cuppa tea and a scone on the seafront was on my menu, and a walk in the morning sun. It was so nice to just be still for a while and have nothing planned, at least until tonight.

"Good morning, Mr. Seagull, how are you on this fine day?"

"Why, I'm very well Mr. Hill, I just caught a herring for breakfast out on the bay."

"Jolly good, my friend, now you fly off and have a good day!"

After spending a full day walking and relaxing around Cardiff Bay, it was time to pick up Melody and Gay.

"Hurray!" Gay shouted, as she got into the car. "No making tea or doing dishes tonight – we are going over to Grandma's for tea!"

"And no drying dishes for me!" Melody exclaimed, with almost the same amount of enthusiasm, "and Grandma makes the best afters!" And we were a happy bunch as we arrived at Helen's.

Helen had made a roast beef dinner with baked potatoes, vegetables and her own special gravy. The food was so good that there was hardly a word spoken, only noises of gratitude that came from three hungry people, while Helen continued to watch her figure and ate only a garden salad. Melody was the first to finish and she waited for afters to arrive like a child on Christmas morning.

"It's coming, Melody," Gay said. "You and Dad are almost drooling at the mouth." And we were.

"I don't mind drooling," Helen said, "as long as no one wags their tail or barks like a dog."

Melody barked, and we all laughed. And it was all worth drooling for! Helen had made one of her signature bread and butter puddings, with raisins and hot custard; and Melody and I continued our noises of appreciation until we were… well, shall we say, bursting. It was so good!

After tea, Gay and I helped Melody with her class project – The Adventures of Nan's Nan and her Family. Melody wrote in her diary all about how Nan's Nan had kept us safe during the thunderstorm, and then we shared more with Helen about the treasure chest and how we had carried it from the castle path and all the way across the golf course to the car.

Helen laughed as she pictured our feat, and then she asked if anyone had seen us….

Tuesday

"Only a few golfers," Melody replied nonchalantly.

Helen laughed louder now, and said "You must have looked like you were committing a crime carrying a big trunk across Pennard golf course!" "I'd love to have seen it," she continued, "and you carried it all the way to Bendrick Drive!"

"Yes, like four pirates!" Melody said proudly. "Well, it's time to talk about the house and your move to Pennard," Helen said, as she poured us a nice cuppa tea.

"We are getting the keys and possession of the house on Friday," I reminded everyone, "and I will be taking a small load out to our new house when I pick up the keys."

"And I will pack some boxes on Friday morning, because I've got the day off," Gay said.

"What about me?" Melody asked.

"You're going to school, Melody, because you only have one more week after Friday, and then you will be on Summer Holidays."

"Yah, Grandma, did you hear that? One more week and I'm on Summer Holidays!"

"Yes, sweetheart, I did, and you're pretty excited, aren't you?"

"Excited isn't a big enough word because we are moving to Pennard! I'm over the moon!"

"Then I think we are all feeling the same way, Melody. It's very exciting isn't it!"

"Oh, and Grandpa phoned to invite us all over to his place on Friday evening for tea, and we will be able to open the treasure chest!"

"Yes!" Melody shouted, dancing around the room.

"I hope there is something worth dancing for in that chest, Melody," Helen said, trying to get her to calm down.

"There is treasure, everyone, you just wait and see!" exclaimed Melody.

Gay tried to explain that there might not be gold coins or jewels, but rather another type of treasure, like costume clothes and artifacts, "…or even another diary like Dad found, that tells us about other people's lives who lived a long time ago."

"I prefer gold coins, Mum," said Melody, "so I can buy what I want for my new room at our house in Pennard."

And it was all so exciting as we made plans for the coming weekend.

"The nice thing," Helen reminded us, "is that you can move in slowly after getting the keys, because your house here in Cardiff has only just gone on the market, so you won't have to move out quickly."

And we all agreed that it was a blessing.

So, we had a plan. I would take our first load of fragile breakables to the house in Pennard and pick up the keys. Carol, the realtor, would meet me there at 10 o'clock, and then I would spend the day at our new house getting some things organized, as there was no point in driving all the way back to Cardiff only to drive all the way out to Swansea again in the evening. Gay would start packing some boxes after walking Melody to school, and then after school, Helen would drive Gay and Melody in her car out to Dad's for tea. We would all rendezvous at Dad's at 6:00 pm, and then open the chest.

I was up and had the car packed early on Friday and was soon on my way to our house in Pennard. And what a wonderful feeling it was, to be moving into my beloved Grandma

Tuesday

and Grandpa's house! Oh, the wonderful memories that came flooding through my heart and mind as I got closer and closer to Swansea, and then on to Pennard. I was surely a blessed man! And as I drove along, I thanked my God for his kindness and love that he had lavished upon my family and I!

I arrived in Pennard at 9:30, which meant I had half an hour to spare before meeting Carol for the keys. I sat across the road at Pennard Stores, and I had a cup of tea and something to eat in the courtyard while I waited for Carol to arrive. There were several people I recognized having their morning coffee and reading their newspapers at the courtyard tables, which were really the outside part of what was now a thriving little restaurant. It had been just a little tea and grocery shop when I had moved away from Pennard, but that was more than twenty-five years ago. Friends and acquaintances had grown up and had families of their own now. Some people stared at me as if they knew me from somewhere. And they did! But I was just content to sit and watch and feel, as this small village of my boyhood began to put its arms around me and welcome me back as its long lost "Son," back to its charm and generous heart. And I wept with joy as I looked across the road at our wonderful home and heritage, that I could never have hoped to attain! But I did! Thank you, Lord, for blessing me more than I could ever have dreamed of or hoped for.

And as a car pulled into the driveway, I walked across the road to meet Carol. Within minutes, she had given me the keys and any information about the house that I needed to know. And then I stood in my own front garden, in my beloved Pennard, as the new owner of my beloved Grandma and Grandpa's house on Southgate Road!

What shall I do? Sing or dance? I did both, and then I went into the back garden where my brother and I used to play in the old air raid shelter, and Grandma would bring us tea and biscuits and tell us stories of my dad's childhood during the war. Honeysuckle still hung from the trellis over the back door, while bees buzzed, and butterflies danced from flower to flower. And I danced with them, celebrating the past, the present, and the future all together!

And I said to the seagull on the roof: "This is something to celebrate, isn't it!"

"Oh yes," he said, and he flew in a circle and squawked his approval.

After bringing in the items I had brought with me from Cardiff, I visited each room as long-lost friends and I conversed intimately with each of them. And it was as if the past, present, and future all conversed with me, and became a part of this dream coming true. And I spent the afternoon revisiting the village and having lunch in the pub before heading to Dad and Mary's house for the evening.

Dad, Mary and I had a toast of apricot brandy before the others arrived, and we'd have another one when they came. "Congratulations on the house, Kings!" said my Dad with pride in his eyes. "You've come a long way from your days of riding wild horses and living in caves."

"Yes, I have," I responded, "but to me it seems like it was only yesterday when I lived in a cave and was called the Caveman of Bacon Hole."

Suddenly the doorbell rang, and Helen, Gay and Melody arrived.

Tuesday

"Come in!" Dad shouted, as Mary walked down the stairs to meet them. I sat in the living room, relishing the smell coming from the kitchen and listened to Dad's old wooden stairs creak as the girls walked up the three flights to the living room.

"What a wonderful old house!" I heard Helen comment, as she climbed the last of the stairs.

"It belonged to the owner of a coal mine," Dad replied, "and I restored it to its original design."

Dad had done an amazing job restoring the house, which was over two hundred years old, and which was haunted on the second floor. The rooms have high ceilings with artwork on the plaster, and the living room windows are arch-shaped with seventeenth-century embroidered curtains. The second floor is like an antique shop, with all Dad's restored furniture and his artifacts from his metal-detecting adventures. I'm sure the ghost is a Viking wanting back his sword!

"Come on in," Dad said, getting up from his leather chair and shaking hands with Helen, and then hugging both Gay and Melody. "Did they tell you about the treasure chest, Helen?" he continued. "We brought it back from Pennard on Monday."

"Yes, I've heard all about it," she said, "and we're all looking forward to seeing what's inside."

"Tea first," Mary said, sticking her head around the corner of the kitchen door. "Please sit yourselves down and I'll bring it in."

Helen went to the kitchen to help Mary. "We haven't all been together like this since Kings and Gay got married on the beach," Mary said, putting the gravy and mashed potatoes on the table.

"Oh, a cooked meal," Gay said, "what a treat! We've been so busy with the packing and organizing that we've seldom sat down for a meal."

"And congratulations!" Mary said. "I'm sure you all know that the house belonged to Roger's mum and dad."

"Yes, Kingsley has been so excited about living in his grandparents house."

"It's a good size house too," Dad added. "It's five bedrooms, isn't it, Kings?"

"Yes, it still has five bedrooms and three bathrooms, just as I remembered it, and the old fireplace where Grandma would make her coal fires is still there. I take our first full load over there tomorrow!"

"Then we certainly do have something to celebrate," Dad said, and we toasted the house and whatever we might find in the chest.

"Cheers! Here, here! To the house and the treasure!"

"And we must not forget Nan's Nan," Melody said, lifting her glass of orange squash. "It was she who led us to the chest."

And then we were all preoccupied with Mary's delicious roast beef dinner.

"A wonderful dinner!" we all said to Mary, as she went to the kitchen to get the afters.

"Oh, my favourite!" Helen exclaimed. "I love treacle pudding and bird's custard!"

"Yes, thank you, Mary!" we all chimed in, lifting our glasses to the cook. Mary grinned happily as she cut the treacle pudding and then poured the steaming hot custard on top.

Melody leaned over and whispered in my ear: "I'm glad the others only had small pieces so we can have more!"

Tuesday

"Me too," I whispered back. "It's fun eating like Farmer Brown's pig." Melody laughed loudly, and Gay gave us her look of "you're up to no good." And we were! We ate until we hurt, while Helen and Gay were most ladylike. "Alright, now let's go and do what we've all been waiting for!" Dad announced. "Let's go and see what's in the chest!"

"Yeah!" Melody shouted for all of us. "Let's go and see what's inside!"

We all creaked down the stairs to the ground floor and then followed Dad through the back garden to his workshop. And as we all sat silently in anticipation around the chest, I said to Helen: "I agree with you. I think not knowing, and then waiting to open the chest is the most exciting part!"

Dad slowly tried to lift the top of the chest. "I'm putting a lot of pressure on it, and it still won't budge," he said.

"Why won't it open?" Melody asked, with a concerned look on her face. "It's not that we can't open it," Dad replied. "It's that we need to be gentle with it. Remember, it hasn't been opened in hundreds of years – maybe even a thousand, and if I pull too hard, I will probably break it. I think the top is stuck with sand and mud, and it's acting like a seal or glue because the chest has been stuck in the clay for so long."

"How did you remove the clay off the outside of the chest?" Helen asked.

"An archaeologist friend of mine made up a concoction that removes the hard clay but won't damage the wood. And as you can all see, it has cleaned up the sides nicely, but if you brush it under the lid, then you risk getting moisture inside the chest."

Dad now used what looked like a large, flat paint scraper, but with a rubber edge on it, and he slowly applied an even pressure as he moved it along the front of the lid. The lid began to make creaking noises, then Dad moved the tool to the side of the chest and it began to loosen. Now we could see a minute gap, opening at the front, and as we held our collective breath, you could hear a pin drop.

"I think we are almost ready to open it now...," Dad said, breaking the silence. "Melody, you were first to see Nan's Nan digging in the sand, your mum told me, so, I think you should open the lid."

Melody beamed with excitement at her grandpa's words.

"Lift gently...," we all said, encouraging her. The lid creaked louder and louder, and it began to open.

"That's it," both Helen and Gay said, "keep going."

Then it wouldn't open any further. "It's stuck, it won't move anymore!" exclaimed Melody.

"Stop for a minute then," Dad replied. "I think it's just stuck on the one side." And he gently pried again with the paint scraper.

Suddenly, there was a loud pop! And then he was able to slide the flat edge along the whole side of the chest.

"Okay Melody, I think it will open now!"

The moment had arrived! What would we find? To think that it had not been opened for hundreds, maybe even a thousand years, gave me a strange and yet wonderful feeling that I could not explain.

And I imagined a person putting the last item into the chest and then closing it. What could they have known? Would they have considered, even for a minute, that it would be lost under the sands for hundreds of years? Did they bury it in faith that one day it would be found? Or was it buried to hide from enemies, and then lost in the sands of time?

Melody continued to pull, and the chest squeaked as the wood rubbed together.

"It's like an announcement," Gay said. "The fibers of wood are calling out to be heard!" "Its opening, its opening!" we all shouted. "Come on, Melody!"

A heavy stillness descended on us like a blanket, as we peered into the open chest and we could see what appeared to be a faded piece of velvety material that covered whatever was underneath.

Dad said that we should lift the fabric very slowly in case there was something wrapped in it, although it looked completely flat to me.

"Let me help you, Melody," Dad continued, and they both lifted the velvety fabric from the chest.

Underneath what Dad now described as a type of woven wool, and not velvet, were several different artifacts, and we decided to take turns lifting them out. Dad said that after himself and Mary, Helen was the most senior member of the family, so she could go first.

Helen lifted out what looked to be six metal candle holders of various sizes and designs, and they were tied in the middle with a leathery-type twine. She placed them on the table so we could all examine them.

"They look like they are bronze or brass," Dad said, examining them closely. "Look, this one has a type of wax on it, like that of a burnt candle, and it still has a faint scent." We each smelled it.

"And look at the designs on them!" Helen proclaimed excitedly. "These two have faces on the front, like watching eyes!"

"Creepy!" Melody said, handing them to me.

"Look at this one," Gay said. "It has the design of a bathing woman on it, and it's taller than the two with the faces and staring eyes. And it's got some ancient writing on it." She handed it back to Dad.

"It's similar to the writing in the diary that we are trying to translate," he said, "but I am not familiar with these words."

The other three candlesticks looked to be made of iron and they had designs of people on the front of them. One had a cloaked man with some sort of face covering over his head, and a dagger in his hand. Another one that was almost identical in size and design, had a partially naked woman wearing what looked like a large thong around her waist and she had bare breasts. The last of the candlesticks had been made in the shape of a dagger and it had an angry looking face on the front of it.

"This is scary looking," Melody said, quickly handing it back to me. And it was the darkest looking face!

"I wouldn't like to meet him in real life," I exclaimed. "I think he's had a bad day."

Melody giggled, which helped to lighten the serious mood around the table.

"Your turn again, Kings," Dad said, as I pulled out a small but heavy item wrapped in animal fur and tied at the top with the same type of leather twine that was around the candlesticks.

"Help me untie it," I said to Gay, and we both pulled at

the knot, which disintegrated. "That's a sign that something is very old when it falls apart like that," Dad said.

"Or made in China, like my dolls," Melody added.

"Yes, indeed, they make a lot of rubbish over there," I said. "But I can assure you that none of this was made in China." It was my turn, and I opened the animal fur to find what looked to be an ancient metal bell.

"It's a bell!" Melody exclaimed, "and it's in the shape of a sheep with horns."

"It's a ram," I said, "and look! It still has the small gong inside it, so it might still ring." I gently shook it, and the ring was deep and low pitched – "like it is announcing something," I said, looking at dad. He nodded in agreement and said that it sounded like the announcement of an event.

"Like a ceremony or ritual," Helen suggested.

Gay pulled out the next items. They were also wrapped in animal fur and they appeared to be items of clothing. And there were two robust looking pieces of leather, with metal straps and thick leather pieces that hung off the large thick garments.

"I believe they are pieces of ceremonial clothing," Dad said excitedly! "And look at these other items of ancient clothing. There are three waist ties or belts with a type of metal buckle on them. And this one has a precious stone woven into its middle. I think it is a sapphire!"

At this point, Melody glanced at me with a disappointed look and whispered in my ear that there were no gold coins or treasure.

"Let's wait and see," I encouraged her. "There are more items to come out of the chest yet."

"Look at this gown!" Mary said. "It's made of a thick lace material, and there's something wrapped in the middle." "My gosh, it looks like a veil or a type of head covering," Gay said from across the table. Underneath the lace gown was a small leather pouch, which was heavy, and we all passed it around to feel the weight of it.

"Open it, Gay," I said, handing it back to her.

"It might be gold coins!" Melody said, as a look of anticipation returned to her face.

Gay slowly opened the pouch and lifted out some items one by one. First was what looked like a thick metal bracelet with a marking on it.

"This is too heavy to go on someone's wrist," Helen said, as she held it in her hands and rubbed her fingers over the strange markings. "It must be a type of ankle bracelet, and the marking on it makes me think it is some sort of identification piece."

Gay seemed particularly interested in it and she insisted on holding it next. "Yes, I can feel the energy of it," she said. "It's an identification bracelet – you're right, Mum!" Dad thought the marking on it might be a number of some kind. As the conversation continued, I began to get a picture in my mind of the person wearing it as being a type of "slave" but I kept my thoughts to myself.

The next item to come out of the pouch was an identical bracelet, but the identification marking, or number was different. "It sure is heavy," Melody said, putting it down next to the other one on the table.

Gay now pulled out a type of ring. "This is a precious metal," Dad said, as we handed it around the table. "Feel the

Tuesday

weight of it!" He went and got his magnet and moved it over the ring, which repelled the magnet. Melody watched in amazement and asked if gold was magnetic. "Not pure gold," Dad answered. "If something like a ring or pendant has some metal in it, then it is not pure, and the magnet will pick it up."

"You mean like if Mum or Grandma's earrings were only gold plated and had some other kind of metal under the gold?"

"Yes, that's exactly what I mean, well done! But look at this, Melody, the magnet is repelling the ring – so its pure! There is no other metal with the gold!"

Melody's face lit up like the morning sun. "Its gold, Mum! Look, Grandma, it's gold!"

"Dad, we did find treasure after all!" she exclaimed. And I was glad that she had found her treasure.

"What type of ring is it?" Helen asked.

"This also has a marking on it," Dad said, looking at it through his appraisal loop. Dad knew a lot about jewelry and precious metals, and he was often asked to do appraisals at his antique business, so his opinion held a lot of weight. "I don't think this is a finger ring, but a toe ring," he said, putting down his looking glass. Gay was so excited! She pulled out the last item from the pouch and it was another ring! And the design was almost identical to the previous one, only this one was bigger. Dad confirmed that it too was gold, and that it was worn by someone with a larger toe.

It was Melody's turn to take out an item, and she pulled something out that was wrapped in a type of material, not unlike the velvety texture that had first covered the contents of the chest, but this had more of a soft leather feel to it.

"Unwrap it, Melody," Helen said, wishing it was her turn again. To our surprise, it was a pair of shoes with a design on the sides. "Can I hold them, Melody?" Gay asked eagerly. And Melody handed them to her mother.

"Look, there is a ram's head design on the sides, the same design as on the bell!" said Gay. She held them against the bell, and the design was identical. "And feel how soft the slippers are inside," she said, rubbing them with her fingers.

"They feel like they are lined with squirrel or rabbit fur," I said. "It's the same feel as my rabbit pelt jacket."

"I can't help thinking about Taliath's grandfather, who made shoes and slippers for his clan," Gay said. "What do you think, Dad?"

"These are no ordinary shoes that a person would wear day to day," he replied, "and look at the soft soles. They were probably worn indoors for a special occasion, certainly not for walking or hunting; and the design on the sides gives them a type of status, I would think. I don't know for sure, but I would say they were probably worn as part of a ceremonial dress, along with some of the other items of clothing."

At Dad's words, Gay's expression changed. It was an expression that I had seen only once before. It was the same expression that had come over her face when I had been talking to her about my experiences with Nan's Nan, when we were driving home from our weekend at Port Eynon. I had thought she was just overtired. But I recognized the expression today as one of uneasiness, or even fear? And it was the way she was looking at the artifact. It was as if she recognized it, having seen it before. As Gay put the item back on the table, she lifted her head and our eyes met, but her eyes quickly retreated, and she looked away. What was going on with my Gay?

There was still more to come, and it was Mary's turn again. She pulled out another pair of shoes. These, however, were not like the soft leather boot design that Melody had pulled out; they were a type of sandal. And there was a piece of leather that separated the large toe from the other toes and helped to hold the shoe on, just like our modern sandals do today. The bottoms were of thick animal hide and had the appearance of having been worn often. The most interesting thing about these shoes was the pottery button that was woven on to the top of the leather strap on each sandal, and they had a picture of a ram's head on them, just like on the side of the other shoes.

"The ram is obviously significant to these people's culture," Helen said, "and I think it might represent a clan or a tribe."

"It's too early to come to any conclusions," Dad said, "but I agree with what Helen is saying. The ram represents something important or sacred to these people."

It was my turn again, and I pulled out what I felt was the most appealing piece of clothing of all. It was an animal fur cloak. And it was not like my rabbit pelt jacket that I had made when I lived on the cliffs. This was made with different furs and it had the shape of a ram's head burned onto the front of it. The fur had been burnt off to the skin to make the design, Dad affirmed. "And it appears that there are three different types of animal fur woven together to make this garment."

"Put it on, my love," Gay said, and I did. "It was small on me, and Helen remarked that it had likely been worn by a woman, so I asked Gay to put it on. It fit over her shoulders, and then draped over the front of her body to just below her waist.

"It's beautiful," she said. "I wonder if it was worn by a Clan Queen like Taliath talks about in her diary."

"It was certainly worn by a woman of status," I exclaimed, looking at Gay and calling her my Queen.

"And I am your Princess, right Dad?" Melody spoke loudly, not wanting to be left out.

"Of course, you are," I smiled.

We were down to the bottom of the chest now, and only a few more items remained. Dad pulled out a type of dagger, which was made with a bone handle, and it had a blunt metal edge, like it had often been used. "This was not a decorative piece," Gay explained, feeling its energy. "It feels dark, like it has taken lives, and it belonged to an evil man!" Dad now looked across the table at me, as Gay projected what I could only describe as "a familiarity and an authority" in her understanding of the artifacts and what they were used for. Dad was not the only one to see the strange relationship that Gay had with the artifacts. Helen could see it too, and she looked uncomfortable.

"That dagger gives me the creeps," Melody said, looking at me. "Maybe it belonged to a pirate," She suggested.

"It might have." I smiled, trying to lighten the heaviness that was growing around the table. But I really thought it had been made long before any pirates came to the Gower.

The last items in the chest included a wooden carving of a ram's head.

"It looks like something the ancient Celts might have worshipped in some of their ceremonies," Dad said. There were

Tuesday

also two pieces of wood and what looked like a leather whip with sharp bones attached to its strands.

"I have no idea what the pieces of wood are. Maybe something that's worn on the body in some way?" he suggested. "And that cruel looking whip is certainly what it looks like – a tool of punishment." We all looked around at one another and agreed that it was of a cruel nature! Then right at the bottom of the chest were what looked like three wooden hair barrettes, and each had a design carved into it. Melody and Helen tried them in their hair, and it seemed that indeed that was what they were.

"I will look after the dagger and a few of the candleholders," Dad said, "and keep the empty chest here at my workshop for a while, until you have moved into your home in Pennard. But take the other artifacts with you, and look at them while you're doing your translation of Taliath's diary – maybe you will make some connections?"

Gay and I were thrilled to be taking the artifacts back to our place. Even with all our packing going on, we wanted to examine them more closely. Dad reminded us that we were to keep our finds quiet and not to tell anyone about them. "Not even the people at the museum should know, not until we can determine their full significance, and their possible relation to Taliath's Diary and the settlement around St. Mary's Church and the Castle. I was half expecting Helen to ask if we were going to keep the artifacts for ourselves or eventually give them to the museum. But she said nothing and seemed to respect Dad's thoughts on the matter. I had often told her about my exploring and about finding artifacts with my father, and today she had seen it firsthand.

It was getting late – time to head back to Cardiff. Helen said she did not feel tired and offered to drive. I would leave my car at Dad's and pick it up tomorrow.

We said goodbye to Dad and Mary and were soon on our way. Wow! It had been worth the wait, and we discussed the items we had found all the way back to Cardiff. Helen dropped us off and helped us to carry the artifacts inside.

"Bye Helen, thanks for driving, and we'll see you on the weekend."

"Bye, you three, and don't forget to take your project to school tomorrow, Melody."

"I won't, Grandma. See you on Saturday."

Thursday morning arrived and we reviewed Melody's project at the breakfast table. She had written an excellent account in her diary about Nan's Nan, and the mare's family lineage, and the events of last Sunday when Nan's Nan had protected us during the storm at Pennard Castle. Both Gay and I felt confident that she would get good marks from her teacher Mrs. Jones.

Gay would drop me off at the train station to go to work, and then she would walk Melody to school.

"See you tonight, my girls, and don't forget about your project, Melody."

"I won't, love you, Dad. " "Love you too Melody."

It was hard to believe that it was Thursday already. The week was going by so quickly, and as the train flashed past the fields and hedgerows and I made my way towards Swansea, it would soon be the weekend again. Gay had the day off and was packing for the load that we would take out to our new house on Saturday, and I was glad that Helen was coming to help. She

Tuesday

would be visiting her friend in the village in the afternoon, but she had offered to help us in the morning. Owning Grandma and Grandpa's old house in Pennard still felt like a dream, but every so often, the reality of the blessing would hit me, and I would get so excited! Much as I enjoyed riding the train, I would not miss the long commute from Cardiff to Swansea. And although Helen would still be up in Cardiff at least for a while, Gay and I would not have to make the long drive so often.

I arrived at Swansea station, and David was there to meet me.

"Hi David, I wasn't expecting you to meet me this morning…"

"Thought I'd save you walking or catching the bus to the church," he said.

"Thanks, that's nice of you." "How was last weekend, Kings? I didn't get a chance to ask you earlier in the week."

"Oh, it was great! We were down on the Gower as usual."

"You all love the Gower, don't you, and it won't be long before you move into your new place. It's this month, isn't it?"

"Yes, we are moving some items in already, and then we have the big move at the end of the month."

"That's great, Kings, and don't forget to let Jackie and I know if we can help in any way."

"I will, David, thanks."

My day at work went slowly, and I was glad that I was going over to Dad and Mary's for tea before driving home to Cardiff.

When I arrived at Dad's, he was still excited about the chest and the artifacts, and he said he had been able to meet with his archeologist friend, Steven Mills, that morning.

"Steve thinks the chest is at least nine hundred to eleven hundred years old, Kings. It is oak as we established before, and it was the mud and clay that preserved it, and they protected the artifacts from extreme temperature changes and moisture. Otherwise, the items of clothing would not have survived and been in such good condition. I am still puzzled as to whether this is the chest that Taliath talks about in her diary. If it is, it certainly traveled a long way from where we dug the holes near the tree, where the coordinates of her map said it was."

"Who knows, Dad, maybe there was a mudslide, or a flood that moved it."

"We won't know, Kings, unless the diary makes a connection with it as we continue our translation. One thing we should do though, once you have moved into Grandma and Grandpa's place, and things have got less busy for you – we should do some metal detecting on the slope where you found the chest – and focus on the cliff drop in front of the castle. It's pretty steep ground, but it's the least likely area where people would have been looking for artifacts, I think."

"Yes, you're right, Dad, that would be a great idea. Did you talk to Steven about the candle holders and the dagger?"

"Yes, I did, and he thinks their age range is consistent with that of the chest, so the artifacts are a genuine find! Not as in the case where people find an old chest or box, and more modern items are found inside."

"That is great, Dad! Gay is still excited about the finds, and she'll be pleased to hear what Steven said."

"How about Helen, Kings? What did she say about things? I wasn't sure if she would get upset about us keeping

Tuesday

the artifacts and not letting the museum people know that we had found them. She's a librarian, isn't she, and she has studied a fair amount of British history."

"Yes, Dad, and I was thinking the same thing. But she didn't say anything, other than that she enjoyed being there and taking part in opening the chest."

"Good, I didn't want to offend anyone with our 'pirating ways,' shall we say."

"I'm sure you didn't, Dad."

"Well, let's go and have some tea. Mary has made a shepherd's pie."

"Great, I'm hungry!"

"And I think she also made another one of those treacle puddings."

"Oh, that's very good!"

After eating until I hurt and enjoying some fun conversation and laughter with Dad and Mary, I got ready to head back to Cardiff.

"Bye, Kings, I'll keep going with the translation and I'll make copies for you and Gay. And please keep me posted if you come across any connection to the artifacts in your translations."

"We will, Dad, and thank Mary again for the nice tea."

"Okay Kings, see you soon."

"That was a great evening," I said to my stomach as I drove away, and I wondered how Gay had done with the packing.

When I arrived home, it was late. Melody was staying at Helen's for the night to get away from the chaos of half packed boxes.

"Come here," Gay said excitedly, as she took my hand and led me into the living room. She then poured us both a large glass of wine.

There on the floor, she had laid out all the artifacts that we had brought home from Dad's. The candlesticks were positioned around the room with candles in them. And she wanted me to look at the leather garments that she had tried on. "I've put them on, and I know how to wear them," she said, now blushing. "They fit perfectly!"

Recognizing her blush, I said, "Is that all, my love? Do you have something else to tell me?"

"Yes," she whispered, "you know me very well, my Prince, and I do have something to tell you, but I'd much rather show you."

"What is it?" I asked, getting more excited.

"Here, you must read this first," she said. "I translated it from Taliath's diary this afternoon, and now I am going to wear the leather Surth for you."

"Leather Surth – what's a Surth?"

"I will show you in a minute," she said, her face now red as a rose, "but you must read the translation first; otherwise, you won't understand what it is." And she picked up one of the leather garments from the floor and went into the bedroom.

"Alright," I said excitedly, "I'll read it."

"Tell me when you're finished," she called out from the bedroom, and I began to read.

Tuesday

(Dear Reader: Due to the complexities in the translation of certain words in the ancient Celtic language, and for you to be able to understand Taliath's feelings and emotions at the time of her diary entries, I am writing in a dialogue form. This will capture the expression and essence of her experience at the time, and of the character of the persons she hereby records. Some of the more graphic words have also been cut out but the full publication of the diary will be released at a later date).

♪❋

ENTRY FROM TALIATH'S DIARY
[MY FIRST LOVE CEREMONY]

I was fifteen when I first entered the Temple of Ceremonies. Two of my elder sisters, Gwenhwyfar and Arlais, had entered a few years before me, and it was the stories of their experience that pressed upon the pages of my mind as I waited to enter this both sacred and terrifying place! I tried not to think about my sisters' stories, but to focus on my mother's instructions. Her words seemed to calm and guide me as they battled with my sisters' warnings and advice, which frightened me.

I would try and create my own story as much as I could in this, "my first Love Ceremony."

Mother told me to be bold and confident, but I could feel my palms sweating, and my feet twitched in my sandals. I took some slow, deep breaths as I waited for my ceremonial partner to arrive and escort me to the Waiting Chamber, where I would prepare my body for the ceremony.

Finally, he arrived. He was tall and rugged looking with a lot of hair on his face, and he wore a brown ceremonial belt. We had only set eyes on each other once before when we were introduced by my mother before the temple priest. My mother's reluctance to introduce me told me that our introduction was not voluntary, but rather a suggestion by the powerful priest of our clan. The priest's suggestions were almost always "threatening orders" of self-interest and a hidden agenda, which he tried to mask with his forced smile and eyes that reflected the evil intent of his deeds.

My partner's large rough hand engulfed my small trembling hand as he led me to the Preparation Chamber, and then left me to prepare myself for the ceremony.

I tried to think of positive things, and stories that I could tell my sisters, even if they did not happen. I was going to lose my virginity and become a woman today, although as far as I was concerned, I had already become a woman when I was twelve. Becoming a woman was something to celebrate, wasn't it? I would not just feel my anus fill with the warm seed of the clan's "Poporahh Boys" as my elder sisters quite often did. Today I would feel the penetration of a mature clan man thrusting into my vagina.

Tuesday

I sat in the coveted "Seat of Ceremonies" and began my ceremonial dress. I had been assigned a body maid just for the occasion. A body maid is called a "canthola." My canthola's name was Sirrieez. She stood before me with her bare feet and unpainted toes upon the cold stone ground. And I shivered as I stared at her bare feet. She read to me from a scroll regarding the sacred attire that I was required to wear, and the order during the ceremony that I would follow implicitly, or face serious punishment, or even death.

Firstly, Sirrieez disrobed my trembling body by standing behind me and untying the straps on my shoulders. Slowly, my robe fell to my feet, and I stepped out of it and stood naked before her, wearing only my sandals, which she seemed to stare at with envy. I had been chosen to participate in a love ceremony, whereas she would probably always be a body servant. But as I heard again, in my heart, the uneasy tone of my mother's voice as she agreed to the priest's request of me, I trembled even more. And I wished I could change places with Sirrieez.

'Stop shaking,' she scolded. 'If you don't stop, you won't be able to participate in the ceremony.' She was right. I had to calm myself and not show any fear. Mother had told me to be bold and confident. Easier said than done, Mother, I whispered under my breath.

'Stop talking to yourself!' Sirrieez ordered. So, I began to take some more deep breaths. Next came a hard knock on the large heavy door that stood like a guardian between me and more of my fears that shouted out from its other side.

My body tensed instantly as the evil priest poked his head around the door, his searching eyes quickly scanning me from head to toe. He then handed Sirrieez a measurement cane that he would use to measure me and my partner before we participated in the ceremony. And I could not believe my good fortune as the priest asked Sirrieez to take my measurements rather than him doing it. Apparently, he was running behind schedule and needed to prepare the candles in the ceremonial room.

That meant I would not have his cold evil eyes watching me, as I so often had seen him looking at my mother in our village. I had heard my mother talking to my eldest sister, Gwenhwyfar, telling her how the evil priest would always touch, and try to intimidate my mother when he was taking her measurements to fit her Surth. But I would have Sirrieez attending to me, and I began to relax.

She measured me from my toes to the top of my head. 'You are five feet and nine inches,' she said sternly, 'tall enough to be a Clan Queen!'

'Don't taunt me!' I snapped. 'That is the last thing on my mind.'

'Do be quiet girl and let me finish measuring you.'

Tuesday

But the truth was that I did dream of becoming a Clan Queen one day, and I had done so since I was a young girl. Doesn't every girl want to become a Clan Queen and have some control over what happens in her life?

'It is time to measure you for your Surth, so keep still!' I kept as still as I could, as she measured from the side of my vagina, around my buttocks to the cleft of my anus, and then took the same measurement from the other side. These were the measurements needed for me to be fitted with the Sacred Ceremonial Surth. The Surth covered two of the three entrances to my body – my vagina and anus. The other entrance being my mouth.

The priest now returned and asked Sirrieez for my measurements, and then gave her my partner's measurements to compare. My ceremonial partner was almost the same height as me, at five feet eight and a half inches. One of the ceremonial laws of the love ceremony requires the woman to be at least four inches taller than her male partner. So, I would be required to wear my hair up high upon my head, which would give the appearance of me being taller. I would also be wearing Ceremonial Sandals, which were part of the dress requirements for ceremony.

At fifteen, I knew little about why us women were required to be taller than the men during ceremonial practices, other than what my mother and grandfather had told me. 'It is the woman's body that is to be given the place of honor in our ceremonies. And the man is to take on the role of humility,' and he is even dishonoured if he fails to meet the desires of the participating woman. But back to my first love ceremony…

Sirrieez now brushed my hair as I continued to sit in the revered "Seat of Ceremonies," and I thought of how many of us women had sat upon this sacred seat… hundreds? Maybe thousands over the years of the Established Clans? Probably only hundreds in our clan, as we had been almost destroyed two times in our history, having then become an Unestablished Clan, and having had to fight for our survival to become an Established Clan again. Few clans ever are re-established after being conquered and pillaged as ours was. This is a great honour to our clan, my grandfather said!

My mother and sisters had sat here before me, and now it was my turn. Sirrieez did not have to remind me that I was sitting in a place of privilege, as she jealously jagged the comb through my long hair. Being a body servant, she was not allowed to wear her hair long, and I could feel her spirit of envy as she brushed harder and harder. 'Ouch!' I cried, as she jabbed my scalp painfully, 'Must you be so rough?' 'Shush girl!' she retorted, 'and be quiet.' Finally, I shouted, 'Stop! You're hurting me!'

I had never had my hair cut as far as I could remember, so there was a lot to brush and prepare for the ceremony. Sirrieez now rolled my hair over a "Bashzon" which is a specially designed piece of wood, for rolling and

Tuesday

holding a woman's hair to sit high upon her head during ceremonies. Sirrieez told me that it had been worn by four successive Clan Queens, and that I should be proud to wear it. 'I am!' I said, trying to be convincing, but my trembling voice told her otherwise. 'You have so much hair,' she said, 'you are going to look a foot taller than your ceremonial partner. And I'd love to see that man's face when he sees your ravenous body all prepared.' I smiled and tried to laugh, but my voice was tight and nervous.

Suddenly, Sirrieez reached down to my waist and gently pushed the lips of my vagina apart with her fingers, and then pushed another finger deep into the entrance of my sacred place. 'What are you doing!?' I protested. 'Seeing if you're wet,' she replied. 'You are nice and moist. Good! You will need to be when you are inspected by the Pilliahh, who are the Senior Ceremonial Clan Women. If you are dry, it can be uncomfortable when they inspect your vagina and anus.' I remained quiet as Sirrieez rolled the last of my hair around the Bashzon, and then pushed a wooden peg through it, to hold my hair in place. Sirrieez then held a mirror behind me so I could see how I looked. My hair was high and elegant, and as I stood up, I looked about a foot taller. I could feel my confidence growing, and for a few minutes I forgot about the evil priest. I reminded myself that I had been 'chosen' to participate in my first Love Ceremony. It was my body that was going to be celebrated! Today I would become a woman in the eyes of my clan. 'Just be confident and bold.' My mother's words echoed again in my heart. As Sirrieez and I waited for the priest to return, I began to think of why they call this ceremony a love ceremony. How could it be a love ceremony if your ceremonial partner has been chosen for you? I don't know this man. I have only set eyes on him once before. No, you love someone who you choose yourself. 'I think they need to change the name of the ceremony, to the 'coming of age ceremony,' I said to Sirrieez. 'Hush Girl!' she whispered. 'You could lose your head by saying that if the Priest or Balla ever heard you! Sometimes the priest listens from behind the door to what is said.' I felt a lump in my throat again, and my vagina tingled.

Suddenly the priest appeared again and chased my mother's comforting words out of my heart. He handed Sirrieez my ceremonial Surth and robe that I would soon be wearing. And before leaving the room, his lustful eyes stared again at my naked flesh. No wonder my mother and sisters hated him so much. As my frightened eyes met his, I could feel the darkness in his soul.

'It is time to fit your Surth, and then put on your ceremonial gown,' Sirrieez said. 'Now stand up and face me.' I turned and faced her while she sat on a low stool to fit me. I stood tall and tried to look confident, but inside I was shaking like a leaf. She started to fit the Surth around my waist, and I squirmed as she pulled the cool leather flap up over my vagina. 'Now turn around,' she said, as she held onto the main strap

Tuesday

around my waist, and then pulled a fitting up between my buttocks. It had a thicker piece of leather around the middle that flopped over my anus.

'If you think you're nervous, Taliath,' she said, 'you should think about this: if your Surth does not fit you, the priest will slit my throat with a dagger and kill me because I got your measurements wrong!'

'Are you serious?' I gulped, feeling a lump in my throat.

'Yes, I am serious! That priest murdered my mother!'

'Murdered your mother?' I squeaked.

'Yes, she was measuring a new Clan Queen for her Surth, and the priest and the balla said she measured wrong. Not my mother! She never made a mistake with her measurements. The priest wanted her dead because she refused his advances after a ceremony in the temple.'

'I'm sorry, Sirrieez, I really am, and I believe you. I know that priest is evil, just by the way I could feel him looking at me.' Sirrieez began to weep and said nothing more about her mother.

My body squirmed as I felt Sirrieez's cold hands on my skin, and she slowly made the final adjustments to the Surth. 'Keep still,' she said, 'and tell me how it feels? It looks good and not too tight.' 'Yes, it's fine,' I replied, 'and at least I have something on my body now, before the priest returns.'

'That's true,' Sirrieez replied, 'but the Senior Clan women will have to remove it again to inspect you, before you are able to enter the temple.'

'I know,' I said, and I began to feel nervous again as my sisters' stories of probing fingers and tongue consumed my thoughts.

'Here, you can put this on now,' Sirrieez said, handing me my ceremonial gown. And I tried to think of my mother's words again. 'Just be bold and confident!'

'I'll try mum,' I said, to encourage myself, but her words didn't seem enough as Sirrieez left me alone in the room to wait for the senior clan women to arrive. And I could feel my body shaking again, and I don't think I'd ever felt so alone and vulnerable as I did then.

Suddenly I jumped out of my skin as there were several heavy knocks on the door. Was it the priest returning? I hoped not. Before I could have another thought, the heavy door thumped open! Good, it wasn't the priest! It was the Senior Clan Women. Or was it good? I would soon know if my sisters' stories were true.

'Oh, I wonder who we have here then,' said one of the women with a raspy voice. 'We will soon find out,' the other said with a cruel smile, and they chuckled.

'Take your gown off and let us have a look at you!' I didn't know whether to run or cry. There was nowhere to run to, so I wept.

Tuesday

'Oh, stop weeping.' the one with the cruel smile said. 'Don't you know how fortunate you are to be participating in a love ceremony?'

'Yes, I mean no. I don't know!'

'Well, you should know, girl! Now cheer up,' the other woman said. 'You get to have all sorts of wonderful things happen to you, if you have been a good girl, that is, and stayed pure. Now let down your gown and step out of it. And stand still while I remove your Surth.'

Hesitantly, I undid my gown straps and began lowering it to the floor.

'Hurry up!' the cruel woman said, as she tore my gown down to my ankles, and it caught on my ankle bracelet. I stepped out of it and stood in my sandals and Surth. Another knock came on the door, and this time it was the priest. He quickly looked me up and down with his cold dead eyes, and said, 'She's tall.' Both the women laughed at his remark, and he left the room again.

The cruel-looking woman now knelt in front of me and removed my Surth. She then began looking at my vagina. I didn't know where to look! So, I stared at the cruel faces on the stone walls, and they stared back at me with no mercy. I could feel her breath on my tender skin, as I looked straight ahead and tried to think of something nice. Anything I could look forward to, that would take my mind off this intrusion upon my body. I thought of the last Sunday when my sister, Tanwen, and I went on an outing outside the castle grounds with our aunt. We took some food with us and some wine, and we watched the wild horses playing on the hills. And my aunt was planning to take us out again this Sunday.

Suddenly I felt a finger, and then another, pushing aside the lips of my sacred place. I shuddered, as she pushed in a finger and felt around. I could feel my own tightness, and she laughed and said, 'Enjoying it, girl?' The other woman cackled and then knelt behind me. What was she going to do? Wasn't this enough! She pulled my buttocks apart and then stuck her finger inside me, pushing it in and pulling it out slowly as my tight little anus gripped her finger. 'Have you been behaving yourself?' she cackled? 'Yes,' I replied feeling her finger pushing deeper and deeper. And I vowed in my heart, that if I ever became a Clan Queen or a woman of authority within my clan, I would kill these two vermin bitches!

'You have been behaving, haven't you.' she said, removing her finger harshly.

'There's no sign of any entry into her anus,' she said to the cruel one, who still knelt in front of me exploring my vagina. 'There's nothing here either,' she said disappointedly, finally pulling her fingers out of me as she fixed her envious eyes on mine, and I felt she would slit my throat if she had the chance.

The door thumped open, and there stood the priest. I never thought I would say this, but just for a few

Tuesday

seconds, I was glad he was there, so I was not alone with these hardened bitter women who had violated my body and soul! Gwenhwyfar and Arlais had been right! These women were cruel bitter cows and bad to the bone!

The priest then asked them: 'Is she clean or defiled?'

'She's clean,' they answered together in their brash and raspy voices, and I breathed a sigh of relief. If a woman is found to be defiled while she is being prepared to participate in the ceremony, she is immediately reported to the balla, who is the executioner, and she is put to death.

'Wash her then,' the priest said, and he left the room.

My vagina was now streaming wet with anticipation, or dare I say it, excitement, or maybe both? What else could I do but try and imagine what was to come?

If it were too horrible to bear, I would travel somewhere else in my mind, back to my grandfather and I making shoes together when I was a young girl, or to the happy valley below the castle where my aunt took my sisters and I. But maybe I would enjoy what was to come? I could only wait and see. I was going to be bathed next – that might be nice. And as I waited for further instructions from these bitter cows, another warning from my eldest sister, Gwenhwyfar, came to my mind and heart: 'Whatever you do, Taliath, do not forget to take your sandals off when you enter the Sacred Altar Room, and keep your veil on until your ceremonial partner removes it when you are standing before the Sacred Ram.'

As I read this latest translation of Taliath's diary, I was reminded of the ram's head we had found in the chest. Could that be or represent the Sacred Ram that I am just reading about? Just then, I heard Gay calling out from the bedroom, "have you read it yet?"

"I am almost finished," I called. "Make sure you read it all," she shouted, "and then come and meet me in the bedroom."

Gay had clearly spent a good part of the day translating this, and she had left some of the obvious words in their original language form. Dad and I had calculated that, on average, it takes 30 hours to translate just 10 pages of the diary. It is a lot of work, but of course well worth it.

When I first read this latest insert from Taliath's diary, with all its rawness and passion that evokes such response and awareness from my own human condition, I was hesitant to include it in my book. Why? Was it because of the fear of what people would think, and how I would be judged as a writer? Is it because of the awareness of my own intrinsic emotional response to Taliath's desperation, fears, victories, and passions from her experiences? I do not know. Maybe it is in part the sum of them all, the relation of our human bonds within her experiences.

I have decided to include it in my book, to uphold the promise I made to my father – that I would tell Taliath's story, and share the truth of her life, and the life of her people within the world. So, I give you, dear reader, the continued story of the life of Taliath Saren.

Tuesday

♪✻

My eldest sister, Gwenhwyfar, had reminded me of how a priest conspired with a balla, in a neighbouring clan, to trick a woman participating in a Love Ceremony into not removing her sandals before entering the Sacred Altar Room. She was then immediately taken to the high priest, who ordered her execution. 'Don't let that happen to you, Taliath,' she said, 'because priests can be corrupt, especially when they don't get their way with you. I want you to celebrate your body and enjoy the ceremony, not get executed!'

Well, back to the story of my first love ceremony...

After standing and waiting with the Senior Clan Women for what seemed like hours, I was finally led away from the preparation room, through a long dark corridor that had candles burning every so many yards, and behind the candles were frightening stone faces that seemed to stare right at me.

'Where am I going?' I protested. 'Be a quiet girl,' the cruel woman replied, and she slapped my back with her hand. 'Come on, move along! We don't have all day,' the other woman barked.

I continued to stare back at the scary stone faces as we walked along. Was I going to be secretly murdered? I asked myself, as fear began to grip me more tightly, and all the faces on the wall shouted, 'Yes! You're going to have your throat slit and bleed to death on the cold stone floor.'

My fear now shouted so loud that I stopped and demanded to be told where I was going!

'Get going, girl!' the women shouted, both slapping me hard on the back. 'You don't get to ask questions! You obey and do what you are told!' I stopped again, not because I wanted a confrontation, but because I was becoming numb with fear, and I found it hard to walk.

Finally, one of them answered me. 'You're going to be bathed. Didn't you hear what the priest said? You need to be washed before you take part in the ceremony!'

'Alright, stop shouting at me,' I said, bursting into tears. These women had hearts of stone! And the manners of pigs!

I shivered and ran my hands over the goose bumps on my legs. 'Stop touching yourself and keep walking,' they snorted, and one of them whipped me from behind with the leather Surth that I would soon be wearing.

Eventually we reached the end of the long corridor and came to a small room. I could see steam and smell the fragrance of lavender. 'Go on, in you go,' one of them said. 'Don't just stand there.' And I went inside.

The whole room was full of steam, and the strong aroma of lavender filled the air. Large candles burned

Tuesday

before friendlier faces carved on stone statues. Some were faces of beautiful women; others had symbols on them of instruments and weapons used by the clans.

Hope began to enter my soul, as slowly I began to see, through the thick steam, a sunken pool surrounded by white stone slabs in the middle of the room. I think the slabs and the sides of the pool were made of marble. At least that is what my grandfather had told me.

'Go on, in you go,' the impatient voices reminded me. I stepped out of my sandals and hung my robe over one of the statues. I could see now that there were three steps leading down into the pool, so I slowly stepped in until I was almost up to my waist. The bottom of the pool felt like rough stone underneath my feet until I reached the middle and then I stood on a smooth slab. Oh, the hot cleansing water bubbled around my body and helped me to feel clean again where those awful cows had defiled me with fingers and tongue.

The callus cows hung my Surth upon a large metal stand and then took off their sandals. And they sounded excited as they each took a washing skin from a stand and then stepped into the pool. They were pleased to be standing in the hot water, but their words remained harsh towards me as they washed my back and breasts.

And that was all the translating Gay had done today.

Once I had finished reading it, I called out to Gay in the bedroom. "I've finished reading it, and it's fantastic!"

"I will be right there, love." Before I stood up to go to the bedroom, Gay returned to the living room.

She was wearing her hair high on top of her head and it made her look about a foot taller. 'What have you done to your hair?' I asked. 'It looks wonderfully sexy.' She smiled, and I could see that she wanted to tell me something as her beautiful slender body walked across the room. Her feet were in the sandals we had found in the chest, and she had one of the gold toe rings on the middle toe of her left foot. Her breasts hung free, her brown nipples taut and erect.

Around her waist she wore the 'Surth,' the thick leather garment she had taken into the bedroom. It covered her vagina from the front, and a strap fitted between her buttocks, with another round piece of leather flapped over her anus. It was exactly as Taliath had described it in her diary! And as I continued to watch her prance around the room, exuberant and uninhibited, my desire for her became immense. This was not the shy blushing lady that I had come to know.

She finally stopped her intoxicating strut and faced me. "These artifacts that we found in the chest are connected to Taliath," she said in her excitement. "I'm wearing the Bashzon, made of ewe wood, to hold my hair up high. And this is a 'Surth,' covering my sacred entrances, and I am wearing the 'Sacred Ceremonial Sandals' that are worn in the Love Ceremony."

At her words, I could hardly hold my desire any longer!

She had tried to duplicate everything she had translated from the diary. In the bedroom, candles were lit, and the scent

Tuesday

of lavender filled the room. And there was a scroll of paper rolled up and tied with a bow. It was a list of what I was to do to her body to make sure she was not defiled.

"Read the script, my Prince. It contains the orders from the dark priest. You must do to me what the Senior Ceremonial Women did to Taliath, and thus make sure that I am pure and not defiled, so that we can participate in a love ceremony together. When you have explored my sacred entrances, you must bathe me."

She had prepared a hot steaming bath and she was burning lavender oil.

I made her stand still as I opened the scroll and read it aloud. And as I explored her sacred entrances, she moaned. "Take your sandals off and step into the bath," I ordered, and I slapped her with the leather Surth.

"I shall ring the Ram's Bell when I'm ready to come out, my Prince. You go back to the bedroom and get my Surth ready, and don't forget to read the rest of the script."

After a short time, the bell rang, and I returned to Gay with her Surth over my shoulder, and her veil and towel in my hands. "Step out," I ordered sternly, and she stepped onto a towel I had placed beside the bath. Slowly, I began to dry her trembling, pulsating body as she moaned again to my touch. And as I dried her from her slender neck down to her freshly painted toes, she kept saying, "Oh, that feels so good, my Prince, dry every part of me and get me ready."

With her body washed and dried, I now fitted the sacred Surth around her waist, and she was streaming wet as I attached the straps to her front and rear. Our eyes met and danced, and we desired each other in a way that was intoxicating.

"Now step into your ceremonial sandals and let me put on your veil."

"You must lead me back to the living room now, my Prince, where we both must bow before the Sacred Altar."

'Sacred Altar?' I wondered. I can't remember reading about that in the translation. Maybe she translated more of the diary than she gave me to read?

Regardless, I was having too much fun to stop and ask any questions. Gay was my Queen, and I was her ceremonial partner. I wanted to untie her high hair that made her look so tall, and pull her back to the bedroom, but I remained disciplined because we were in a sacred covenant together in our first Love Ceremony!

"Don't forget to keep my face covered with the veil," she said, "and remove my sandals before we enter the altar room. Otherwise, the evil priest will put me to death by slitting my throat in front of the altar!" And as we entered the living room, I feared we might wake up Melody with our noise, but then I remembered that she had gone over to Helen's for the night. Now there were no inhibitions.

Gay had lit two candles and placed them in the candleholders with the frightening faces and staring eyes that we had found in the chest. Then she put them on the stands behind the Ram's Head that she was using for an altar. "We must bow down to it," she said, "before commencing our ceremony."

"Stop and take your sandals off," I ordered, "before we enter the room, and let me put on your ankle bracelet that identifies you as property of the Coastal and Black Mountain Clans of Wales."

Tuesday

We stood now in front of the burning candles that kissed our almost naked bodies with their heat. I lifted Gay's veil as the solemn Ram stared down at us. Gay's eyes met mine with love and lust, and we could not remain composed any longer, evil priest or not!

I pulled the wooden pin from her hair and her long curls fell to her waist. Then I removed her sacred Surth, and grabbing her wrist sternly, I pulled her to the bedroom and pushed her onto the bed. Our eyes met and danced again, and I ravaged and kissed her breasts. Her vagina flowed like the Nile as I drank from her raging sea of love, and then plunged my exploding manhood inside her. We rolled and kissed and banged and moaned until our bodies were spent, and the evil priest came and killed us!

Gay and I had never needed any help with our love life, but I could not remember such wonderful lovemaking since we had stayed in bed for those three days straight when we went on our honeymoon adventure around the Gower.

And we both said, thank you to Taliath Seren. "You may have lived a thousand years ago, but you were with us today!" And we fell asleep in each other's arms, and I felt like the richest man in the world to have such a wife with all her scintillating charms! My gosh, dear Taliath, I better stop writing like this, before they change my genre to erotica!

Chapter Eleven
It's 11 a.m., Lets Go!

We woke up Saturday morning still glowing from our night of romance and fantasy, and we made love until the phone rang. It was Helen, who informed us that it was 11 a.m., and that she and Melody were on their way over to help us load the car with boxes to take to our new home in Pennard.

We quickly showered and dressed, only to hear the doorbell ring and Melody racing up the stairs. Gay had put the packed boxes in the spare room, and we carried them downstairs and into the two cars. Helen and Melody would ride in Helen's car, and Gay and I would take hers. We had both cars packed and were on our way within the hour.

After helping us carry the boxes into the house, Helen left to go and meet her friend in the village as planned, and Gay, Melody and I unpacked the boxes. It was a wonderful feeling to have the three of us in our new home together, and we enjoyed putting each item in its chosen place.

Once we had finished unpacking, Gay and Melody walked across the road to Pennard Stores. "We will bring you back

It's 11 a.m., Lets Go!

something for lunch, love," Gay said, leaving me in the front garden to reminisce.

It was still hard to believe that we were moving into Grandma and Grandpa's old house, and as I walked in the garden, the gentle winds of memory stirred – of such wonderful times spent with my beloved grandparents. The stone birdbath stood in the middle of the lawn where it had stood for sixty years, and it whispered stories of Grandma and I cleaning it out and scrubbing it each spring, and then filling it up with water and watching the birds take their baths. First the blackbirds would dip their wings, and the smaller birds would hover and flutter above the bushes nearby, eagerly awaiting their turn. Sparrows drank happily, and wagtails balanced on the sides of the birdbath with their long tails. Grandma and I would sit in the sunroom with a cuppa tea and biscuits and watch till all the birds had taken their bath. Now I walked over and inspected it, and it was still in good condition. I looked forward to teaching Melody, and Samantha when she arrived, all about the garden birds that Grandma had taught me so much about.

The old rose bushes had buds and would soon be blooming, and there was our sacred mauve rose bush that Grandma and I had planted one Mother's Day when I was six or seven. It was a big plant now, and it gave cover to many of the smaller birds that frequented the garden. In the corner by the fence was the old fishpond, where Grandpa and I used to watch the goldfish on sunny days, and in the early spring, when the frogs spawned between the waterlilies, we'd watch for the tadpoles to be born.

Grandma had a large glass bowl which she allowed me to keep some of the tadpoles in, and we would watch them grow little arms and legs, and eventually they would lose their tails and become frogs. Then Grandpa and I would take them to the little stream that ran across the golf course and let them go. This was something I could do next spring with Melody, I thought, as I went and inspected Grandpa's greenhouse. It was still standing, although it looked like it had not been used for some time. Weeds were growing in the vegetable beds, and a few of the windows were cracked. Grandpa had taught me a lot about growing tomatoes, and I looked forward to growing my own. In late winter, he and I would take a wheelbarrow and walk across the cliff tops, and we would follow the ponies until we had a wheelbarrow full of manure for the greenhouse. Grandpa would then dig it into the soil, all ready for when he transplanted his tomato plants from the house, which he grew from seed starting in early February. Each year he would keep seeds, which my grandmother carefully extracted from the juicy tomatoes, drying them on a cloth before putting them away until the following season. I remember, after the long grey winters in Pennard, getting excited and looking forward to spring when I saw Grandpa putting his little seeds in containers and watering them on the windowsills.

I saw that the old pole Grandma used for her clothesline was still standing, and even the little wheel pulley was still on the tree. That would be one of my first jobs once we were all moved in – to set up the clothesline again and dry our clothes in the sweet summer air. I can remember my clothes smelling like Grandma's lavender as she took them off the line. "Mm, smell your shirt, King, but don't blow your nose on it."

Grandma would clean the mats by hanging them over the clothesline and giving them a good smack with one of her saucepans. She gave my brother Fraser and I a saucepan each to bang her large carpet with, but we often turned it into a game and chased each other around the garden beating each other about the body. "You bad boys!" Grandpa would say, but we still had treacle pudding and custard for tea.

Just then Gay and Melody returned from the store. "Here you are, Dad, we got you a Cornish pasty and a dandelion and burdock." "Thanks, my girls," I said, sinking my teeth into the pasty, and we spent the rest of the afternoon exploring Grandma and Grandpa's house, and deciding what pieces of furniture would go into each room. "We need to make a list," Gay said, "so we can tell the movers what to put in each room." Our big move at the end of the month was coming up fast.

Just before five, Helen returned from visiting her friend in the village, and we returned to Cardiff. "I can't wait for us to be all moved in," Gay said, "and we can sleep in our own beds in Pennard."

"Yes, that will be so nice," I agreed, "and not having to drive back to Cardiff on the weekends." Over the next few weeks, we got all our small items moved in; and Helen, along with Dad and Mary, helped us a lot with our long drives from Cardiff and out to the house in Pennard. Now we were ready for our final haul with the movers, and that was happening in a few days. There was, however, something concerning going on with Gay. It had been fun when it started, and I had enjoyed it as much as she had. But now it was getting too much!

Gay was becoming "consumed" with Taliath and her family's lives. We were not just translating a diary anymore. I understood that we had found a unique piece of history in the diary and in the artifacts that we had discovered in the chest. They were an incredible find! But the artifacts were no longer something of the past for Gay. It was now something that she lived with and related to in some way or another every single day! Every time we made love, she wanted it to be part of one of the Celtic ceremonies. They were wonderfully sensual and intriguing to take part in, but the ceremonies and the amount of time she was spending translating the diary was now at the expense of other things.

Melody had come to me on several occasions and said, "Dad, what's wrong with Mom? All she seems to want to do is talk about Taliath and her people, and not what is going on in our family. I'm interested in finding out about history, Dad, but Mum isn't spending enough time with me, and when she does, it's like she's not really interested in what I'm doing because she's too occupied with Taliath's clothes and the other things that we found in the chest."

"Yes, I know what you mean," I said. "Let me talk to her, sweetheart, and figure out what's going on."

After I thought about it, I decided to go and talk to Helen first, and run things by her, and then I would talk to Gay.

I called Helen and arranged to go over to her place. I made the journey to Cardiff promptly and rang the doorbell. Helen answered with a look of concern on her face. "Everything alright?" she asked.

"I don't know," I replied. "but I'd really appreciate your thoughts on a concern I have about Gay."

"What is it, Kings?"

"I just felt I needed to talk to you and ask you a few questions about Gay. Was Gay interested in local history and the Celts when she was a young girl, before I met her? And what do you know about your ancestry, Helen?"

"Kingsley, in hearing you talk, one thing seems obvious, namely that Gay hasn't told you that she was adopted."

"No," I choked out in shock, "she hasn't, and she tells me everything, or at least I thought she did!"

Seeing that I was upset, Helen came over and sat on the chesterfield next to me, and taking my hand, she tried to reassure me. "Don't take it personally, Kings. Even her sister Pearl doesn't know. When we told Gay at twelve years old, she asked my husband and I to never tell anyone, and the three of us made a covenant that we never would unless Gay changed her mind one day when she was older."

"But I think you should know, Kingsley, because knowing about Gay's ancestry will help you to understand her better."

"Thank you, Helen. I so appreciate you telling me, and I will definitely not mention it to Gay. But I do have some questions..."

"Of course, go ahead."

"Do you know anything about Gay's birth parents? You, of course, are her mother, and nothing will ever change that."

"Don't worry, Kings, I am at peace with things, and I'm happy to tell you what I know."

"Thank you so much..."

"Gay's biological father is believed to be dead, although no records have been found, so perhaps he is still alive somewhere. Unfortunately for Gay, not knowing where her father is, or if he is still alive, has haunted her for years. Her mother is very much a gypsy, and she lives in a Celtic commune up in

West Wales. My husband John and I would stop in there once every year or so, on our way to Cardiganshire, where we spent our holidays when Gay and Pearl were young."

"We kept an eye on her biological mother because Gay wasn't adopted in the usual way."

"Not in the usual way?" I parroted back.

"No," replied Helen. "When we were in our twenties, my husband and I went to live in the Celtic commune. It was a whole way of life, away from mainstream society, and we loved it! It was at the commune where we met Armes, Gay's birth-mother, who was, and as far as I know still is, a prophetess there."

"A prophetess?" "Yes. She foretold events in people's lives. She was also a great teacher of the Celtic culture and the laws and traditions that we tried to live by in the commune. As far as I know, it was Armes who started the commune."

Helen looked at me and said, "You probably need a stiff drink while you're hearing this. I know I do in telling you." She got up and poured us a large apricot brandy.

"Please continue," I said, after taking a few sips, which went straight to my head.

"Right, where were we?" Helen replied. "Yes, Gay's family of origin. As I said, my husband and I went to live in the commune, and Gay's mother, Armes, had given birth to Gay sometime around the time she was first setting up the commune, and she had apparently left for some time to give birth in a hospital."

"How do you know this, if you and John arrived at the commune after Gay had been born?" I asked.

It's 11 a.m., Lets Go!

"Another couple, who had been at the commune since its beginning, told us this shortly after we arrived. Gay was two years old when my husband and I first met her at the commune. Gay's mother had a boyfriend who was one of the members living at the commune, and he was very jealous that Gay did not belong to him. He became abusive toward Armes and Gay. Other people in the commune witnessed the abuse, but because Gay's biological father wasn't around to protect them, the boyfriend continued on with the abuse, and nobody did anything about it."

"Why not?" I asked. "Abuse is abuse!"

"Well, the problem, Kings, was that Armes and her partner were like royalty in the commune, and what they said was law! If they didn't like someone, or if anyone questioned their authority, that person was excommunicated very quickly. My husband John and I saw this happen several times."

"I still don't understand why someone didn't step up and protect Armes and Gay," I said. "Armes should have kicked the boyfriend out of the commune and protected herself and her daughter."

"I agree with you completely, Kings," Helen replied, seeing that I was getting upset. "But not everyone is as brave and protective as you. Armes felt trapped, and she believed that if she got rid of the boyfriend, she might lose her status at the commune. Another brandy, Kings?"

"Yes please."

"Anyway, things only got worse. So, it came down to either Armes leaving the commune with Gay, or else staying and retaining her almost 'royal' status, which would also mean staying with the abusive boyfriend and giving up Gay. For me, it was obvious what she should do, and that was to get away with Gay to safety! But Armes chose to stay at the commune and give up her daughter."

"I'll never understand how any mother could do that," I said, sipping on my brandy. "That just shows she shouldn't have been a mother."

"I'll tell you what happened," Helen continued.

"At the time, my husband and I were trying to conceive, and we had been trying for four years with no success. I was Armes's best friend in the commune, and one night she came over to John's and my hut, with little Gay in her arms. Armes had bruises on her face, and she was afraid that her partner was going to kill her and little Gay. He had told her to get rid of Gay or leave the commune. That night, Armes asked us to take Gay and bring her up as our own. And that is what we did, and I have been Gay's mother for almost forty years. So, you can see, Kings, that this sort of adoption does not happen every day. After living in the commune, John and I moved to Pennard, and our friends and neighbours just assumed that Gay was ours."

"And of course, she is," I replied, and after finishing another glass of brandy, and being given an equally strong kiss from Helen, it was time I was on my way.

Wow! I hadn't been expecting that! Gay had been adopted in a unique way, and Helen and her husband had lived in a Celtic Commune. And I thought I was the adventurous one!

I had always perceived Helen as being very strait-laced and predictable, a real mummy's girl, who's naughty girl antics would be wearing her high heels on a weekday instead of just on the weekends, which was the rule. Or wearing bright red lipstick when her mother had bought her plain gloss. Kissing

It's 11 a.m., Lets Go!

a boy behind the bookshelf in the library, and maybe arriving home half an hour after her curfew, if she was being very naughty! But not leaving mainstream society and going to live in a Celtic Commune with alternative-living sinners. One never knows, do they?! But I had grown to love Helen. She was no longer the stuck-up, cow that took my Gay away from me when I was a teenager.

No, Helen is a beautiful, kind, and vibrant woman. Helen keeps her "lovely lady" status in my eyes, no matter what she may have done in the past or does in the future.

The weekend was coming quickly, and after an exhausting few days, we were moved into our new home in Pennard. Thanks Helen, and thanks Dad and Mary, for all your help. It feels great to have all our belongings under one roof, and not to have to go back and forth to Cardiff with any more loads.

Friday was Melody's last day at school before the summer holidays, and also the day when she would get the results of her school project which she had done on Nan's Nan. I had taken the day off work to go with Gay and Melody to Melody's school in Cardiff. Melody's teacher, Mrs. Jones, had called us earlier in the week and told us that this was a special end of year assembly, and that Gay and I were invited. I had called Helen and she would come and meet us there.

Each Monday and Friday, Melody's class took part in the school assembly, where they sang hymns and the headmaster Mr. Evans either brought a short devotional or told a story of inspiration to the pupils.

Sitting here today reminded me of my school days at Pennard Primary School on the Gower, where another Mr. Evans read us devotionals or told us stories. Gay wore my favorite green and white dress with her green high heels, and Helen wore a long blue dress with white heels. Melody looked so pretty in her flowered dress and white tights. And "I felt honoured sitting in the presence of three lovely ladies," I told them, as the last hymn came to an end. Mr. Evans then presented a devotional on "kindness," which made us all think of how we could be kind to other people over the summer holidays. He then said he had three awards to hand out for school projects, and all the children looked around in anticipation and wondered who the lucky three children were going to be?

"I hope she gets an award," Gay whispered in my ear. "She's worked so hard, and she deserves to get something."

"Yes," I replied, "it would mean the world to her."

Melody looked at me with her nervous smile, and I smiled back.

Mr. Evans began to call out the winners while children and parents whispered. "Quiet please," he said sternly.

"In third place, for his excellent woodworking project in Mr. Davies class, please join me in honouring Master Neil Heath!" There was a loud round of applause as Neil got up from his seat and climbed up the stage to get his award.

"It's a big glass trophy," Melody whispered. "Neil is two classes older than me."

"Next, we have our second-place award, and ladies and gentlemen, boys and girls, this is the first time that we have given an award for writing and journaling, and our winner is from Mrs. Jones' class. Please give a big round of applause for our youngest winner, Miss Melody Hill! Yes! Well done, Melody!"

Mrs. Jones and her whole class stood up and applauded Melody.

"And all of us here at Bute Street School want to wish Melody all the best as she moves to her new school in September," Mr. Evans continued.

Melody waved to us from the stage after shaking hands with Mr. Evans, and then curtsied to the rest of the audience.

"I'm so proud," Gay said, as Melody carried a large wooden plaque back to her seat.

"Look!" Melody said excitedly, "It's got a gold-coloured pen attached to the side, and there's my name, Mum and Dad – Melody Hill."

"That's wonderful, Melody," we all said. "You worked so hard and you really deserved it."

We stayed and listened to Mr. Evans read out the first place finalist, and then went back to the school dining room for cake and juice. Melody's whole class came up to congratulate her and to wish her well with her move to her new school.

After celebrating at the school, we said goodbye to Helen and made our way back to Swansea, and on to our new home in Pennard.

On the weekend, Gay and Helen had planned to visit Gay's sister Pearl in Bristol. Pearl had married and moved away while I was living in Canada. Melody was supposed to stay with me at the house, so that we could get her room organized after the move. But it was decided at the last minute that Melody would go too and spend time with her cousin in Bristol. All of a sudden, I had the weekend to myself.

The conversation I had so recently had with Helen, and finding out that Gay had been adopted, was still pressing upon my heart, and I decided to go and find Gay's birth mother.

I did not understand why I would want to meet Armes, considering that Gay and I had Helen in our lives, and she was all we needed, wasn't she? But for some reason, I knew I had to go and meet Gay's birth mother.

Does she have some wisdom or understanding that I need to know? Or am I just being curious as to who she is, and I just want to meet her? I pondered, but I didn't know the answer.

Helen had said to me, that she was telling me about Gay's birth mother so that I could understand Gay more. Maybe I would discover something from Armes that would help me to do just that…

After breakfast, the girls left for Bristol, and I started driving towards Cardiganshire. I did not know exactly where the Celtic commune in West Wales was, but in a conversation with Helen, she had mentioned the little village of Eglwyswrw, and that it was near Cardigan Bay. Interestingly, my mother and father had taken my brother Fraser and I camping on a few occasions to Eglwyswrw when we were young boys. And later, when we were older, Mom and Dad bought a caravan in Cardiganshire where we would go on long weekends and summer holidays. So I knew the area quite well, but I had never heard of a Celtic commune in the area. Oh well, it was a beautiful day for a drive to West Wales, and even if I did not find the commune, it would be an adventure, and I could go for a swim at Poppit Sands, which was a lovely beach.

It was a beautiful drive through the mountains, and the fields and meadows of the farms along the way smiled and sang and made music with my memories, that danced all the way to Cardiganshire. I drove through the little village of Eglwyswrw, and then I walked up one of the hills to stretch my legs and have a snack. The air was fresh and sweet, and the birds sang of the glories of the season, and I ran and danced with a Red Kite, that dived and circled over a little bubbling brook that was making its way to the distant sea. After stretching my legs and saying goodbye to the Red Kite, I drove around with a map not knowing the way, but what a beautiful day!

I had reached a dead end, or so I thought, and the sign read "Private Property, Keep Out." But as I looked over the wooden gate, the buildings across the field did not look like a farm. They looked like a camp or a community, and a large stone lodge or house stood in the middle of what looked like smaller stone huts. "Can I help you?" said a voice from behind me. Startled, I turned around.

"Sorry to have frightened you," said a woman who looked like she had walked out of The Middle Ages.

"Yes, perhaps you can help me," I said, still staring at her strange clothing. "I'm looking for a Celtic commune, and I'm trying to find a woman named Armes."

"May I ask who you are?" the woman replied. "And what is your association with Armes?"

"You know her?" I asked enthusiastically. "Yes," the woman replied, "and I live in the commune."

"I'm Kingsley," I said reaching out my hand.

"And I am Arwydd," she said, and we shook hands.

"I am a friend of a lady named Helen Tripp who used to live here at the commune and was friends with Armes," I explained.

"Follow me," Arwydd replied, "and I will take you to meet Armes."

I couldn't believe my ears! It wasn't luck. I don't believe in coincidences, only divine appointments.

She led me across some fields that had sheep and cows in them just like a regular farm, but there in the middle of one of the fields was a large oak tree, and there were people who appeared to be holding hands and dancing around its trunk. As we got closer, I could see that they were women, and apart from what looked like leather thongs around their waists and wildflower chains in their hair, they looked completely naked, their swinging creamy breasts illuminated as they danced in the afternoon sunlight.

"I know about trees and their importance to Celtic culture," I said to Arwydd.

"And what is it you know?" she asked.

"When a Celtic Tribe cleared the land to build a settlement, they always left a great tree in the middle of the land that they had cleared. This is where the Chieftain would be inaugurated – for the tree, with its roots extending to the lower world and its branches reaching to the upper world, connected him both with the power of the heavens and with the elements. And in warfare, the enemy tribes would try to destroy the Mother Tree, to strip the tribe of their identity and cut them off from the source of life. Thus, they would be truly conquered."

"How wise that you should know and understand this, Kingsley. Are you a Bard, or something?" Arwydd asked, as we continued to walk across the fields.

"No, my father taught me that," I replied.

"What else do you know of our culture?" she asked, as we now walked side by side.

"Your name, Arwydd, means Sign. And the first Celtic

alphabet was Ogham, a system of strokes across a horizontal line in which each letter was associated with a tree. The first three letters were Beith, which is Birch; Luis, which is Rowan; and Nuin, which is Ash. The wood from each tree was accorded a practical, medicinal, and symbolic value."

"My favourite is the slim and elegant birch, with its silver bark," I continued. "Beith can be made into shoes and baskets, and it was even used to make boats. It is celebrated as a female tree and is associated with the "Lady of the Woods.""

Arwydd, gave me a gentle smile and a blush, but remained quiet as if contemplating what I had said.

We now came to what I would describe as a very primitive little settlement of fifteen stone huts and three larger buildings that were also made of stone. One had an old thatched-roof, and the others had plain grass or sod growing on top of them. There seemed to also be a type of wooden barn, and a few wooden buildings that were all painted a very dull pink colour. People walked around the settlement in similar clothing to Arwydd, both men and women, but mainly women, it seemed, as we passed by a well, and an open fire pit where several more women were sitting together, knitting and spinning wool. Everyone acknowledged us by a bowing of their heads, and I wondered if Arwydd had some sort of tribal status.

"Should I bow?" I asked, but instead of answering me, she turned and bowed to me, and two other women came to meet us. Arwydd said something in the Celtic language that I didn't understand, and the two women now smiled and bowed to me.

"They will take you to Armes," Arwydd said, and I followed them to the large stone building that stood in the middle of the settlement. One of the women rang a bell which was to one side of the door of the building, and we waited for a while for someone to open the door.

To my surprise, two other women came to the door wearing only thongs or sandals on their otherwise naked bodies.

I followed as they led me along what appeared to be a long corridor, with burning candles that were positioned along the walls every few yards, giving off just enough light so one could see one's footing along the rough stony floor. Angry-looking figureheads on stands, seemed to watch me as I walked quickly past, and I felt a cold, unfriendly energy coming from them. Then the corridor turned a corner, and there was a full statue that stood in the middle of our path. It was a robed man holding a dagger, with murder in his eyes! The women passed to one side of it, and I followed more closely until I passed it, and then I looked over my shoulder to make sure it wasn't following us! Good, it wasn't! "That's the last time I want to meet you on a dark road, mate. You give me the creeps!"

Finally, we came to a room with a large wooden door, and I tried not to stare at their bodies as they stopped and then rang a large bronze-coloured bell that stood on its own in a metal frame to the side of the door.

It seemed that we had been waiting a long time, and I wondered who would come to the door? Would it be Armes, or somebody else?

The large door creaked open, and a rather delicate looking woman with a slight build stood in front of us. And I was tempted to say, "Who are you? I was expecting a knight!" But I held my tongue, just in case this woman was really Armes, Gay's birth mother. She stared at me with her piercing blue eyes, as if trying to discern who I might be inside. My guides now bowed to the woman, and then turned and lowered their heads to me. I bowed my head and said, "Thank you," and they turned and walked back down the corridor.

"I'm Armes," the woman said. "Please come, follow me." She led me to what I would describe as a Medieval dining room or waiting area. There were massive wooden candle holders as tall as men, with various size candles in them, but none were alight. There were however, small candles burning on an ancient-looking oak table, giving a dim light to the room. A coal fire burned in a fireplace that was built into one of the stone walls, and the air was heavy and warm, unlike the drafty corridor. There were animal skins on the wall, and thick woolen mats on the floor with various Celtic designs on them.

"Sit here," she said, and I sat in an old wicker chair that had a high, rounded back, and it was quite comfortable. Armes sat on what looked like an 18th century chaise lounge. I was familiar with the design, as Dad had restored similar looking ones to sell in his antique shop.

"So, tell me why you are here, Kingsley," she said. "You knew my name and you asked to come and see me. Are you interested in joining our commune? Or are you here for another reason?"

"I'm here for another reason," I said, thinking about what I should or should not say. "What is the reason for your visit?" she asked. "If you're here to learn more about our way of life in the commune, then I want to know your intentions."

Armes came right to the point in her communication with me, or at least that was the case with her speech, but she also had a good energy about her, which made me feel more comfortable in sharing why I had come to see her. She smiled and waited for me to speak my intentions.

So, I told her that Helen Tripp had told me about her and about the commune. And also that I had found Celtic artifacts in an ancient chest a few weeks ago, and that I was interested in learning about them.

"Helen! You know Helen?" she asked. "Helen used to live here at the commune and was my best friend. Kingsley, I would like to talk to you more, but I have a commitment to read tea leaves for an hour or so. Can you stay until I am finished, and then we can talk? You can have lunch here in the commune while you wait."

"Alright," I said, feeling embraced by her warm countenance. She reminded me of my Gay.

"Why don't you stay where you are," she said, "and I will have some food brought to you. We have just harvested our corn and we are celebrating 'Lammas'. Would you enjoy roast chicken, potatoes and corn?"

"Yes, that would be nice," I replied, feeling hungry.

"Please stay in this room," she said, "and I will send Ceridwen with your food." "Thank you."

While I waited for my food to arrive, it gave me some time to reflect on what had happened so far. It had been a great experience for me already, and there would be so much more to learn – I was sure of that. The people I had met so far seemed to resemble Celts or Druids. Each of which I had some understanding of, as Dad had studied them extensively. So, let me think…. they are celebrating Lammas. What do I know about Lammas?

Lammas, also meaning "Loaf-mass" was celebrated

by the ancient Celts on August 1st. It is during the height of summer, when the crops are ripening, and the people are about to reap what they have sown. In Ireland, big horse fairs and marriage markets are also held at this time. My father told me that in the old days, couples could "hand-fast" at Lammas for a year and a day. This was a trial marriage and could be dissolved if the couple didn't get along or were not able to conceive a child. And I wondered if Armes and her people practiced that tradition here?

Lammas is also known as "Lughnasa" the feast of Lugh, the solar god who is said to be master of all skills. This was a time that the Celts celebrated their talents in friendly competition.

"I am happy with my God," I thought, "He is the creator of the heavens and the earth, and no other god compares with Him!"

Ceridwen arrived with my lunch. She placed the tray of food before me and bowed.

"Thank you," I replied, and I lowered my head. These women are sure polite, I thought, and I turned my attention to my food. Then shortly after I had finished my chicken and corn, Ceridwen returned with a sweet-tasting fruit loaf covered with strawberries and a thick yogurt topping. "This is lovely," I said to myself. "I've never tasted anything quite like it."

What kind of status did Armes have in the commune? I pondered again. She was obviously revered, and the people obeyed her. Helen had spoken of her as a type of enchantress. A bit exaggerated, I thought; I see her as more of a Bard or Seer.

Celtic society had great respect for people who could see beyond what was visible and use their special powers to benefit others in their community or tribe. My father told me that these wise and gifted people had public roles as druid priests and lawgivers, or as bards who held in their memory the history of their clan. When I think of bards who are able to hold in their memory the history of their clans, I can't help but think of my Gay! – who relates so spiritually and emotionally to Taliath and her diary – as if they are her own people. Maybe they are? Is this what is going on with Gay as we continue to translate the diary, and now have the artifacts that we found in the chest? It was all very mysterious, and there was an awareness being birthed in my soul that I did not yet understand.

Armes returned from her tea leaf reading and invited me into her living quarters.

"I trust you enjoyed your lunch," she said, as I followed her into another room, which was concealed behind two of the very large wooden candlestands. "Do come in and take a seat." She beckoned with her hands and I sat in another large wicker chair, only this one had a thick quilted cushion on it, making it far more comfortable. Armes lit several candles and then sat across from me in a similar-looking chair, but with an animal fur draped over the back of it.

"How was your tea reading?" I asked. "It went well. It's a group that I teach once a week."

I nodded.

"So, tell me more about Helen and what your relationship is to her. Are you her friend or an acquaintance?"

"I'm more than a friend," I said. "I'm married to her daughter Gay."

"Oh," she said, a little taken aback, "can you excuse me for a minute?" And she went behind a large purple curtain that divided her room, and she lit some incense on a fragrance burner, and a faint smell of lavender began to come from behind the curtain. It reminded me of Gay burning lavender when we had had our love ceremony the other day.

"I won't be long," she called out from behind the curtain, as the smell of lavender began to fill the whole room. Now came the sound of water being poured into a container. What was she doing behind there?

Suddenly she reappeared wearing a long Celtic gown, and she had taken the sandals off her feet. She then lit the burner on an old oil-powered stove, and she put a pot of water on the stove to warm. As far as I had seen so far, there was no electricity in any of the buildings. It must get cold here in the winter, I thought, especially in these stone buildings.

After checking the heat on the stove, she went behind the curtain again. "Just relax, Kingsley," she called, and then she reappeared with two clay goblets. "Elderberry wine," she said, "made here in our clan," and she handed me a goblet. I drank some and it tasted full and sweet, and I wasn't prepared for what happened next.

Armes asked me to follow her behind the curtain, which I did.

We walked past her bedchamber and what looked like an old oak canopy bed with embroidered material covering the top of the canopy. She opened the door of a small room and I followed her inside. "Sit here and finish your wine," she said, leading me to a large, cushioned chair.

As I sat back and sipped my wine, I felt stimulated by what had happened, and I contemplated what would happen next. Armes now brought a metal bucket of hot steaming water and placed it in front of me, its scent rising to my nostrils. She then knelt and undid my sandals, and gently lifted my feet into the hot scented water. She began washing my feet with a sponge, and slowly she rubbed and washed the soles of my feet and between my toes.

It was a humbling experience, as she was like a servant to me, without me uttering a word. Her warm caring presence seemed to fill the room, and I felt only peace and humility.

Leaving my feet soaking in the water, Armes stood up and rang a small hand bell that she picked up from a table. Two women soon appeared, dressed only in thongs and sandals. They looked to be the same women who had walked me through the corridor to meet Armes. "Hello again," I said, but they just lowered their heads in respect and attended to me. One of them carried more hot water and proceeded to pour it into my pail, which made the water piping hot again. The other woman filled our goblets with more wine. Then both women bowed to Armes and turned and bowed to me before leaving the room.

Armes sat for a while in silence and just sipped her wine and smiled at me. I also said nothing, but my heart said many things. And I felt her listening to me in the silence, and I opened my heart so she could look inside. "I can see you," she said. "I know," I replied, and awareness sang a song.

A beautiful lifetime had passed, and another began as Armes placed a towel in front of the pail, and she lifted my feet one at a time and gently dried them. After she had finished drying between my toes, she let down her hair, which she had been wearing up in a bun, and she rubbed my feet with her silky soft hair. And I became completely engulfed by her spirit that spoke gently, and then loudly, and then shouted! And I answered and our spirits danced!

Armes now spoke as she rubbed my feet with oil. "Tell me about my daughter," she asked, almost in a whisper. And I shared Gay's and my story, of how we had met as teenagers and fallen so deeply in love. And then how we had lost contact for over twenty years, and both lived different lives, but then we found each other again!

"True love searches…" Armes replied, "searches until it finds what it has lost, or for what it has never known before. And it doesn't stop until it has found what it knows to be love."

"You love my daughter, Kingsley, and her love has found you."

"Yes," I said quietly, "Gay's love has found me again."

Armes looked up at me and smiled. "I am glad," she said, "and I have found you, my Son."

"You have," I said, and I knew that my soul would love her always.

After she had finished oiling my feet, I followed her back to the first room that I had entered in the building, and we talked some more.

"Gay is interested in Celtic culture," I shared, and she has been trying to learn about some artifacts that we found in an ancient chest. We think the artifacts belonged to a Celtic clan."

I did not tell Armes about Taliath's diary, at least not for now. Maybe one day I would, as she might be able to help us understand more about Taliath and her family's way of life.

"What other things were in the chest?" she asked. "I know you briefly mentioned candle holders, and items of clothing, and a dagger, when we first spoke. And that reminds me, Kingsley, I have some artifacts too, which I found buried in the sand dunes at Pennard many years ago. Would you like to see what I found?"

"Yes," I replied, "I would!"

Armes opened an old wooden box and pulled out three ankle bracelets that looked exactly like the two that Gay and I had found in the chest. "Do you know what these markings on the anklets mean?" she asked.

"No, I don't, but Gay and I found two exactly like these in the chest, and they have similar markings, but we don't know if they are numbers or letters."

"Let me show you. These markings here are letters in the "Ogham" which is the first Celtic alphabet, and the letters read the word "Maeve" which represents the goddess of sovereignty and intoxication. The symbol of Maeve is the cup or goblet. And these markings here are numbers, and they read one hundred and seventeen. This number identified the individual within the clan, and the individual's details – age, sex, family name, and social status – were recorded by the Clan Priest in what the Celts called the "Covenant Book of Laws.""

"That's wonderful," I said. "Thank you, Armes, that has helped me to understand a lot, and I can't wait to share this with Gay. And I hope that we can also translate the meanings on the anklets that we have found."

"If you are not able to make sense of them, bring them with you next time you come, and I will translate them for you."

"Thank you, Armes, I am learning so much."

"Could you tell me more about Maeve?" I asked.

"Yes, I will. Here in Wales, and especially on the Cardiganshire coast, we have always had a special connection with Ireland. It is only the Irish Sea that separates our lands or joins them as some of our ancestors believed. My Grandmother told me of an Irish Legend…"

"Each new king of Ireland would have to "marry" Maeve to assume the throne. A priestess, taking on the role of the goddess, would offer a cup containing the "ale of cuala" to the new king. By drinking from the cup and by sleeping with the priestess – he signified his willingness to marry the land and become its guardian. To drink from the Celtic cup means not that you just commune with the one who offers it, but that you dedicate yourself to the service of the higher powers that it represents."

"Each new member here at the commune is required to drink from the Celtic cup as part of their inauguration ceremony. We also drink from the cup as part of some of the other ceremonies that we perform here."

"What do you drink from the cup?" I asked. "Wine?"

"Often we drink wine, but also what we call "Magic Drink" which contains lime-flower, chamomile or meadowsweet, and sometimes a little whisky."

"The magic drink is offered to your ceremonial partner, or friend, in the spirit of love and empowerment. First, you give the cup to the other person to drink, and then you take the cup and drink yourself. This is a simple daily ceremony that we practice here at the commune. It signifies a promise to be true to what is best and most noble in your relationship."

Armes was an encyclopedia of Celtic knowledge, and I ate it up! "How did you learn the Celtic alphabet and language?" I asked.

"My Grandmother gave me a document that had been handed down for many centuries, down through the generations of clans, and my mother taught me how to read the Ogham and to sound the letters into words. It is a great heritage for me to be able to understand our ancient language and culture, and to teach it to others."

I could hardly believe what Armes had told me; it was all so enlightening and wonderful! My whole experience here at the commune had been this way.

"I don't have much more time to talk, Kingsley, as I am overseeing an inauguration ceremony at our temple. We have three new members joining our commune today, and I'm not able to invite you to observe, as only members of our commune may attend."

"I would like to see you again, Kingsley, and please bring Taliath, I mean Gay, with you if you can."

"Did you say 'Taliath'?" I said, "I thought I heard you say Taliath." Just for a moment, Armes was taken aback by my words and appeared nervous.

"It's alright," I assured her, "whatever you say to me will go nowhere else."

"I can see that name means something to you, Kingsley, so I will share one more thing with you."

"Gay's birth name is Taliath. I named her after a distant ancestor of mine, about whom my grandmother told me stories. She lived in one of the Welsh Black Mountain Clans."

I was flabbergasted at Armes' words! No wonder Gay had this connection to the name!

Still in a daze, I listened to Armes continue to talk.

"Us clan women don't take the surnames of our male partners, like they do in modern times," she said. "It is the woman's maiden name that is handed down through the generations, not the man's."

Armes then gave me Gay's birth certificate to read, and it read: female, Taliath Saren, born July 5th 1981, at Singleton Hospital, Swansea.

It was time for Armes to leave for her ceremony.

"Goodbye Kingsley, I must go now to perform my duties at the temple. Give my love to Helen and tell her that I've never found another friend like her. And when the time is right, I would like you to tell Gay of our visit, and that I love her."

I was then escorted back through the settlement and through the fields to my car. It was only 6 p.m., and the summer sun was still quite high in the sky. The girls would not be home from Bristol until tomorrow evening, so there was no rush to get home.

Haunted by what I had just discovered, I decided to go for a walk along the clifftops between Fishguard and Newport Bay, and if I didn't wander too far away from my car, watch the sunset. I needed to think about Gay's birth name being Taliath Saren and what this could mean!

I drove through the little villages of Eglwyswrw, [try saying that backwards after a few pints in the pub and you have instant entertainment, and the English can't even say it frontwards!] I continued on to Velindre, and then Newport, where I parked the car.

Much of the cliff tops are thick with thorn, bramble and bracken, and you must choose your path, but there are wonderful stretches where the walking is easy, and there is rarely a time when the coast is not worth exploring. Whether on mild December days, or blustery March, or on through the summer months, its beauty is new each day and it renews one's soul. October is one of my favourite months, with the pale grasses and fading heather seen through a filter of evening mist, and it is also the best time to see the young seals wallowing in the bay. The cliffs have a sun-soaked stillness – melancholy to the soul as one stares across the wide and rugged expanse of the calling headlands, and the iron rocks that guard the bay from the angry shouts of the sea.

Towards the end of May and in the first half of June, flowers carpet the cliffs in tens of thousands. Constant pruning by the south-westerly winds cause those that survive to be strong and healthy. As in the human realm also, the winds and rains that batter against our lives can make us strong, gentle and true; and we appreciate the sun so much more as it leaves its pavilion behind the clouds and smiles its way across the sky.

This evening, I was greeted with yellow ladyfingers, moon daisies, and sea pink, contrasting with the grey blue rocks and their brilliant orange lichen, and my heart sang a song with the smiling yellow gorse with its coconut smell. And I sat on a rock and breathed in the air from the sea that rode upon the talking winds, while the sun finished his circuit upon the shadowing hills above my blue shining day. And it was time for me to walk back across the cliffs and be on my way.

And I drove my way through the winding hills to Newcastle Emlyn, Carmarthen, and on to Kidwelly, Burry Port, Llanelli, and over the bridge at Loughor, just to name a few of the places that dreamed with me on this wonderful day.

It was dark when I arrived home in Pennard, and I sat in my lounge chair and reminisced more about the day.

My time with Armes had been wonderful, and I would look forward to visiting her again. The fact that she had found artifacts, and could read the Ogham, the first Celtic alphabet, could help Gay and I with our translation of Taliath's diary, and help us understand more about our artifacts that we had found in the chest.

What I found most fascinating about my visit with Armes, was to learn that she had been taught the Ogham and the Celtic culture and laws by her mother and grandmother, and it had been this way for numerous generations. In Gay's and my translation of the diary, we had discovered that Taliath had learned the culture and laws of her people from her grandfather, the shoemaker, not from her grandmother. Her grandmother was mean and nasty, a real "cow" according to Taliath and her sisters. But her mother, who was the "Clan Queen," taught Taliath's eldest sister Gwenhwyfar the ways of Queenship for when she would take over her mother's reign. There was no Clan King, and it didn't appear so far in our translations that there were any male figures involved in teaching the customs and laws to the people, other than Taliath's grandfather. The Princes and the Nobles made and implemented the laws along with the Priests and Balla, but as Taliath wrote in her diary, "The Princes, who make the laws, are so far removed from the people."

The more I tried to compare Armes' teachings that had been handed down to her from her mother and grandmother to what Gay and I were discovering about Taliath's life from her diary, the more questions I had. So, I concluded that there was far too much to learn and understand before trying to make comparisons, and to just enjoy this wonderful journey of learning about the life and culture of the Celts.

Then there was the gobsmacking discovery of Gay's given name being Taliath! And her mother's maiden name is Saren! And when Armes showed me Gay's birth certificate, it read Taliath Saren. The very same name as the Taliath Saren whose diary we are translating from 970 AD!

Considering this, and Armes' connection to the ancient Celtic Clans, it is no wonder that Gay has this connection to Taliath and her people's way of life.

But what is the sum of this connection? What does it mean?

Saturday night turned into Sunday morning, and I spent the whole of Sunday morning thinking about this.

Obviously, Gay has a connection to her mother Armes, and her ancestry before that. But what else?

I was tempted to share my experience at the commune with Dad – maybe he could shed some light on things.

But if I told him, he would want to visit the commune and meet Armes, no doubt about that. So, I decided not to tell him, at least not for now.

And what would I tell Gay? I anticipated her feeling betrayed that I had gone to meet Armes behind her back. I didn't want her to be the last to know. But she hadn't told me that she was adopted, and I was trying to convince myself that I had a right to know. Maybe I did? Was our relationship not safe enough for Gay to be able to tell me? Is she hiding her wound? Obviously, she hasn't dealt with this issue in her life, and Helen had told me that the situation with her father had haunted Gay for years.

In the afternoon, the phone rang, and it was Samantha. She would be finishing her traveling in a few weeks, and then would be coming and stay with us. I began to get excited at the thought of seeing her, and I couldn't wait to show her our new home in Pennard.

The girls arrived home in the evening, happy and refreshed after their time in Bristol and a nice visit with Gay's sister Pearl.

Before Helen returned home to Cardiff, I asked if we could have a talk. I wanted to share with her some of my experiences at the commune, and meeting Armes. "How about tomorrow," she said, "I won't be driving home to Cardiff tonight, so we can talk in the morning." I said that would be fine.

After breakfast, Gay took Melody into Swansea to pick up her new school blazer that had been on order, and to get another pair of sandals. This gave Helen and I the house to ourselves.

Warming her hands on her teacup, Helen smiled at me in anticipation of what I was going to say. And I felt almost shy as she read me with her big blue eyes.

"Let me guess," she said. "You went to meet Armes at the commune in West Wales?"

"How did you know?" I asked.

"I felt that once I told you about Gay's ancestry, you would want to find out more, and you have."

I felt a little surprised at Helens word's, but not shocked. She had always been intuitive.

"Don't be concerned, Kings," she said. "If I hadn't wanted you to know more about my daughter, I wouldn't have told you. And as I have shared before, I love you and I trust you implicitly."

I felt both humbled and esteemed by this lovely lady of such rare quality and substance.

"What did you find out about Armes?"

"She is indeed a woman of presence and knowledge," I shared. "And as far as I could see, she is respected and even revered by the other commune members."

Helen giggled and said, "I was wondering what words you would use to describe her. Presence and knowledge? Yes, I would agree with those attributes. How about sexy, sensual, and humble, or what she would present as being humble?" And Helen and I both looked at each other with knowing smiles and laughed.

She continued to read me with her blushing face, and then said, "Oh Kings, you are truly lovely. Always watching over our hearts, and don't think I don't see it. You wouldn't tell me anything if you thought it might hurt me, and us girls love you to bits." She then came and sat next to me on the chesterfield, took my hand and kissed my cheek.

"That was lovely," I replied. "You said what we both feel, and this chesterfield is becoming our special seat."

Helen blushed, so lovely, and she laughed like a young girl trying to hide her heart.

"I love you too, Kings, and sometimes I'm jealous of my own daughter, but I do get to share you, don't I? And that means a lot to me."

"Yes, you do," I answered, and I reached out and found her hand.

Over a pot of tea, I shared with Helen nearly all my experiences at the commune.

It's 11 a.m., Lets Go!

"Armes asked me to give you her love, and to tell you that she has never found another friend like you."

"Did she ask about Gay, Kings?"

"Yes, she asked me to bring her to the commune one day to see her, but that's something I don't see happening very soon. I would like Gay to tell me about Armes first."

She began to cry in my arms, and said, "I know that Gay will want to meet her birthmother one day, and I think that day is coming soon. I love you Kings, and thanks for taking care of me."

"I love you too. And remember that Armes could never take your place in Gay's life."

∽

Over the next few weeks, we began to settle in and get organized in our new home, and we met a few of our neighbors. Samantha also arrived and it was a wonderful feeling to have her under my roof again, and she was soon settled in and the months of being apart soon melted away into the closeness we had always shared.

Melody had made friends with the girl next door, Beverly Ace, and she spent less time with Gay and I. On the weekends, she would go for sleepovers at Beverly's, or Beverly would spend the night at our house. It was great to see Melody making friends and enjoying being more independent. And we hoped that it would be the same for Melody at Pennard School when she started next week. Her school in Cardiff had been very challenging when it came to making friends and being happy at school. But it had ended on a positive note with her winning the award for her project on Nan's Nan.

Pennard School was the same school that I had attended when I was Melody's age, and I looked forward to walking her into the schoolyard on her first day. It was a short drive to Pennard School from where we lived on Southgate Road, and after her first few days she would be able to catch the school bus with Beverly. The school bus stopped right outside Pennard Store, which was just across the road.

One Saturday morning, Gay and Samantha and I took Melody shopping for the rest of her school uniform and supplies, and I remembered a day when Samantha was ten years old. I had always walked her to school from where we lived on Vancouver Island, and she would take my hand and we would skip along the pavement like two best friends, and we were. Then one day we arrived at the playground of Pacific Christian School, and she let go of my hand as usual to go and play with her friends, but she turned around and said to me, "Dad, I don't need you to walk me to school anymore." And I can remember standing there crushed at her words! I can remember another parent coming up to me and saying, "Are you alright, Mr. Hill? You look a bit lost this morning."

"I'm not alright," I said. "Samantha doesn't want me to walk her to school anymore, and I have to grow up." The parent smiled and said, "I know exactly how you feel, and it's hard! But you will get used to it, and soon you will be enjoying your daughter's next phase in growing up. And your next phase." she said as she smiled.

She was quite right, and I have been through it three times now, including with my boys Jonathan and Benjamin. Only we didn't hold hands as much as kicking the soccer ball to each other until the final bell rang to start class.

It's 11 a.m., Lets Go!

And now it would happen with Melody one day. She was already almost 11. But that is the way of things and I was going to enjoy every moment of the wonderful experience of being a dad.

Since Gay had got back from visiting her sister in Bristol, I had noticed a change in her. She seemed to be more balanced in the way she was dividing her time with Melody and I, and with interpreting Taliath's diary. She even asked to have a family conference again, which included Helen. "This is good," both Melody and I said to each other. "We haven't had a family conference since we moved from Cardiff."

"I'm sorry I was so preoccupied," she said, "and I know that I neglected you all."

Melody went and sat on her mother's lap, and of course all sins were forgiven.

Now that we had most things organized at the house, we invited Dad and Mary over for supper more often, and we spent time metal detecting at Pennard Castle. Helen learned to use a metal detector and quite enjoyed the excitement of digging up treasures, even when they were only old bottle caps and coca cola cans. And we searched the slopes in front of the castle, as Dad had wanted us to, but we found nothing worthwhile, not even some old shillings or pennies or a fifty-pence piece. But it was fun trying, Helen reminded us, as our newest enthusiast. And Dad assured us that we were just not at the right place, and that there were more artifacts to find nearby. We will keep looking once a month, we all agreed, and start searching in new areas that we haven't tried before.

Samantha had found herself a Welsh boyfriend named Glynn, and she said, "He's just like you, Dad." And after she brought him home to meet Gay and me, I said she had my approval, as long as he didn't live in a cave, ride a wild stallion, or steal the milk money from the milkman. "He doesn't do any of that, Dad, but he's hoping to learn from you."

"That's alright then," I said, and we both laughed.

Chapter Twelve

Summer's Gold

It was late August, and the high spring tides were upon us. Each morning, Samantha, Melody and I went body surfing at Pobbles Beach. We swam and rode the waves for hours, and after we got cold, we built sand boats and castles before the incoming tides. On the far hill of Cefn Bryn, that always seemed so near, the green bracken of spring and summer began to turn to brown, and the songs of the skylarks were of their memory's past. I looked up into the hills and wondered what the autumn season would hold, and like the elusive rainbow, I had found my pot of gold – Samantha, Melody, and Gay were mine to hold, and this summer of 2019 in my arms I will always hold, and through the years you will never grow old, my beautiful summer – summer gold.

We now approached the last weekend before Melody started her new school and Gay and I returned to work. It was Helen's birthday on Saturday, and as far as Gay and I were concerned, there was only one place to take her to celebrate, and that was to our caravan at Port Eynon. We took a vote, and Samantha and Glynn were in too.

We booked a large caravan with four bedrooms, and the Birthday Girl would have her own room.

Helen came down from Cardiff on the Thursday evening and stayed the night, and we left for Port Eynon on Friday afternoon.

Gay and I were up at the crack of dawn on Saturday, and we decided to go for a walk on the beach before anyone else woke up. As we strolled across the sand, we looked back at our footprints, and ours were the first of the new day. Man and Woman, God made us, and hand-in-hand we felt like the first people that God had put in this Garden of Eden. And how lovely it was to have Gay's hand in mine.

Suddenly, the sun rose above the headland, making the sands glow gold. "Come, my darling," Gay said, and we took our shoes and socks off and ran to the dunes. There we made love, as the sun climbed higher and warmed our naked bodies. The sea was silver all the way to Oxwich Point, and a gentle breeze carried the fragrant smell of summer's breath to our nostrils, and I pulled Gay back down to our sandy blanket, and we lay there and kissed as the seabirds called good morning from out on the bay.

"The tide is coming in again, my love," I whispered, as our passions spent their last breath.

"I love you, Kings, and your love fills my whole soul." And I wiped the sand from her body and dressed her.

"Come on," she said, and I chased her to the waves.

And we walked back with the sun and the sea breeze, and we stepped in each other's footprints until we reached the pebbles and walked along the path to the caravan.

Helen and Melody were up making breakfast, and

Summer's Gold

Samantha and Glynn were just getting dressed. "You two were up early," they said, and we felt like we had lived a whole day already.

After breakfast, Gay and I told Helen that she wasn't to do any more cooking or cleaning for the rest of the weekend.

"You're the birthday girl, and you get to relax!"

"If you insist," she said, smiling, and we all answered, "We do!"

Gay and I packed lunches and we all headed down to the beach to play. The tide was coming in quickly now across the flat sands, and the girls decided to make a sand boat, and like pirates, defy the waves.

Glynn had never been bass fishing, so I decided to teach him how I caught them off the rocks.

"First, we need bait, and it is best with bass to use something live, like lug or rag worms, or my favourite, soft crab. There aren't any lug or rag worms to dig, but I know where we can find some soft crab."

Glynn carried our rods, and we walked around the curve of the beach to the point.

"Do you think we will catch one?" he asked.

"I think it's quite likely," I replied. "The conditions are right. We have an incoming tide, and August is a good month for bass. Plus, there is only a light breeze, which means we can get close to the water's edge and safely cast out from the rocks. The water is deeper around the rocks, and you don't have to cast far."

I showed Glynn how to set up the rods and tie the treble hooks.

"I'm using treble hooks to help hold the crabs," I explained. "The shells of the crabs are quite soft – a real delicacy for a hungry bass. If you only use a one-prong hook, you can lose the bass when they strike. But if you use a treble hook, you have three prongs holding the bait, and the crab stays intact longer after a few bites or with the heavy pull of the tide. The only disadvantage in using a treble, is that the bass will often spit out the hook without it getting caught in its gullet, so you have to watch your rod tip carefully, and only pull the rod tip lightly when the fish strikes." Glynn listened intently to my instructions, and then sat and watched me turn over rocks in one of the shallow gullies.

"Here's one," I cried, as I grabbed a scampering soft crab from underneath a rock. "Feel how soft his shell is," I said to Glynn. "It's a real delicacy for salmon bass."

"I want to try to catch one," he said, taking his shoes off and joining me in the gully, and we each turned over rocks and caught about ten crabs.

"It's time to head to the rocks at the point," I said. "The current from there will take our bait a fair way out into the tide." And I showed him how to push the shank of the hook into the bottom of the crab, and then gently position the three points of the hook.

"Two into the flesh right up to the barbs, and one sticking out to the side, which hopefully will get stuck in the mouth of the bass. You can also wind your line around the crab once or twice, which again helps to keep it on the hook."

Glynn was a natural, and he was soon putting on his own crabs. His casting was good too, and I only had to show him twice how to hold the line in his hand and then let it go at the same time as he made his cast.

"One of us should fish close to the rocks," I said, "and the other cast further out." Glynn cast his line just beyond the nearest gully, while I cast mine out into the waves about fifty yards out. "Watch your footing!" I said, as we each held our rods and anticipated a strike. His rod bent first, and he shouted, "I think I've got a strike!"

And indeed, he had, but the fish had thrown the hook. "Leave it out for another few minutes," I said. "Your bait is probably still intact, and he might have another go at it."

Meanwhile, there was a strike on my line, and he was hooked! I let some line out as the bass darted to get away.

"You've got one, you've got one!" Glynn shouted, almost as excited as me.

"See how I'm letting him run?" I explained, "but I'm keeping enough tension on the line so it's difficult for him to throw the hook. He's moving his head from side to side, and I can feel him trying to throw the hook. It is important that I keep the tension on him as best I can, while not pulling so hard that I pull the hook out of his mouth."

After a minute or so, I called out to Glynn again. "You can see now that he's not pulling as hard, and he doesn't seem to have the energy to make another run for it. That means I have tired him out as best I can, so I'm going to bring him in now. Remember, you keep the line tight and don't give him any slack, and you pull him in nice and smooth, not jerking the rod, otherwise the hook can still come out of his mouth."

Suddenly, his dorsal fin broke the surface, and he had the strength to make a final run for freedom. I kept the line tight, however, and smoothly wound him in. I landed a nice salmon bass, about five pounds.

"I'm impressed," Glynn said, and by the look on his face, I almost wished that he had caught it. Almost, that is! It's hard not to be selfish when you're winding in a fish, and I took solace in my brother's words: "if you've got a fish on, it's your fish! And you mustn't feel guilty if the other person hasn't caught one!"

But I did want Glynn to catch one – he was so keen and trying so hard. "The next fish is yours, I said, either on my line or yours."

Now he was smiling, and we both cast out a fresh soft crab. We fished for another hour and no bites, but then suddenly, my rod tip bent, and I gently lifted my rod. It felt like it was hooked good, and I handed my rod to Glynn.

"Don't forget to keep the tension on," I reminded him, and don't jerk the rod. That's it, nice and smooth, now reel him in, and if he runs, stay with him or he'll shake the hook."

Glynn played the bass like a pro, and when he landed it, it was about four pounds. He smiled all the way back to the beach where the girls were already fighting the waves that were breaking into their boat.

We quickly put our gear down and covered our catch with my jacket, and then we jumped into the waves to help the girls try and save their ship.

"Come on, Dad!" Melody shouted. "Put some more sand on the sides, otherwise we'll sink!"

Gay and Samantha were busily throwing fresh sand onto the walls that were quickly crumbling. Helen stood in the waves at the front of the boat, trying to make a human shield, but the rollers were coming quick and fast, and it was time to shout "abandon ship!"

And I grabbed Helen's hand and pulled her into our boat. The walls caved completely now, and the waves came crashing in!

"There's pirates!" Melody shouted. And we all abandoned our posts and jumped into the conquering waves. What fun we all had!

We all ran back up the beach, as the girls shivered, Glynn and I displayed our proud catch. Then it was time to head back to the caravan and warm up.

Once we had changed our clothes, we sat at the picnic table at the campsite, and we decided to have fish and chips as a special birthday lunch for Helen. Samantha, Glynn and Melody walked back to the chip shop at the seafront to pick up our food.

"There's nothing like good old British fish and chips with salt and malt vinegar," Helen said, making our taste buds impatient.

"Plus, tartar sauce and Heinz ketchup," Gay said, as we tried to wait patiently for our food to arrive.

Our three musketeers arrived back with fish and chips wrapped in newspaper, and the smell of hot chips and vinegar filled the air.

"Sorry, Mr. Seagull, these aren't for you," I said, and he glided off. And everything was alright in our world. We had fish and chips, and each other – what more could we want? "Happy Birthday, Helen!"

"Oh, this is so wonderful!" she exclaimed, wolfing down her chips in a way that only a refined lady can. And between 'yums' and other noises of pleasure, there was little other conversation. Mr. Seagull returned and sat on the caravan roof, waiting to see if he could give us a hand with the dishes, though I had my suspicions that he would only clean and not dry.

It was time to bring out the cake! Melody blindfolded Helen with our checkered pirate towel, and Gay and I brought out the cake as the "Happy Birthday to You" echoed around the caravan site. The sun, now westering, tipped his hat between the clouds, and then shone brightly upon us, and it was a very happy birthday for Helen, with many returns of the day.

"Thank you all!" she exclaimed, smiling radiantly. "This has been so very special, and I love you all."

Helen spoke most often through the little things she did for you, like warming up the teacups before she poured the tea, or covering your hard-boiled eggs with little cozies on their heads. And most of all, she offered her encouraging smiles and gentle nods of approval when you had the wonderful privilege of basking in her presence. So, when she did speak, her words were meaningful and true, and one could set a course of goodness by just listening to her wise and gentle words. "Happy Birthday, Lovely Lady!" We sat at the campsite until the sun put down his cap upon an orange cloud that glowed with the stories of our day. Pour me another glass of blackberry wine and talk to me with your smiles.

Helen read Melody a story, and Samantha and Glynn retired for the night.

"It's a lovely night, my love," Gay said quietly. "Let's go for a walk on the beach."

As we walked across the sands, the tide had washed away the footprints that told the story of our morning, and I was reminded that at the end of each day, only our memories are

Summer's Gold

left in our hearts to take into another day – some happy, some sad, as each of us try to find our way. And I felt glad that today we had made many happy memories, that through the years would somehow stay, and in our hearts, we would remember and celebrate yesterday.

"Look, Love, the big sand dune! Let's go and play!"

And I followed behind my undressing Gay, as we ran up the dune to play, and I lay in the soft sand and made love to my Gay, and we shouted, "Hurray! Hurray! for our love and the day, and forever in your arms my love I will stay!"

Then we lay cooling in the sea breeze that brought goosebumps to our skin, and we held each other tight again, and shared our secret hopes, dreams and sin.

After I had run down the dune and back, and collected Gays clothes, she said she had something to ask me.

"What is it?" I smiled, pondering what it could be. We always talked about everything, from love to mermaids in the sea. "There is something I haven't told you about me, Kings, and it's not that I haven't wanted to tell you. I just haven't wanted to tell myself."

"What is it?" I asked, reassuring her with a hug. "I'm adopted. Helen isn't my birth mum."

I pretended I was surprised. I was surprised that she had told me here and now. I had felt sure that I would have to ask her one day a long time from now. But I was glad she had told me on this day. I didn't say anything; I just held her in my arms and caressed her fingers, which told her what my heart was saying: Thank you, thank you for telling me.

And I wished I had told her that I knew, but I didn't feel guilty because it was something that I had needed to do.

We sat on top of our sand dune and watched the sunset fade over the bay, and then she asked me something that was more colourful than the day!

"Would you be willing to spend some time with mum and get her out and about a bit? She hasn't gone out to meet people since my stepdad died. She just has her one friend, Mandy, in the village, and otherwise she doesn't really know anyone else."

"She's lonely, Kings, and she loves you, and I don't think she's ever known what it's like to have the love and companionship that we have. It would be wonderful if she could meet someone special, or even make some new friends. She won't come out with me, I've tried, but I know she would enjoy your company," Gay commented.

"I was thinking that you could take her out next Saturday night. Melody and I are going to visit Pearl in Bristol, and there is a speed dating event happening in Mumbles on Saturday evening." "Speed dating, what is that? I have never heard of it," I replied.

"It is a way for single people to meet in a non-threatening environment without having to go to a bar or pickup joint in order to meet someone," Gay continued. "Everyone meets at a local restaurant or pub. You spend a short amount of time with one person, and then move to another table where you meet someone else. You only spend a short time talking to each person, just enough time to know if you would like to get to know more about them. If you don't have any interest in the person, then you only have to spend that five minutes or so with them, so it's not too uncomfortable."

"Mm, that does sound like something Helen would be willing to try," I said, "so what happens if you like someone, and you want to see them again?"

"If you like someone you have talked to, then you tick their name on the list that the organizer gives you at the start of the evening. If the feeling is mutual and the person you are interested in wants to meet you too, then they tick your name on the list."

"That sounds like a good way to meet someone," I replied, "but how do you find out if a person is interested in you? Surely you don't have everyone's phone number on the list, otherwise you will get people who you are not interested in contacting you," I said. "No," Gay replied, "only the organizer has everyone's contact information, and if you are a match with someone you ticked on the list, then the organizer emails you their contact information. They don't give out phone numbers, only emails addresses."

"I would be happy to try and encourage Helen to go," I replied, "and I could drop her off and pick her up after." "You might have to go with her, my love, you know how she is about meeting men. Go with her!"

"I don't know about that," I though out loud, "and besides, you have to be single to go, don't you?" "Yes," Gay answered, "but you can pretend to be single and watch over Helen. please, Kings," she pleaded! "My friend Jane met her husband at a speed dating event, and I just know that mum won't go on her own."

I pondered the idea for a few minutes, and then said yes, "I will go because I love Helen, and it would be wonderful if she could find someone special in her life."

"Really Kings? You would go with her? Oh, that would be wonderful, thank you my love, it would mean so much to me if she could meet a nice man who would treat her like the wonderful woman she is. I will book you guys up for the speed dating for next Saturday when we get home from our weekend." I was happy that Gay was so excited about it, but I wondered inside what I had got myself into!

As Gay and I walked down to the sea, she thanked me again.

"It's alright," I replied. "I care for her very deeply, and we both love your mum."

"Thank you, Kings, I love you."

"I love you too," I said, and kissed her.

Gay and I paddled our way back in the waves, and we watched the fluorescent colours of the breakers as they crashed upon the sand. And it felt so good to have our love held in each other's hands. Only the waves and the wind could understand, how deep is our love, as we walk across the sand.

When we got back to the caravan, our fire was all ready to light. We had promised Melody that we'd have a campfire, and Samantha and Glynn had brought some hotdogs and marshmallows to roast. Samantha helped Melody light the fire, while I cut some roasting sticks off the trees behind the caravan site. I used my Bowie knife, the one my dad had given me for Christmas when I first went to live on the cliffs all those years ago. That was when my great adventures started, I thought, as I hacked the branches from the trees.

We sat around the fire and told stories as we roasted our hotdogs and marshmallows, and it was my turn to tell a story. "Tell us the one about the sea monster you saw at Foxhole Bay, Dad," Samantha said, her eyes wide in anticipation.

Summer's Gold

"It happened early one morning when I was on my way to go mackerel fishing at Eddie Tucker's cove, near Pobbles Beach. I was climbing down the rocks with my fishing gear, and I noticed a movement on the otherwise completely calm water. About thirty feet from the rocks was what looked like a whirlpool swirling around. I put my gear down on the rocks to observe this strange sight. It was not a seal or a porpoise. Seal's glide and twist and turn when they are hunting prey, and they will most often surface to thrash the fish back and forth in their mouth. The area of water that was swirling around was about twenty feet in diameter, far too big for a seal. As for porpoises, they arch their backs out of the water while they swim and move across great distances quickly."

"This swirling pool stayed in the same place, and its circle of water was getting larger and larger as I continued to watch. Could it be a whale? I thought. My mother had once seen two basking sharks in the bay, but the largest creatures I had seen were dolphins and porpoises criss-crossing in front of Grandpa's boat. This was different, and I could sense that something was about to surface – and it did!"

"Suddenly a long black neck with a large horse-like head pushed up through the water. I couldn't believe it! The creature looked around with its large brown eyes and had what looked to be like ears on the top of its head, and there was hair growing from underneath its chin. It seemed to look right at me, and it was not afraid! Nor was I, as it looked to be a very peaceful creature. I had never seen any animal like this, but I had heard stories of a strange prehistoric-looking sea creature that had been seen over the years around the Gower Peninsula."

"What else did you see?" Helen and Melody asked together.

"Its head and neck stayed in an upright position for some time, and then suddenly several humps appeared behind the creature's neck as it slowly began to swim on the surface. This is when I thought it must be a creature having survived from the age of the dinosaurs…! I kept watching it as it slowly moved further out to sea, and then it dived under the water, again out of sight."

There was silence around the campfire, until Samantha informed us that her days of swimming in the sea were over!

"Me too!" Melody declared.

"If it wanted to harm humans, it would have done so a long time ago," I said, hoping to encourage everybody. "I believe it is a peaceful creature, more scared of us than we are of it. It probably just wants to be left alone to live its life catching fish to eat."

"Or catching people," Melody said, laughing.

It was Melody's turn to tell a story, but my marshmallow was on fire, and there was lots of smoke and laughter.

"What are you doing, Dad?" Samantha asked, laughing.

"I am trying to form another skin on my marshmallow, because I like pulling the skins off and eating them." Melody told Samantha and Glynn her story about sending her message in a bottle at Hunts Bay. Helen, Gay and I remembered, of course, as we had been there. And she went on to share that she was hoping someone would find it soon, and she was hoping it would lead her to someone who would become her best friend.

"It will wash up on one of the beaches one day, and someone will find it," we all said, trying to encourage her.

Samantha had some big news to share. She had been accepted into the extended 2-year program she had applied for at Swansea University – so she would be staying here in Wales even longer! And I can't tell you how happy that made me feel, to know that she was staying here with us, and not going back to Canada so soon.

On Sunday morning, Gay wanted to have a sleep-in and read a book that she had been looking forward to reading. Samantha and Glynn had planned to spend the day together hiking, so I decided to take Helen and Melody spear fishing at the Three Cliffs river. It was an incoming tide and the time of year when the skate came up the river. "They might be there," I explained to Melody, who was already getting excited. "But if they are not, there is always something interesting to do in the valley."

"I'm in," Helen said, also excited to be coming.

We parked the car at our usual place on Bendrick Drive, and we walked along the side of the golf course to Pobbles. As Melody ran ahead of us, Helen and I walked fast to try and catch up. "I wish I had her energy," Helen said, as Melody continued to run and chase butterflies from one gorse bush to the next.

We skipped our way through the warm sand as we followed Melody down the path beside the castle to the Three Cliffs valley below.

Melody took both our hands as we arrived at the banks of the Killy Willy stream.

"You look for the shape of the skate in the riverbed," I explained, as our eyes scanned the bottom. "You'll see the movement of fins flicking around the body of the skate. That's how they bury themselves and hide in the sand. Remember, they can camouflage themselves quite well by changing to the colour of the sand, so it's their movement that helps your eye to spot them, not their colour. Their eyes are also on the top of their head, and their mouth is underneath the head, so you can't see their mouth until after you have caught one."

"There's one!" Melody shouted, as she pointed to a medium-size skate that was resting on top of the sand. "Look, Dad, I can see its eyes on top of its head, and its fins moving in the sand."

"By Jove, you're right! Well done, Melody, good spotting!"

"Now we don't want to scare him," I said. "Otherwise, he will quickly skim away downstream, and we won't see him again. Skates can feel the vibration of us walking on the bank, so we need to step lightly and walk slowly."

"Like we're stalking our prey?" Melody asked. "Yes, that's exactly what we're doing. Well done."

"Now there he is, right across from us!" I said suddenly. "Melody, I want you to kneel here on the bank and watch the skate, while Helen and I go and cut a spear from one of the trees in the woods." And Melody was excited that I had given her the important job of observing the skate. "Now, if he does move, just remember the direction he went, whether upstream against the current, or downstream with the current, and try and follow him to where he stops."

It was time to find a branch and cut it with my Bowie knife. Helen and I found a perfect branch on a tree just inside the woods.

"This is just what we need," I said. "It's about six feet long and an inch thick. Heavy enough to throw, and thick enough to carve a barb on the end."

I hacked the branch off the tree, and we headed out of the woods to return to Melody. As we quietly walked along the riverbank, it looked like Melody had not moved. She was still kneeling and peering into the stream.

"He's still there," she whispered, "but he's pushed himself deeper into the sand."

"Good reading of the situation, Melody. That usually means that he feels safe and is going to stay in that spot for a while, unless something spooks him, of course."

"Now let me show you how to cut a barb in the end of the spear," I said to Melody. "We have to put a barb on, so the skate doesn't wriggle off the end of the spear when it hits him."

Melody giggled and ground her teeth like a little warrior. I cut a deep groove into the spear about five inches from the end, and then sharpened the tip to a point.

"You've done this a few times," Helen said. "I remember Gay telling me about a big skate you speared, and remember when I bought a fish from you?"

"Yes, I remember." I said, smiling. "It's time to spear the fish," I announced, and I got Melody and Helen to lie still on the bank and keep their eyes on the skate, or where they remembered seeing him in the sand.

"Okay, I'm going to slowly stand up and throw the spear," I said quietly.

It was all so exciting, as I hadn't speared a skate in many years, and once again I was the "Caveman of Bacon Hole."

I stood up slowly and I could just make out the shape of the skate in the riverbed. I needed to throw hard and straight and hit it just below the head.

"Here goes," I whispered to the girls. I held the spear firm in my hands, anticipating its weight for a few seconds, and then I threw hard and straight.

It was a good throw! As soon as the spear left my hand, I knew that I had him! The spear plunged through the flesh just below the head where I had aimed, and the skate wriggled against the barb that held him on the spear.

Immediately I shouted, "Yes, I got him!" And I pulled off my shirt and jumped into the river with my shorts on to retrieve my catch. The girls clapped as I lifted him up on the spear and threw him onto the bank, and we all did a tribal dance. And I was the man!

Helen's eyes sparkled, and she said, "You are a wild one, aren't you!" And I answered, "I am."

Next it was time to teach Helen and Melody how to gut a skate.

"The wings of the skate are pure meat, and you cut them off as close to the body as you can."

Melody got right into it, and as soon as I had demonstrated how to cut the wing off, she was reaching for my knife to cut the other one.

"Careful, it's sharp!" I said, and with a little supervision she soon had the other wing cut clean off.

"Look, Grandma," she said, proudly holding it up to Helen.

"Well done!" exclaimed Helen, "and if you carry on like this, you're going to be a cave dweller like your dad."

"Did you hear that, Dad? I'm going to be living in a cave like you, and spear skate to eat!"

"You are?" I replied. "Then I will have to teach you how to throw a spear too."

Summer's Gold

"Will you, dad? Will you?"

"Yes, I will. But it's going to take some practice before you can put a spear through a skate and retrieve it from the river."

"Let's finish cleaning the skate," I said, "and then we can try tracking another one, and give you a chance to throw the spear."

Melody danced up and down, shaking the spear in her hand. And I said, "You look like a Zulu from Eglwyswrw."

Melody roared with laughter and almost fell over. "A Zulu from Eglwyswrw," she repeated. "That's so funny!"

Helen was laughing as well, and she said we were truly becoming a cave family.

I showed Melody how to cut the remaining meat away from the spine of the skate, and then we threw its frame to the waiting gulls.

"Is that Charlee, the seagull?" she asked, as one of the gulls swooped down and carried the carcass downstream.

"If it is, he's over twenty years old by now – isn't he, Kings?" Helen asked. "Yes, Charlee would be at least twenty by now, you never know, it could be him, because seagulls can live to be fifty years old."

"That's almost as old as me," Helen winked, and I told her that she didn't look a day over forty. And she didn't – she had really taken care of herself, and she smiled at me.

I now showed Melody how to practice throwing the spear into a shallow part of the river, and she looked to be a natural as she held the spear the right way and anticipated its weight. She aimed at a stone on the riverbed. "Five more throws," I said, and she hit the stone three times.

"Well done! Now I will show you how to sharpen the point of the spear."

"Watch carefully – always hold the knife like this and cut away from your body."

"Can I have a go?" Helen asked. And I handed her the spear.

"That's right," I said. "See, Melody, how she's pushing the knife away from her body, so she doesn't cut herself."

"How often do you have to sharpen the point of the spear, Dad?"

"I check it after every throw to make sure it is still sharp. Sometimes it hits a stone or some hard clay, and even the backbone of a skate is hard and can blunt your spear. You want to keep it as sharp as you can so that it will pierce right through the flesh of the skate – otherwise, they will wriggle away and escape."

Once Helen had finished sharpening the spear, we walked along the riverbank in search of another skate.

"What you should remember, Melody, is when you see the skate, you only have one throw of the spear, and if you miss, he's gone."

We walked along the riverbank to one of Killy Willy's curves, and memories of my first spear-throwing days excited my heart again.

"This bend in the river was one of my most productive places for hunting skate when I lived in the wild," I said proudly, "and you can see that the water is deep here. It's like a pool and slow flowing. Quite often you can get a skate resting or feeding here on its way further up the river."

"It's hard to see the bottom," Helen said, "but it looks like a good place where a skate would sit quietly on the bottom."

"I'll show you a secret!" I said, looking up at the sun. "An old man once taught me that being able to see a skate has a lot to do with where the sun is in the sky, and the shadows at certain times of the day." Melody imitated me by looking up at the sun, and she wore a look of wonder on her face. "Mm," she muttered, "sun and shadows, huh? That sounds interesting, Dad."

"Let's climb up the rocks beside the river," I said, "and look down from a height." I took Helen's hand and the three of us scrambled up the rocks.

"How high are we climbing?" Melody called down.

"Stop where you are," I said, "and let's all look down into the pool from there."

There was no glare from the sun on the water from where we stood, as the long taunting shadows from the rocks behind us reached out from the edge of the rocks and across the valley floor.

"It's easier to make out the shapes on the bottom of the pool from up here, isn't it?" I said.

"There!" Helen pointed. "There's one! I can see its shape on top of the sand."

"I can see it; I can see it!" Melody shouted. "Yes, it's a skate," I affirmed! "Now I'll show you what we do."

"It's no good throwing the spear from up here, as it's too far away and we wouldn't hit it. So, we are going to keep our eyes on the skate and very carefully climb back down the rocks. Watch your footing as well as the skate, otherwise you could fall."

"It is getting harder to see the skate the closer we get," Helen commented.

"That's because our angle of light is changing," Melody said, beginning to understand what I was trying to show her.

"I'd never have guessed the visibility in the river would be better from a distance," Helen said.

"It's getting difficult to see it," Melody announced, having climbed down the rocks about twenty feet further than Helen and I. "Come back up to where we are," I said. "We are close enough from here. Can you see the outline of the skate, Melody?"

"Yes, I can still see it."

"Okay, good. Now I am going to get you to throw the spear at the skate. I want you to try and aim just behind its head into the largest part of its back. Always try to aim at what you can see, not what you can't, or what you think might be there, otherwise you're just guessing."

"I can see the widest part of it, Dad."

"Good, that's what you aim at," I replied. "Now feel the weight of the spear in your hand, like you did when we were practicing, and try to make an allowance for its weight in accordance with the distance of your target. Remember, you are throwing down, not across, so you don't need as much distance as if you were throwing across. The height you are throwing from will give you a lot of power, so your main concentration should be on accuracy."

"Okay, Dad."

"Helen and I are going to stand on each side of you, and we will grab hold of you once you throw the spear. So just have your feet apart in a way that you feel balanced for the throw."

"What if I miss, Dad?"

"It doesn't matter, don't worry about missing. Just keep concentrating on your throw."

"Remember that you're throwing from a height, so you only need to put a medium amount of thrust on the spear as you throw it." I added.

"Okay, Dad. I think I'm just about ready."

"Good, Melody, good position. Keep your feet apart for balance and move the spear back and forth with your arm to get the feel of the weight of it in your wrist. You have got plenty of time, so don't rush. That's it, you control the spear by your wrist, and thrust it with your arm. Keep your eye on your target."

"I'm ready, Dad," she said, with a serious look on her face. "Good. Remember – long and smooth, don't jerk your wrist, and just follow through like you did in practice."

"I'm going to count down from ten," said Helen, "and then you throw…. Five, four, three, two, one, throw!"

Melody's throw was smooth and strong, and she pierced the skate through one of its wings. It immediately turned on its side and tried to wriggle its body off the barb. Helen took Melody by the arm while I scrambled down the rocks to retrieve the skate before it reached the faster flowing waters beyond the bend.

Quickly stripping to my waist, I jumped into the pool with my knife, just as the skate was about to wriggle off the spear. I plunged my knife into its flesh and dragged it to the riverbank. It was a large skate, a lot bigger than it looked from up on the rocks.

"You did it, Melody! Well done!" Helen and I shouted. "Look at the size of it! It's got to be fifteen pounds," I said. And Melody grinned from cheek to cheek like a Cheshire cat.

After cleaning all the meat off the skate, and putting it in my backpack with the rest, it was time to head back to Port Eynon to meet the others.

"Wait till Mum hears about this!" Melody exclaimed. And we all held hands in celebration as we walked back up over the dunes and across the golf course to the car.

"Can I keep the spear?" Melody asked, as she took a break from singing her celebrative chorus of "I'm a Zulu from Eglwyswrw" and we arrived back at the car.

"Yes, you can keep the spear, Cave Girl, and when we get home, we can hang it on your bedroom wall."

"Did you hear that, Grandma? Dad said we can hang the spear on my bedroom wall!"

"Yes, Cave Girl, I heard."

"Dad, do you think I could live in a cave like you, now that I've speared my first skate?"

"Yes, I'm certain of it!"

And Melody stood taller than when we had left this morning.

When we arrived back at the caravan, the others had made another campfire, and we sat and shared stories of our day. Gay had finished the book she had been looking forward to reading, and it was all about the ancient peoples of Gower.

"You have to read it, my love," she said. "It starts off from Neolithic times, and then goes on to cover the Celts and Druids in Wales, and the first Viking landings on Gower."

Samantha and Glynn had been on a wonderful hike, having climbed up to the top of the cliffs, and then followed the cliff path to Oxwich Bay. They had spent time in the village and visited Oxwich Castle, and then taken the lower path to the old Church, and then walked as far as the point before climbing back over the headland to Horton and back across the beach to Port Eynon.

When Melody told her story of how she had climbed up the rocks and speared her skate, we all cheered. She walked around the campsite proudly shaking her spear, and we cooked the skate over the fire. Its white meat was soft and flavorful, the kind that melts in your mouth; and Samantha had picked up some chips from the chip shop that were still wrapped in newspaper and warm. So, skate and chips with tartar sauce and ketchup was the order of the day. And to crown our wonderful weekend, Helen surprised us by making a treacle pudding with bird's custard.

What a wonderful weekend and birthday celebration for Helen. But the best news for me was knowing that Samantha had been accepted into her extended program at Swansea University. She would start her first semester in September, and I was ecstatic that she would be here with us in Wales.

My boys would not be here until Christmas, but God was working all things out for the best in his good and perfect time. This was one of life's lessons that I was learning, and I was so thankful.

Chapter Thirteen

Number 8 and Number 12

Monday was a big day for us, as Gay went back to work and started her commuting from Swansea to Cardiff, and I took Melody to her new school. Her first day was only a half day at school, and after meeting all her teachers and some of her new classmates, she was able to come home. The teachers seemed nice and looked forward to welcoming Melody into their classes.

We had given Samantha the largest of the three spare bedrooms at home, which she seemed happy about. It was a lot bigger than her room where we had lived on Vancouver Island. Melody was thrilled about it, as Sam's room was next to hers.

"We can sneak into each other's rooms at night," Melody said, with a mischievous look on her face, and Gay and I were happy that Melody was enjoying her big sister so much.

Helen would remain in Cardiff, and it would feel strange not having her so close and not being able to go over to her house for tea during the week. At least Samantha could babysit when she was not busy with Glynn, so Gay and I could go out. And Helen would continue to come down on weekends and stay in one of the other spare rooms.

In the afternoon, when Melody and I got home from the school, she went over to play with her friend Beverly next door, which gave me time to call Helen, as planned, so we could arrange to spend some time together. Gay had called me on her lunch hour and told me that she had already booked Helen and I up for speed dating on Saturday, but I didn't say anything to Helen, not yet anyway. I would tell her in person when we saw each other on Saturday morning.

"Gay and Melody are going to Bristol on the weekend to visit Pearl, and Samantha is staying over at Glynn's until Sunday night. Why don't you come over on Saturday about eleven? That will give us most of the day together, and then you can stay over until Sunday night."

"Wonderful. Kings, I will see you then."

"Bye Helen, see you then," I said as I put down the phone.

Melody and I made tea and we surprised Gay when she got home from work.

"How was your commute?" I asked.

"The train was very relaxing, much better than driving all the way to Cardiff, and I was able to park my car in Swansea at my friend Jane's. She lives close to the train station, and she said I can park at her place anytime, so that will work out perfectly."

"That's wonderful, my love. Now I think Melody has something to show you…."

"You do?" "Yes, Mum, and you must come up to my room to see what Dad and I have done."

"Okay, Princess. Let me finish having tea with Dad first, and then I'll come up and have a look."

When Gay went up to Melody's bedroom, I could hear her exclaim "Wow! Is that your spear? The one you speared your skate with?"

"Yes, Mum, and I can look at it each night before I go to sleep."

After reminiscing about our day, it was time for Melody to go to bed. Gay had some homework to do, so I agreed to tell Melody a story.

"I'm sad, Dad," she said when I entered her room.

"Sad! Why are you sad, Princess?"

"Well, I don't know … I hope you don't think it's silly."

"Anything you tell me isn't silly, you know that. Unless you want to be silly, and then I can be silly too."

She smiled for a minute and then said, "No, this isn't silly, Dad."

"Okay, out with it. What are you sad about? Come on, tell me, or I'll be sad too."

"Do you think anyone will ever find my message in a bottle, Dad? I am feeling sad because it has been a long time since I sent it. Remember, Dad, that was back in the spring when we sent it from Hunts Bay, and now it's almost the end of the summer and no one has answered me back."

"I can see how that must be hard for you, waiting and wondering if anyone is ever going to find it."

"Yes, it is."

"Remember the story I told you about when I was a young man living in Bacon Hole? I think it will encourage you if I remind you of what happened."

"One night I was feeling very discouraged because a lot of things had gone wrong in my life, and I didn't know what to do. So, I prayed, and I asked for God's help."

"The very next morning I went for a walk along Hunts Bay, to reflect on the time I had spent living in Bacon Hole. I was getting ready to go and live in another area, in another cave where I thought I might feel better."

"As I was walking on the beach, I found a message in a bottle, and stuck to one side of the bottle were barnacles. I picked up the bottle and held it under the water in one of the rockpools, and the little tentacles of the barnacles were moving in and out of their shells. This told me that the bottle had been in the water for a long time – long enough for barnacles to form and grow on the bottle. And the fact that they were still alive told me that the bottle had not been sitting dry at the top of a beach somewhere; otherwise, the barnacles would have died. The bottle had been traveling along in the sea and had not spent much time, if any, on land."

"Now, if I had gone down to the beach on any other day, or even at a different time of day, I would have missed it, and it would have been taken out to sea again on the next tide. What do you think about that?"

"I think you were meant to find it, Dad."

"That's right, I was! And do you know why I was meant to find it?"

"No. Why?"

"Because of what was written inside the bottle. There were four Bible verses, and each verse said something to me that my heart needed to hear. And those words changed my life!"

"So, who do you know sent me the message in the bottle?" I asked.

"Why, God, of course!"

"That's right! And do you know what I believe?"

"What, Dad?"

"I believe that God is watching over your bottle, and when the right person comes along who is supposed to find it, then God will bring it to shore. Maybe he is just waiting for you to pray, Melody, and ask him to bring your bottle back into shore. Or maybe it has already reached a shore somewhere, and the person who is meant to find it has not come along yet…".

"Will you pray with me, Dad, so we can ask God to help the right person find my message?"

"Of course, Sweetie, let's pray."

"Dear God, Melody has been waiting for what seems like a long time for someone to find her message in a bottle. Please make sure that the right person comes along to find it."

"Is there anything you want to ask God, Melody? He's listening."

"Yes. Dear God, please make it so that the person who finds it will be my friend. We have just moved to Pennard. I have Beverly but I need to find a best friend."

"Well done, Princess. I know that God has heard your prayer. You wait and see. He answers our prayers if we keep trusting."

"I am trusting him, Dad, and I love you."

"I love you too, Princess. Nite nite, and don't let Nan's Nan bite."

"I won't. Nite nite, Dad, and don't let Nan's Nan bite."

The rest of the week went by quickly, and it was soon Saturday morning. Gay and Melody started packing for Bristol after we had finished breakfast, and I spent time relaxing in the garden as we waited for Helen to arrive. "I think we should have told her sooner," I said, "rather than leaving it to this morning." "There is a reason to my madness," Gay replied, "If I had told her any sooner, she would have had too much time to think about it, and say no. But because I have already booked you to go, she is more likely to agree." "I don't know," I replied, "I don't think she likes surprises of this nature so much." "Believe me, I know Helen," Gay said, "it is better this way." We would have to wait and see, I thought, I would much rather Helen go on her own, and I could drive her there and pick her up after.

Helen arrived just before 11:00, and I carried her suitcase upstairs to her room. As I came back down the stairs, I could hear Helen and Gay talking in the kitchen. Helen was hesitant and nervous when Gay told her what she had done. "You should have asked me if I wanted to go," Helen said, "or at least told me sooner! I don't want to go," she said, as I walked into the kitchen. "Are you in on this too?" she said, giving me a look of disapproval? "No, I mean yes," I replied, "Gay and I want you to be able to meet someone who will see you for the wonderful woman you are and treat you the way you deserve to be treated." "Oh Kings, you are such a charmer, you lovely man!"

"We just want you to get out and about a bit," I continued, "so that you will have the opportunity to meet someone." "Well, if you insist," she said, giving me a half smile and looking less nervous after hearing my words. "But I want you to come with me, Kings." Gay smiled at me as if to say, I told you so. And I told Helen that I would go with her.

Gay and Melody left for Bristol before lunch, leaving Helen and I to enjoy the afternoon together. It was a nice afternoon, and Helen helped me in the garden until it was time for us to get ready for our speed dating adventure. "I must be mad, agreeing to this," Helen said, as she put on her makeup. "Not at all," I said, "how else are you going to meet someone if you don't go out?" "Oh, Kings, it's not like it used to be when I was young, when you met people at the local village market or at the young farmers dance."

"You look lovely," I said, as I opened the car door for her to get in. "Do I really look lovely, Kings?" she asked. "Yes," I replied, "otherwise I wouldn't have said it." "Now I know your lying, Kings, you would never tell me anything else other than how nice I look, you lovely man." "I mean it," I smiled, "you really do look lovely. I like your dress and your matching shoes, and what is that scent your wearing?" Helen's eyes filled with tears at my words, and she leaned over and kissed me. "It is called misty violet," she smiled, and we drove on to the pub.

The event was being held at the Mermaid Pub in Mumbles, not far from Swansea. I parked the car and Helen took my arm as we walked to the pub. "Why don't we go out for the evening ourselves," she laughed, "we are dressed for it, and no one would be the wiser." "Come on." I smiled, "you never know, sparks might fly if you meet someone nice." "I'm already with someone nice! You better protect me from those wild beasts that go to speed dating." "I will," I laughed, and we each filled in an information sheet at the door where there were two ladies checking us in. "The only rules we have are that you are not married, and that you will be respectful to all other participants," one woman said, "even if there is no connection between you and the participating person, remember they are probably feeling nervous too and we want this to be a positive experience for everyone. This is meant to be a fun and relaxing event," the other organizer said, and both Helen and I agreed to the terms. I did feel a bit guilty, because I am married. I whispered under my breath, "I told you Gay, it's only for single people." But since we were told we got drinks and appetizers, I looked forward to a good pint of beer.

Helen and I were now given a participant list and a badge with our first name and a number on it. I was number 12, and Helen number 8. "Come in, number 8," I joked as Helen and I found a table to sit at. "Do not forget to sit at the table with the person who has the same number as you," Christine, one of the organizers said after introducing herself, and her teammate Tina. "There are 12 women and 12 men," Tina said, "and you each have five minutes with each person. I am then going to ring a bell, and then the men are to move to the next table. You ladies are to remain sitting at the table you are sitting at now for the duration of the event. We are going to have a break halfway through," Christine said, "and you can get a drink and an appetizer at the bar using the ticket you were given when you registered at the door. You have a half an hour break to have your drink and food, and when you hear the bell ring for the end of the break, you must go directly to your next table." Sounds good, I thought, as I felt inside my pocket for my meal ticket, I was hungry already.

"Everyone get seated," Christine said. "I am going to ring the bell in two minutes, and remember you only have five minutes at each table otherwise we will not have time for you to meet everyone. So good luck everyone, and do not forget to have fun!"

∽

As I waited for the bell to ring, I thought what it was like to be single again, and I looked at the woman sitting opposite me at table number 12. She smiled at me nervously and then looked away, and I thought to myself, I am glad that I am not single and having to go through all of its challenges again, although some of it was fun.

Suddenly the bell rang, and both the woman and I jumped out of our skins. "That is a loud bell," I laughed, "I guess they want to make sure we all can hear it," I said, "and you must be Maxine," I said, looking at her badge. "Yes," she replied, nice to meet you. And you are Vince, I can see. So, tell me a bit about yourself, Vince."

"Well," I replied, "I am Vince, as the badge says, and I love the outdoors, camping and fishing and exploring new places," and I am married. No, I did not say that I was married, that would really put the cat among the pigeons as I flew from table to table. I can imagine what the women would say, "look out for number 12, he is married," and I had a chuckle inside as I thought about it. "I am Maxine, as my badge says, and I like dancing and going to movies." "What are you looking for in a man? I asked, pretending to be interested. "I am looking for someone who is honest and fun loving, and someone who appreciates family life as I have children." "Me too," I said, "I mean I have children too and they are growing up fast."

Number 8 and Number 12

By the time we felt comfortable talking to one another, the bell rang, and it was time for me to move to the next table. "Bye," I said, as I walked away, and I quickly glanced across the room at Helen who had survived her first introduction at table number 8. She smiled, so she must not be feeling too uncomfortable I thought, as I sat down at the next table.

The next lady was called Ffion, and she was an extremely attractive woman with long auburn hair and lovely green eyes. 'I could get used to this,' I thought, 'I don't mind spending five minutes with a lovely looking lady like this.' "I am Ffion," she smiled, and I smiled back. Unfortunately for Ffion there was an instant attraction between us, and I thought, this isn't fair to her as we enjoyed a nice flowing conversation, about history and literature, and multimedia art, and I began to enjoy myself. "I am going to tick box number 12," she said just as the bell rang for us to end our time. I felt like a fraud. Oh well, I was doing it for Helen, I told myself, as I walked over to the next table. I met three more women and then it was time for a break.

I started to walk over to Helen who had already ordered a drink from the bar, but there was a man already talking to her, so I made myself scarce, and stood at the end of the bar. I didn't want to distract her or the man from getting more acquainted with one another. That is what this break was all about, I thought, giving people the opportunity to talk more with someone they feel they have made a connection with.

"What are you having?" the barmaid said, and she took my order. I ordered nachos and a pint of cider, 'I am going to need this I muttered,' as I could see Ffion walking towards me from the other side of the bar. "It was nice talking to you,

Vince," she said, "and do you mind if I call you when this is over?" "No," I said, lying through my teeth, "that would be nice. I think the organizers are going to give us the email address of all our matches," I said. "Then I will look forward to contacting you," she said.

Finally, Helen walked over and rescued me, kind of. "This is Ffion," I said, introducing her to Helen, and Helen was all eyes, and said, "I am Helen, and …Vince… and I came together." "So, you know each other then?" "Yes," I said, answering for both Helen and I, "we do." After exchanging a few pleasantries, Ffion excused herself to go to the bathroom. "That must have been awkward, Kings," Helen said, "she fancies you something awful, I can tell by the way she was looking at you." "I think you women have an extra sense," I said, "knowing if someone fancies someone or not. It is rather awkward," I replied, "but are you having a good time?" "Surprisingly, I am," Helen said. "I thought I wouldn't like it, but it's nice to dress up and meet some people." "Anyone you like so far?" I asked. "Oh, maybe one man named Paul, he seemed sincere and friendly, and he was not bad looking."

"We had better finish our food," I said, seeing that my nachos were getting cold, and I supped on my cider. "Thank you, Kings," Helen said, "it means so much to me that you are doing this for me, I love you Kings, I really do, Gay is so blessed to have you as her husband." "I love you too Helen," I said, "and the man who one day marries you, will be a lucky man." Tears filled Helens eyes at my words, and I said, "don't you compromise by having a man who is not worthy of you, you are a lovely lady, and you deserve someone very special!" "Do I Kings, do I?" "Yes, you do."

Ffion was back from the bathroom now and heading our way. "I will leave you to it…Vince," Helen said, and she walked off to the other end of the bar. "There was another woman in the bathroom," Ffion said, "and she talked to a man named Jeremy. Anyway, this man talked to her like she was a piece of furniture." "You better watch out for that one," I answered, and I scoffed down some nachos as quickly as I could without her thinking I was a pig. Maybe she did think I was a pig, I thought! But I was hungry, and the bell would ring for part two of the speed dating any minute.

Come on bell, I thought, as Ffion squeezed my hand as she was talking to me. Come on bell, ring and rescue me! I was saved from a knockout, and I headed off to the next table. Pour me drink won't you, and I will tell you some lies.

The next badge read 'Hyacinth,' and it was interesting to meet someone with a name from my grandmother's generation. My grandmother told me that many female babies were given names of flowers during and after World War II.

I was looking forward to ending this speed dating experience now, and I am sure the remaining women that I talked to, could pick up on my lack of enthusiasm, much as I tried to come across as interested in what they had to say. And as the end of the evening bell rang, little did I know that I would one day meet Ffion again, but that is a chapter for another time.

Our hosts Christine and Tina came around to the tables and collected our participant lists, and our evening was over. "You can stay in the pub and get to know each other," they said, "and thank you all for coming. Your matches will be emailed to you within a week, and we hope that you had a nice time."

I asked Helen if she wanted to stay and talk more with anyone, she had felt a connection with. She said no, and we headed for the door, before Ffion singled me out to come and talk to me again.

As I drove home to Pennard, Helen thanked me again for coming with her. "I would not have gone on my own, Kings," she said. "I am glad you went," I replied, "and I am sure Gay will want to hear all about it when she gets home."

On Sunday morning, Helen and I enjoyed having breakfast at the Heather Slade Café, and then we went for a walk along East Cliff to Hunts Bay. After a nice walk on the rocky beach and collecting some fossils, we headed back to the village. "Let's have lunch in the Southgate Pub," Helen said, "that way we don't have to cook and wash dishes." "Sounds like a plan," I exclaimed, "that's what weekends are all about, good food, no dishes, and best of all spending time with a lovely lady." Helen blushed and we ordered our drinks.

After a nice meal at the pub, and a walk back through the village, Helen and I waited at the house for Gay and Melody to return home from Bristol.

The End of the Third Book of
the Gower Peninsula Adventure Series

www.ingramcontent.com/pod-product-compliance
Lightning Source LLC
Chambersburg PA
CBHW071857290426
44110CB00013B/1177